Plato
The Republic

OTHER BOOKS BY

RICHARD W. STERLING

Ethics in a World of Power: The Political Ideas of Friedrich Meinecke
Macropolitics: International Relations in a Global Society

WILLIAM C. SCOTT

The Oral Nature of the Homeric Simile
Prometheus Bound: A Commentary
The Musical Design in Aeschylean Theater
The Musical Design in Sophoclean Theater

Plato
The Republic

Translated by

Richard W. Sterling
DARTMOUTH COLLEGE

and William C. Scott
DARTMOUTH COLLEGE

W · W · NORTON & COMPANY · *New York* · *London*

Printed in the United States of America.

Reissued in a Norton paperback edition 1996

This text is composed in Electra, with display type set in Bernhard Modern
Roman. Composition and manufacturing by The Maple/Vail Book Manufacturing
Group.

Library of Congress Cataloging in Publication Data

Plato.
  The Republic.
  Translation of: Respublica.
  1. Political science—Early works to 1700.
2. Utopias.   I. Sterling, Richard W.   II. Scott.
William C. (William Clyde), 1937–   III. Title.
JC71.P35   1985   321'.07   84–20565

ISBN 0-393-31467-7

W. W. Norton & Company, Inc.
500 Fifth Avenue, New York, N.Y. 10110
www.wwnorton.com

W. W. Norton & Company Ltd.
Castle House, 75/76 Wells Street, London W1T 3QT

For
Maud LaRouche Sterling
and
Charles, Ellen, and Alice Scott

Contents

Preface

The act of translation, especially of a masterpiece, is both exhilarating and frustrating. Translation provides the opportunity for close and prolonged companionship with a great author—in this case Plato—and that is cause indeed for exhilaration. Frustration results from the recognition that translation can never reproduce the original. Variances in vocabulary, sentence structure, word order, idiom, and cultural context are not only characteristics that make every language unique; they are also the principal reasons why translation must be a matter of conversion and not mere copying.

If the translator cannot reproduce the original, he can still faithfully convey the author's originality. Intellectual argument and aesthetic purpose can cross linguistic barriers intact, even if the translator may have to reach for synonyms or for alternative sentence structures in order to assure clarity in the language of translation.

Clarity of English expression and fidelity to Plato's Greek in intellect and art are, then, the two overriding obligations of the translator. He must mediate between the two languages in which he works, matching concepts, phrases, and nuances in the original text to the word resources, syntax, and rhythms of his own language. In our version of Plato's *Republic* we have determined not to let the English obscure the Greek, but also—of equal importance—not to let the Greek obscure the English. Instead, we believe that the translator ought to aim for a creative interaction by drawing on the resources of both languages in order to achieve an authentic consonance between them.

John Locke confronted the problem of translating the Epistles of Saint Paul from Greek for seventeenth-century English readers. He steered his course over difficult terrain; the effort caused him to lay down some guidelines for translators in the preface to his work. Locke's principles were a real help to us, particularly his insistence that the means and mechanics of literal translation ought not to prevail over the governing purpose of giving clear and accurate expression to the original author's meaning. Wherever these ends and means conflicted, Locke relied on his own understanding of the whole of Saint Paul's works as the most reliable guide in his choice of English words and phrases. Then, calling his work paraphrase rather than translation, he was able to present his contemporaries with an accurate and intellectually compelling rendition of Saint Paul's works, unblemished by the obscurities that are often the ironic by-products of attempts at word-by-word exactitude in translation.

Our attempt to put into the clearest possible English the thoughts, concepts, theories, metaphors, and assertions of Plato's *Republic* carries a price tag. In order to achieve our goal, we have sometimes combined or restated phrases in order to put the ideas they represent in English as clearly as they appear in Greek. We have often broken a long Greek sentence into shorter English sentences. Sentences within a paragraph have at times been transposed in a quest for greater clarity. English word order has been used throughout the text; hence Greek word order has been converted wherever English usage required it. We have had to forgo the freedom and flexibility available to the Greek language in its use of the participle, which cannot be brought over directly into English.

In the quest for clarity we have never resorted to substantive omissions or to embellishments. We have transmitted Plato's *Republic* from Greek to English in its entirety. We believe that it has come through the conversion intact. We hope that Plato's intellectual power has been made as manifest in English as it is in Greek. *The Republic*, however, is not only a masterpiece of intellect; it is also a work of art. We have sought to give expression to that sense of artistry found in the Greek so that the excellence of *The Republic* in both thought and art might speak for itself. In sum, we claim to be faithful to the text of *The Republic* but not to its every Greek word. It has been our desire to re-create in our version the experience of Plato's audience in Greece.

We have based our version on the Oxford text of Plato's *Republic* in the Greek language edited by John Burnet in 1902. As aids for readers, we have kept in the margin of the text the numbering of the pages and sections of the 1578 edition of Plato's works by Stephanus (Henri Estienne). This numbering scheme has become standard for the works of Plato throughout the world and makes possible ready comparison of texts in different editions whether in the same or different languages.

Though no one is certain that the current division of *The Republic* into ten books originated with Plato—and more than one scholar has claimed that it did not—we are persuaded that each of these books does have a distinctive theme which is developed within the framework of the individual book. Further, we believe that the ten books together can be more effectively understood and interpreted as a unity when each book is comprehended as a thematic component of a larger structure. Therefore, to preserve the integrity of the developing argument, we have kept the traditional division of *The Republic* into ten books without intervening comment (with one exception at the end of Book VI).

Proper nouns and specific references are identified in footnotes if they are necessary to the understanding of the relevant passage. Other proper names are listed with brief descriptions in the glossary.

We have been fortunate recipients of advice and assistance from colleagues during the preparation of the manuscript. We wish to thank Professors James E. Baumgartner, William T. Doyle, Timothy J. Duggan, and Roger Masters of Dartmouth College, and Kenneth E. Sharpe of Swarthmore College, for their counsel regarding some difficult points in the text. The staff of Dartmouth's Baker Library has once again demonstrated its resourcefulness in aiding faculty research. We wish to thank, in particular, Virginia Close, William Moran, and Philip Cronenwett. Eunice D. Lemkul, Catherine Frasier, Gail S. Patten, Susanne R. Putnam, Earl Raymond, and Roxie Roberts were generous with both their typing skills and their patience in the production of the manuscript. Keith Dickey aided in producing the Glossary.

We are grateful to the Egypt Exploration Society for permission to reproduce here the only remaining fragments of the earliest known copy (third century A.D.) of Plato's *Republic* (Book VIII). We also wish to express our gratitude to the directors and staff of the Papyrology Rooms of the Ashmolean Museum at Oxford University for their help in preparing the transparency of these fragments.

We have been aided by a grant from the Research Committee of Dartmouth College. Professor Hans Penner, recent Dean of the Faculty at Dartmouth, generously arranged for a term free of teaching so that the manuscript could be finished on schedule.

RWS
WCS

Introduction

Tell me, Socrates, are we to consider you serious now or jesting? For if you are serious and what you say is true, then surely the life of us mortals must be turned upside down, and apparently we are everywhere doing the opposite of what we should.[1]

Few passages in Plato's writings capture the personality and philosophic intent of Socrates better than these barbed words of Callicles in the *Gorgias*. Socrates and Plato—teacher and student—were for ever urging the world to mend its ways by renouncing all that it was most accustomed to doing. They specialized in upending orthodoxies together with those like Callicles who adhered to them. Revamping old concepts and inventing new ones, they then shunted them about until the obvious began to look doubtful and, finally, to a point where truth and falsehood appeared to change places.

Callicles speaks for many in his objection to being tipped upside down or, more exactly, turned around to admit the opposite of what he had previously believed to be true. His irritation is the greater in that both Socrates and Plato spiced their philosophic dialogue with jest and all varieties of wit from puns and irony to satire and ridicule. Humor was a powerful instrument in forwarding Plato's purpose to make learning like a game. Humor could also divert or placate in cases where philosophic diagnosis or prescription would likely arouse antagonism. But humor can also be powerfully irritating to anyone who thinks he is being made a fool of. And that was precisely Socrates' purpose in his dealings with Callicles in the *Gorgias*.

With or without the humor, the provocative character of message and method in the philosophy of Socrates and Plato is finally rooted in their views on human nature. Their basic proposition about human existence is that men and women can become what they all really long to be, but most fall short because they fear that what they truly

---

1. Callicles in Plato's *Gorgias* 481c. Callicles is Socrates' chief antagonist in the *Gorgias*, among the most renowned of Plato's shorter dialogues. A sophist, Callicles speaks for one of the leading intellectual doctrines of his day. (Translation by W. D. Woodhead.)

long for is illusory. Socrates and Plato declare the human being's true purpose is the happiness that comes from being just. But since justice and happiness so often prove elusive in life, the counter-argument that calls them illusions makes a powerful intellectual and psychological appeal. More appealing still, whoever buys the counter-argument is then free to turn to other purposes as more likely sources of personal and social satisfaction.

What specifically irritates Callicles is Socrates' corollary to the proposition that justice is the highest of human values. The offending corollary asserts that suffering injustice is always better than inflicting it. This affirmation is central to the argument in the *Gorgias* and pervades the whole structure of Platonic philosophy. If Plato had contented himself with a simple statement that justice is better than injustice, he might have elicited a casual assent from a large majority of what are often called law-abiding citizens. But when he has Socrates express the idea in its radical and most basic sense—that suffering injustice is preferable to being unjust—he is clearly making the kind of philosophical waves he conjures up in Book V of *The Republic*.

Plato's way of ranking justice and injustice is only one of a swarm of unsettling propositions he releases from his philosophical Pandora's box. Once it becomes clear that he and Socrates are engaged in unloosing a whole barrage of heretical opinions, it is easier to understand why they were storm centers of controversy in their lifetimes and ever after.

Socrates and Plato were men of revolution. They were enemies of the status quo, of the Greek establishment. They saw the Athenian government and society (along with other governments and societies of their day) dominated by ignorance, pride, envy, falsehood, and irrationality. They wanted to replace these governments and reorder these societies—they wanted to turn them upside down—by introducing a new order, one governed by wisdom, in the name of brotherhood, in humility, and with honesty and reason. Like the best of revolutionaries, then, they wanted to put an end to an old order not because they objected to order as such but because they wanted a new and better order. The new order was to be governed by justice, the very thing whose absence made the old order intolerable.

The Republic is Plato's central testing ground for the new order; it describes a tenacious and protracted struggle between justice and its enemies. This most famous of Plato's dialogues opens with a casual conversation between Socrates and a few companions. But the tone of the dialogue changes almost immediately when Socrates puts the question that is bound to provoke dissension: What is justice? If justice is to replace injustice, must not both be understood as they really are? Socrates' initiative turns the ensuing conversation in Books I and II into a battle of definitions. Five of the company (Cephalus, Polemarchus, Thrasymachus, Glaucon, and Adeimantus)[2] propose more or less elaborate explanations of the nature of justice. All of them are misconceptions, foils which Socrates undertakes to analyze and then discredit. But the foils are formidable and not easily contradicted. Their weakness is in illogic and inconsistency, but there is strength in their persuasiveness. Each in its own way expresses commonly held conceptions about justice whose force derives from an abundance of evidence showing how human beings actually deal with the problem of justice.

Socrates' rejoinder is that all men desire justice, but, like honor, its attainment requires effort, discipline, and risk. The price of justice is high, and many are unwilling to pay it. Hence they are prone to accept counterfeit wares in the form of deceptive definitions. Or, despairing of justice altogether, they refuse it any place among the competing desires for power, wealth, fame, security, and the pleasures of the senses. Glaucon and Adeimantus respond to Socrates by demanding that he formulate a true definition of justice. He replies that both individual and society must be considered before they will be satisfied with his answer. The balance of Book II and much of Book III relate the problem of justice to an analysis of the origins and functions of society and the state.

The chief function of the state, Socrates argues, is education. But his concept of education is not simply what is taught in schools. It includes what parents teach their children, what peers learn from peers, and how the state and society instruct their people to distinguish between friends and enemies, safety and danger, good and evil, respectability and disrepute. State and society are the chief guardians of public tradition, a tradition whose prevailing content consisted mainly of tales about wars, heroes, and gods. The tellers and transmitters of the tales are the poets, among whom the most venerated is Homer.

Plato sees the whole of this educational structure as the prime source of individual and social injustice. His intention is to dismantle and replace it with another curriculum that will educate men to be just. Plato is not against war as such, but he is against a tradition that glorifies war and a world view that celebrates victory as virtue and defeat as vice. Nor is he opposed to heroes. But he objects when poets describe arrogance, treachery, cunning, avarice—and even cowardice—as acceptable traits in a hero. As for the traditional gods, they could be benign, but their chief characteristic was willfulness;

2. Glaucon and Adeimantus are the names of Plato's brothers.

hence they could as easily be malevolent. They used their divine power as a means to gain whatever end they chose to pursue. The result was an unending struggle for power, and the dwelling place of the gods was a place of contention rather than of peace. Cruelty, deceit, seduction, rape, and parricide were part of routine behavior among the gods themselves as well as toward human beings, heroes and nonheroes alike.

Socrates and Plato refused to celebrate such gods, and they castigated the poets, including Homer, for doing so. The result was that Socrates was condemned to death on charges of atheism. Plato, having declared that the received religion must be excluded from the just society, paid a longer term penalty. He has ever after been arraigned on charges of censorship and hostility to free speech and the free circulation of ideas. His defense is simple but often rejected: neither individual nor social justice is possible if the heroes and gods of Greek mythology are permitted to remain as examples and models for divine and human behavior.

Plato's argument with heroes, gods, and poets runs parallel with the initial battle over definitions of justice. Both engage Socrates in the task of dispelling clouds of illusion in order to discover the hidden reality. Only at the end of Book III does he begin to answer the previous question put by Glaucon and Adeimantus concerning the true nature of justice. A just society must be governed by men of reason. Inventing a new social myth to replace the old, Socrates calls those who rule for the benefit of the whole society and not to its detriment golden men; in his myth they rightfully govern the men of silver and bronze.

This is the myth of the metals (415a ff.), the centerpiece of a second accusation that has dogged Plato through the centuries. Plato made clear that merit and not heredity defined the gold man and that gold could be found in all parts of society. Nonetheless, Plato has never yet escaped the charge that he imposes upon society an elitist and authoritarian rule. The charge is pressed even though in Book IV Plato makes justice in the individual the condition of justice in society. Gold, silver, and bronze are only code names for reason, spirit (temperament or will), and appetite. These Plato called the three parts of the soul, the basic components of the human personality and therefore common to all men.

A common human nature, Plato argues in turn, necessarily has a common purpose. Reason must learn how to enlist the resources of spirit in the business of governing appetite. Unbridled appetites—for power, wealth, sex, and all the worldly allurements—are enemies of individual and society alike. But governed by reason, the appetites can instead contribute to the happiness of true pleasure and the freedom that self-government brings to the individual, to society, and to the state. It is when self-government fails that men become slaves to their appetites. Then reason degenerates into cunning, and spirit becomes savage. Both are degraded to the role of servants in the employ of an anarchy of desires. Loss of self-mastery is the loss of freedom. Without freedom, the hope of justice must also vanish.

A just man freely chooses to govern himself by reason. His appetites are characterized by moderation and temperance. So ordered, appetite becomes the servant and not the master. It comes into harmony with the purposes of reason and with the will and spirit which reason must mobilize to gain its end. In the soul so constituted, order wins out over disorder. Reason learns wisdom, spirit learns courage, and appetites are taught how to benefit the soul instead of doing injury.

Who could deny, Plato asks, that men who are wise, courageous, and temperate must also be just? Who could deny that such men are both the best citizens and the best governors? If these things are true, then public virtues and vices are identical to private virtues and vices. The school of justice is the same for the private person and the ruler of the city. Just government in the city, finally, depends on educating as many of its people as possible to be just.

But at this point in the argument Plato returns to an examination of impediments to justice. In Book V he has Socrates make proposals for reform so radical in content that they must provoke radical criticism. Plato likens the anticipated criticisms to giant waves that threaten to drown the philosopher in a tide of scorn and derision. The first proposal calls for the equality of men and women; the second would abolish marriage and private property among the rulers of society. Socrates spins out the implications of his proposals by joining plausible rationales to such bizarre and unlovely consequences for both individuals and societies that his audience must surely be repelled. But Socrates makes no waves; among the company of his listeners no one ventures to criticize.

Only with his third proposal does Socrates succeed in arousing opposition. It is a proposal which Socrates, with mock irony, confesses he has long hesitated to bring forward because he anticipates it will surely be swept away in a flood of invective. Forsaking the elaborate and fantastic social rearrangements described in the first two proposals for reform, Socrates ventures the suggestion that a single change, or perhaps two—or, at least, a very small number of modest changes—would suffice to reform badly governed societies (473b–c). Urged on by Glaucon, Socrates then offers his new plan for good government: either philosophers must become kings, or kings must become philosophers. What the just society requires is a marriage between political power and the wisdom of philosophy.

The storm wave of abuse foreseen by Socrates now rises in full fury. Glaucon prophesies what the critics will do. Led by the politicians and intellectuals, they will unsheath their weapons and attack Socrates with all the force at their command, and he will suffer dreadful consequences (473e–474a). Having escaped even a hint of censure in response to his earlier experiments with the grotesque, Socrates must now pay the penalty for daring to suggest that wisdom be placed in the seat of government. Plato's lesson is clear: men are prone to give credence to all kinds of nostrums, however odious or lunatic, as plausible prescriptions for a better life. But the argument that wisdom should replace folly, that justice should take the place of injustice, is bound to arouse the fiercest skepticism and resistance.

Why should this argument provoke such protest? Because wisdom and justice call upon individual and society to abandon meanness of spirit for generosity. The self that is yoked to selfishness must yield to another kind of self: one that finds fulfillment in harmony with an encompassing humanity. Self-discipline must replace self-indulgence. Self-government must be preferred to government imposed by external authority (443d–444a). These "modest changes" implied in Socrates' third proposal and reiterated throughout *The Republic* are the most radical changes of all. They upend the world of convention in order that a different world might emerge right side up, one in which human beings would choose to trust the better part rather than the worse within their own natures, within themselves.

Opposition to the imperatives of genuine reform can be summed up in one overriding objection. They require the impossible. Plato seeks to disarm the opposition with arguments that take up the final part of Book V and all of Books VI and VII. Once again the subject is education: the training of the philosophic nature. If it is possible to educate some men to philosophy, then it must be possible for all men to recognize the compelling truth of wisdom and justice and so live and understand, or at least revere, the philosophic life (518b–d). To establish the Muse of philosophy as the governor of society is difficult but not impossible. If it were impossible, Plato argues, then we would be daydreamers. But, he says, we are not daydreamers; we do not speak of impossibilities (499b–d).

The education of the philosophic nature characteristically begins by addressing both the strengths and vulnerabilities of aspiring philosophers. It culminates in the lessons taught by the divided line (509d–511e), the allegory of the cave (514a–521c), and the dialectic (534b–540c).[3] Those who master the curriculum will have mastered

---

3. See also the translators' diagram and note at the end of Book VI (p. 203).

themselves: the indispensable requirement for rulers in a just society. Government by such rulers Plato calls an aristocracy. Whether it takes the form of a monarchy headed by a philosopher-king or a body of philosophers in council is for Plato a matter of secondary importance. What does matter is that power should be wielded by those who exemplify the precise meaning of the word *aristocracy:* a government of the best.

Nothing human is perfect; even the best of governments is vulnerable to corruption. In Books VIII and IX, Plato records those melancholy truths. Among the aristocrat-philosophers some will eventually yield to temptation by putting their own interests before those of their city. Building and defending the best city gives way to tearing it down. The harmony of justice in state and society is eroded by disharmony among the classes of citizens and, as Plato tells the story, among parents and children.

After the principles of the best government have been abandoned, the long descent begins toward the worst. On the way, Plato examines forms of government to which he ascribes a disruptive mixture of virtues and vices: timocracy, in which the soldierly ethos predominates; oligarchy, or rule by the rich; and democracy, where the citizens (or majorities) rule to suit themselves. Each runs parallel to the false conceptions of justice advanced by Cephalus, Polemarchus, Glaucon, and Adeimantus in Books I and II.

Tyranny is the worst form of government, and Plato sets it far apart from the vices besetting the governmental forms he has just described. Tyranny is unmitigated evil because the tyrant is an enemy of the city he rules by force. He obeys no law nor serves any need of the city. He pursues only what he deems to be his own self-interest. Consumed by unjust desire, he will commit any crime that promises to serve his tyrannical will. He is the counterpart to the concept of justice proposed by Thrasymachus in Book I: justice is nothing more than the interest of the stronger. Earlier, Socrates admonished Thrasymachus that such a conception of justice could only bring unhappiness to both individual and society. Now Socrates depicts the tyrant, the enemy of his ruined city and a slave to appetite and fear, as the unhappiest man of all (576c–580c).

All existing governments, Socrates concedes, exhibit the noxious characteristics of one or another of the defective forms he has described. None, to his knowledge, is just. But it makes no difference, he argues, whether or not a just society can be found anywhere on earth. The philosopher must not shun politics. Circumstances may bid him hold his peace; but if he encounters a society that might be stirred to reform, he must serve the highest cause that justice commends: to rescue his city as well as himself (496d–497b).

Book X serves as a somewhat unsettling coda to what has gone before. In the first part Plato revives Socrates' quarrel with the poets whom he had symbolically exiled from the city. But the dispute yields to a declaration of love for poetry and an emotional invitation to the poets to return, but only on condition that they abandon their attachment to the old order of false gods and false heroes. Then the mortal and immortal consequences of justice and injustice are weighed anew. The verdict is that the just man will never be deserted by heaven, whose principles he among all men has most sought to make his own (613a–c).

The coda ends with the myth of Er. It describes a short but spectacular foray into the afterlife. But the mythical drama of judgment, of rewards and punishments, of redemption and renewed life, has less to do with heavenly activities than with the familiar problems of earthly existence. Human choice is the central issue in the drama acted out in heaven and on earth. The supreme choice, freely made in both the world and the afterworld, is between good and evil.

And now, says Socrates, the tale has been told. We have been delivered and are not lost.

Plato
The Republic

Socrates and Plato were both natives of Athens. Socrates was born in 469 B.C. and was executed by order of the Athenian court in 399 B.C. Plato was born in 429 B.C. and died in 347 B.C. Both men lived through the Peloponnesian War (431–404 B.C.). Their teaching must be seen against the background of this debilitating war, which resulted in the fall of the Athenian empire and the end of an era of unequaled artistic, intellectual, and political achievement. Plato was Socrates' student and commemorated his teacher by making him the chief spokesman in his dialogues.

Principal Characters in *The Republic*

Socrates
Adeimantus
Cephalus
Glaucon
Polemarchus
Thrasymachus

Book I

Yesterday I went down to the Piraeus with Glaucon, Ariston's son,
to offer my devotions to the goddess.[1] I also wanted to see how their
new festival would turn out. Our own citizens staged a fine parade,
but even the Thracians were good.

Once we had made our devotions and seen the whole festival, we b
started home. But at that moment Polemarchus, Cephalus's son,
saw us hurrying on and had his boy run to stop us. He grabbed my
cloak from behind and said that Polemarchus hoped that we would
wait for him to catch up.

I turned and asked the boy where his master was. He said that he
was only a little way behind us, and once again he asked us to wait.

We'll wait, said Glaucon.

Soon, Polemarchus joined us along with Glaucon's brother Adeimantus, Nicias's son, Niceratus, and a few others who had apparently marched in the procession.

Then Polemarchus said: Socrates, it looks as though you and
Glaucon are hurrying to leave us and return to Athens.

That is a good guess.

But do you see how many there are of us?

Of course.

Well, you are going to have to choose between staying here peace-
fully or fighting us if you try to get away.

How about a third choice in which we persuade you that you
ought to let us go?

But could you persuade us if we don't listen?

Obviously not, said Glaucon.

Then you might as well know right now that we won't listen.

Now Adeimantus broke in. Don't you know about what's going on
tonight? There will be a horse race in which the horsemen will carry 328
torches in honor of the goddess.

---

1. The Piraeus, about six miles from Athens, was the seaport for the city. As such it was open to
many exotic influences. Socrates is present for the festival of Bendis, a moon goddess whose cult
was imported from abroad.

Now that's something new. Do you mean a relay with horses in which the riders will pass on the torches to one another in sequence?

Exactly, said Polemarchus. And the festival will continue all night. After dinner we will go out and see it and then meet with some of our friends and have a really good talk. Don't refuse. Do stay with us.

It looks like we had better change our minds, Socrates.

Well, if you say so, Glaucon, I suppose we must.

So we went to Polemarchus's house. Polemarchus's brothers, Lysias and Euthydemus, were there. So was Thrasymachus of Chalcedon, as well as Charmantides the Paeanian and Cleitophon, the son of Aristonymus.

Cephalus, Polemarchus's father, was also at home. I hadn't seen him for a long time, and he seemed to me to have aged greatly. He sat on a cushioned chair and was wearing a garland, for he had been offering sacrifices in the courtyard. So we went and sat down near him in chairs that had been arranged in a kind of circle.

Cephalus greeted me as soon as he saw me. My dear Socrates, you don't come to see us here in the Piraeus as often as you should. Of course, if I were strong enough to make the journey to Athens, you wouldn't need to come here, for I should come to see you. But, as it is, you really must visit our house more often. My bodily pleasures are rapidly diminishing, but my desire for the pleasures of good conversation grows just as rapidly. So don't refuse us. Regard us as your good friends. Please feel at home in this house, and be a companion to these young men.

Cephalus, I count conversations with very old people among my greatest pleasures. We ought to learn from them as from travelers on a road we have not yet taken but which most of us, sooner or later, are destined to follow. What is it like? Is the journey rough and hazardous, or are there pleasures and satisfactions on the way? How does it look to you now that you have reached what the poets call "the threshold of old age"? Is being old difficult to bear? What kind of report can you give us?

Socrates, I will tell you exactly how I feel about it. Some of us old ones who are about the same age see each other often, reenacting the old proverb that like seeks out like. Most indulge themselves in lamentations for the lost pleasures of youth. Feasting, drinking, women, and all the rest of it crowd their memories; they are peevish because they believe that all the best things have now been taken away.

The majority sentiment has it that life was once sweet, but that now it is not worth living. Some complain that they suffer indignities from friends and kinsmen and then continue on with a long list of misfortunes for which they blame old age.

But, Socrates, I believe they put the blame in the wrong place. For if old age were the real cause, I too would have suffered those woes, and so would all who reach old age. But in fact I know some among the old who feel differently. I remember the poet Sophocles in particular. I was there when someone asked him about sex and whether he could still make love to a woman. "Hush," said he. "I c am happy to have left all that behind. I feel as though I have been liberated from a savage and relentless slave master." I thought then it was a good answer, and now I think so even more.

The truth is that old age brings with it an experience of tranquility and release in these and other matters. When passion's pressures abate, one is rid of a whole horde of lunatic slave masters. Fading d sexual powers and snubs from one's relatives are not the serious problems of old age. The real cause of troubles or well-being is to be found in the character of the individual. If he has been generally temperate and cheerful during his youth and middle years, old age is likely to treat him reasonably well. But one with contrary characteristics will find youth and age alike to be burdensome.

These admirable words made me want to hear more. I should imagine, Cephalus, that when you talk about these matters, most e people remain unconvinced. They think it is not your character that lends grace to your age but rather your fortune. They would likely observe that the rich enjoy many compensations.

You are right, Socrates. Most people don't accept what I say. Their objection carries some weight, but not that much. I am reminded . how Themistocles once responded to a man from the small island of Seriphus.[2] The man was being abusive, asserting that Themistocles owed his fame not to his own prowess but to the power of Athens. 330 Themistocles conceded that had he also been born in Seriphus, fame would surely have eluded him. But, he added, the Seriphian would have won no fame in life even had he been a man of Athens. Themistocles' retort offers a good analogy to the case of those who lack wealth and complain of old age. It is true that even a good man would find it rather difficult to cope with old age in poverty. But a bad man, however great his wealth, can never hope that old age will endow him with contentment and a cheerful temper.

Did you inherit your money, Cephalus, or did you make most of it yourself?

It depends on how you look at it. As for success in making money, I stand about midway between my grandfather and my father. My b

2. Themistocles was the Athenian statesman who led the city to devote its resources to the development of naval power in the 480s B.C. Athens's preeminence during the fifth century was due largely to its navy.

grandfather inherited about as much wealth as I now have, and he then multiplied it many times. In the hands of my father Lysanias the family fortune declined below the current level. I hope to leave my sons a bit more, and not less, than what was left to me.

c   I asked the question because you seem to be not overly concerned with money, an attitude generally associated with men who have inherited rather than made their fortunes. Those who make money themselves love it with a double intensity. They love what they earn the same way poets love their poems or fathers their children. Money for them is not merely useful. It is the chief evidence of their own creativity. The result is that they become bores; money is their only enthusiasm.

That is true.

d   Yes, but let me ask one more question. What do you think is the greatest benefit wealth has conferred upon you?

Something that will once again provoke a skeptical response from many people. But let me tell you, Socrates, when death comes near, a man will begin to fear and worry about things that before seemed innocuous. If he once laughed at stories of the netherworld and the punishments said to be in store for earthly misdeeds, his unbelief

e   now retreats before his fears that the stories may be true. Because of the infirmity of old age or the more frequent sightings of an approaching end, he must now wrestle with suspicion and fear. He reflects on his past and ponders what wrong he has done to others. If his burden of guilt is heavy, he will wake up at night in terror, like a child. Dark forebodings will cloud his life. But the man with a clear

331 conscience will have Pindar's "sweet hope" as the constant companion of his age. Pindar's lines are really a beautiful celebration of the old man who has lived justly and reverently:

> Hope, the mainstay of our mortal purposes,
> warms his heart and shares his journey into age,
> his companion and his tender nurse.

This is a fine—indeed, a wondrous—saying. This is the reward of

b   virtue, and the chief value of wealth is to strengthen virtue—if not in every man, then in the good man. Money makes it easier for a man to shun cheating and fraud. Money enables him to pay his debts, so that he need not fear the next world because of what he owes to gods or men in this one. Money obviously has other uses, too. All in all, however, I believe that wealth's chief service to the reasonable man is what I have just described.

You have nobly praised both honesty and honor as essential vir-

c   tues in the good man. But are these the same as justice itself? To tell the truth and pay one's debts—are these invariably equivalent to just behavior? Or may it sometimes be more just not to pay a debt, or not to tell the truth? Consider an example: a friend who is sound in mind and body lends you his weapons. Then, when he returns to claim them, you see that he has gone mad. Would it not be wrong to give them back to him? Would that not be an injustice? Would it not also be unjust to tell your mad friend the exact truth of his condition and situation?

Your questions are to the point, Socrates.   d

Then we must say that telling the truth and repaying one's debts cannot serve as an adequate definition of justice.

Polemarchus broke in. Yes, they can, Socrates. At least that is what Simonides says.

Well, said Cephalus, I think I shall bequeath the argument to you. I must attend to the sacrifices.

I am your proper heir in any case, said Polemarchus.

Of course you are, said Cephalus with a laugh. Then he left the room.

Then tell us, Polemarchus, how the heir to the argument under-   e
stands Simonides on justice and why you think him right.

I think Simonides speaks rightly when he says that justice is giving to each man his due.

Simonides is a man of both intelligence and inspiration. It is difficult to doubt him. Yet I must say that his meaning may be clear to you, Polemarchus, but not to me. Were he to address himself to our recent example, he would certainly not advocate the indiscriminate return of property to someone who had gone mad. Yet the property   332
was on loan and due on demand, wasn't it?

Yes.

But on no account must one return weapons to a madman?

True.

Then when Simonides said it is just to render that which is due, he must have had something else in mind.

He certainly did. He wanted to explain what is due from friend to friend: something good and nothing evil.

You mean that if a friend borrows money from another friend, he ought not to return it if, for some reason, repayment should harm   b
the lender? Would repayment under these circumstances actually violate the rule that only good is due from friend to friend? Is that Simonides' meaning?

Yes.

This proposition evidently implies another: enemies must receive their due.

Of course. Enemies must receive what is owing them, and the debt from enemy to enemy is nothing good but something evil.

c   Then, as poets so often will, Simonides talks in riddles about justice. He seems to have wanted to say that justice requires that everyone be given his due. But what he actually said is that everyone has
the right to collect what is owed him.
      What is the matter with that?
      We shall see what's the matter. Supposing we were to ask Simon-
ides what obligation the art of medicine has to its patients. What is
the patient's due? How do you think he would answer?
      That is obvious. Medicine is an art obligated to provide patients
with proper drugs, food, and drink.
d   What benefits does the art of cooking confer on the materials it
works with?
      It seasons the meat.
      Excellent. Now tell me what does the art of justice properly confer
and upon whom?
      If we are to follow the earlier reasoning, Socrates, justice is an art
that benefits friends and injures enemies.
      So Simonides defines justice as doing good to friends and evil to
enemies?
      I think so.
      Then who is best able to benefit friends and injure enemies in
times of sickness?
      A doctor.
e   Or on a voyage when all aboard face the perils of the sea?
      A captain.
      And how about a just man? In what situation is he best able to
help his friends and harm his enemies?
      In war, Socrates, when he joins his fellow countrymen in battle
against the foe.
      I see. All this leads me to conclude that when we are well and
safely on dry land, we have no use for doctors or captains.
      True.
      But how about justice? Will it be useless in peacetime?
      I don't want to say that.
333   Then justice has its uses in times of peace?
      Yes.
      Just like farming and shoemaking?
      Yes.
      Just how is justice useful in peacetime?
      It is useful in business, in drawing up contracts and in forming
partnerships.
      But if you were competing in a game, whom would you prefer as
b   a partner? A skillful player or a just man?
      A skillful player.
      Just as you would prefer partnership with a mason if you were

laying bricks or with a musician if you were making music?

Yes.

Then for what kind of partnership is the just man best suited?

In a partnership involving money.

But surely not where money is changing hands. If we wanted to buy or sell horses, it would be better to have a canny judge of horse-flesh as our partner. If ships were the commodity, we should want a shipbuilder or sea captain on our side.

No doubt.

Then in what kinds of money transactions will the just man be the best partner?

When one wants to deposit money for safekeeping.

You mean that the just man is useful only when money lies idle?

Exactly.

Justice is useful when money is useless?

Apparently.

Then it must follow that justice is useful whenever you want to put things in storage, whether they are pruning hooks, shields, or harps. But when you want to put these things to use, you apply the art of viniculture, of warfare, or of music, as the case may be.

Yes.

So, it must be the same with everything else: justice is useful when things lie unused, but it becomes useless when they become useful.

It looks that way.

Then justice can't be worth much. But let us try another approach. The boxer who is most skilled in offense will also be most skilled in defense. The doctor who is most capable of protecting us from disease is also most capable of infecting us. The soldier who guards the fort well will also be good at raiding the enemy's camp. Would you agree?

Yes.

So one who guards well is also good at stealing? The just man, who guards money well, will also be good at stealing it?

Evidently.

Then it seems we have revealed the just man to be a kind of thief. That is one of Homer's lessons. Homer often stressed his admiration for Odysseus's grandfather Autolycus, extolling his surpassing skill in "theft and perjury." Apparently you agree with Homer and Simonides that justice sanctions even the art of stealing so long as a man steals things to benefit friends or injure enemies. Is that what you meant?

Certainly not, although I confess I no longer know what I said. But I am still sure of one thing: the just man is one who benefits friends and injures enemies.

Then another question comes up. Whom do you call friends?

Those you think are good and honest people, or those who really are? And are your enemies really bad, or are they men you only think are bad?

Well, a man's judgments naturally depend on what he thinks and believes.

But don't people often misjudge the good and the bad, so that good people are mistaken for bad and bad people for good?

Clearly.

Then misjudgment can transform good people into enemies and evil people into friends?

That follows.

This also must follow: in such circumstances the just man will find himself defending bad people and injuring the good.

d   Evidently.

Yet the just man is good and would not do evil.

Yes.

But according to your previous reasoning, it is just to injure one who does no wrong.

No, no. That is certainly false doctrine, Socrates.

Is it then better to say that one should harm those who do wrong and help those who are honest and just?

That sounds better.

The truth is that Simonides' definition doesn't work. Someone

e   who is a poor judge of people will often have friends who are bad friends; in this case it turns out that Simonides' definition would have him do his friends injury. Conversely, he will have enemies who in fact are good men; and these the definition bids him support. But now we have come around to the exact opposite of Simonides' original position.

You are right. The error seems to be connected with our use of the terms *friend* and *enemy*.

What error, Polemarchus?

We defined a friend as one who seems to us to be good.

And what definition should we use instead?

A friend is one who is good in fact and not merely in our opinion.

335   If he only seems good, he will be only a seeming friend. The same must be said for enemies.

With this we arrive at the proposition that the good are our friends and the bad our enemies?

Yes.

You add something, then, to Simonides' original definition of justice as helping friends and punishing enemies. Now you want to say that justice requires that we do good to friends who really are good and harm enemies who really are bad.

That clarifies it.   b

But is it right for the just person to inflict injury on anyone?

Of course. He is right to injure bad men who are his enemies.

But what about injury itself? If you injure, say, horses or dogs, will you not make them less excellent animals?

Yes.

Does that not also hold for human beings? If you injure them,   c will they not be less excellent as men?

Yes.

Is justice a human excellence, Polemarchus?

Yes.

So if you injure a man you make him less just?

I guess so.

Now consider musicians or riding masters. Are their purposes achieved if their students become less musical or less able to ride horseback?

No.

How about the just man? Will it be his purpose to behave justly in order to make other men less just? Will the virtuous behavior of   d good men make other men bad?

No.

Then the good cannot corrupt any more than heat can generate cold or dryness water. If justice and goodness are the same, then the just man injures no one. It is his opposite, the unjust man, who inflicts injury on his fellows.

Socrates, I think you are right.   e

So it cannot be wise to say that justice is giving to each his due, if what is due includes injury to enemies as well as benefits to friends. It cannot be true because we have proved that the just man never injures anyone.

I agree.

So if anyone attributes such unwise doctrines to Simonides, or to other revered and intelligent men like Bias and Pittacus, will you be my comrade in arms and combat the heresy?

I'll be your comrade and do battle at your side.

Polemarchus, I think I know where the idea that justice benefits   336 friends and injures enemies originated. With despots like Periander or Perdiccas or Xerxes, or with a traitor like Ismenias of Thebes. Or with some other person so rich and powerful that he thought he could do just as he pleased.

That is likely.

Well, our success in disproving one definition of justice can only lead us to ask whether anyone can come up with another.

Thrasymachus had often tried to break into the argument but had   b been restrained by the others who wanted to hear it to the end. But when Polemarchus and I had reached this point in the conversation, there was a brief pause, and Thrasymachus could no longer be held back. He rose up like a beast and leaped at us as if he would tear us to pieces. Polemarchus and I recoiled in terror.

c   Then he bellowed at us and the whole company. What idiocy is this, Socrates? Why do the two of you behave like dolts, solemnly deferring to each other's vacuous notions? If you really want to know what justice is, you should be able not only to ask the question but also to answer it. You should not try to score points simply by refuting your opponent's efforts; you ought to provide your own definition. After all, there are many who ask but cannot answer. So now

d   say what you think justice is. Say it at last with clarity and precision, and spare us your ponderous analogies with duty or interest or profit or advantage. They produce only nonsense, and I don't put up with nonsense.

I was thunderstruck and could hardly look at Thrasymachus without trembling. Indeed, as in the proverb, I should have been speechless had I not already spotted this wolf before he saw me. In fact, I

e   was watching him all the while his temper was waxing hot, and so I was able to reply.

Spare me your anger, Thrasymachus. If there were errors in the argument, believe me, they were not intentional. Had we been searching for gold, we surely would not have played games with each other and risked letting the treasure slip from our hands. But here we have been looking for justice, something far more precious than gold. How could you suppose that we would waste time pretending to defer to false opinions rather than devoting all our energy to finding the truth? We have been in earnest, my friend, even though our explorations have not been successful. In this situation superior minds like yours should respond with sympathy rather than with scorn.

337   Thrasymachus responded with sarcastic laughter: A fine sample of your famous irony, Socrates. I know how you argue, as I warned everyone here at the outset. Whatever Socrates is asked, he refuses to answer. He will resort to irony or to any other stratagem in order to avoid being pinned down.

With your intelligence, Thrasymachus, you will surely recognize

b   this problem. Suppose you ask a man what sets of numbers go into twelve. But then you tell him that two times six or three times four— or six times two or four times three—are not valid answers, that they are the kind of nonsense that you "won't put up with." If you put the question to him that way, he has no way to answer. Suppose he were to respond with a question: "Thrasymachus, do you really mean to exclude all of those answers, even if one or more are right, and force me to give a false answer?" How would you respond?   c

Your analogy, as usual, is misleading.

How so? But suppose you are right, and the cases are not comparable except to the one who made the comparison. Would he not have every right to speak the truth as he sees it, whether we forbid him or not?

I divine your intention. You are going to come up with one of the answers that I ruled out of bounds.

If due reflection permits me to approve any of them, I might just take the risk.   d

What if I formulate a definition of justice superior to any you have offered? What penalty would you accept?

The penalty appropriate to ignorance: I must make the effort to learn from the wise.·

Very clever, but your effort will also have to extend to paying me a fee.

I will pay when I have the money.

You already have the money, Socrates, said Glaucon. You needn't worry about the fee, Thrasymachus; we shall take up a collection.

Yes, and then Socrates will go through his well-known routine,   e
refusing to answer anything himself but demolishing the answers of everybody else.

But, Thrasymachus, how can anyone who admits he doesn't know the answer then try to answer anyway? The difficulty is compounded if some august intelligence tells him that even the few things he might know something about have no place in the argument. Be more flexible, Thrasymachus. Since you both know and profess to   338
know, it is entirely proper that you should be the teacher and provide the definition. The rest of us are eager to hear you teach.

Glaucon and the others seconded my request. As for Thrasymachus, he was obviously flattered; he was convinced that his definition could not be refuted. He was eager to speak and still more eager for the acclaim he assumed would reward his discourse. After again insisting that I should speak, Thrasymachus finally yielded, but not without one more barb: So this is Socrates' wisdom. He refuses to   b
teach, and though he professes to learn from others, he never bothers to thank them.

I do learn from others. That is true. But it is a lie to call me ungrateful. I have no money; so I pay with what I do have: with praise. I am eager to praise anyone who speaks well. You will be able to verify that soon because I am sure the answer you are about to give us will do you great credit.

Then here is my answer: justice is simply the interest of the stronger.   c

Well, why don't you praise me? But of course you won't.

First I have to understand you. What do you mean by saying that justice is the interest of the stronger? An athlete like Polydamas is far stronger than we are, and it is in his interest to eat great amounts of beef to keep himself in shape. You are not going to argue that we nonathletes have a like interest in such a diet or that it would be good for us to follow it?

Socrates, you are a buffoon. But though your methods are clumsy, you are effective enough in sabotaging other people's arguments.

Not at all. I am simply trying to understand them.

Well, try again. You must know that tyrannies, democracies, and aristocracies are different forms of government.

Yes, I heard about that.

And that governments rule in their respective cities?

Yes.

Now governments use their power to make tyrannical, democratic, or aristocratic laws, as suits their interests. These laws, then, designed to serve the interests of the ruling class, are the only justice their subjects are likely to experience. Transgressors will be punished for breaking the laws and sullying justice. This is why I say that justice operates on the same principle everywhere and in every society. Justice is what advantages the interest of the ruling class. Since the ruling class is also the strongest class, the conclusion should be evident to anyone who reasons correctly: justice is the same in every case—the interest of the stronger.

Now I understand your meaning. But whether it is true or not is something I must still ascertain. I note you used the word "interest" in defining justice, a word you were unwilling to let me use. I admit, however, that in your definition you add the words "of the stronger."

A trifling addition, no doubt.

Trifle or not, our chief business is to discover whether your definition is true. First, I will agree that justice is an interest of some sort. But then you add that it is the interest of the stronger. I question that. We must examine that point.

Go ahead.

I will. Tell me, do you think that it is just and right to obey men in power?

Yes.

How about those in power? Are they always right, or do they sometimes make mistakes?

They will certainly make some mistakes.

Then what they ordain will come out right some of the time and some of the time not?

I suppose so.

When the rulers legislate rightly, the laws will conform to their interest. But to the extent that they miscalculate in their lawmaking, the laws will be contrary to their interest. Is that right?

Yes.   d

The subjects must nevertheless obey all the laws enacted by the rulers? You call that justice?

Yes.

Then it follows from your argument that it is just to serve the interest of the stronger but equally just not to.

What are you saying?

Exactly what you have been saying. But let us look at the matter more closely. You have just made two points. One is that the rulers may sometimes be mistaken about their best interests and that their laws may reflect those mistakes. The other is that justice requires the subjects to obey whatever laws there may be. Did you not make these two propositions?

Yes.

All of which amounts to admitting that it can be just and right to   e
do that which contradicts the interest of the stronger. When the rulers blunder in devising their policies, they damage their own interests. The requirement that subjects must unquestioningly support all the rulers' policies compounds the damage. Now, most wise Thrasymachus, can you see how you contradict yourself? Your indiscriminate equation of justice with what the strong command and the weak obey leads only to its own negation; it actually requires the weak to injure the interests of the strong.

Nothing could be clearer, Socrates, said Polemarchus.   340

If one could believe Polemarchus's testimony, said Cleitophon.

No witness is necessary, said Polemarchus. Thrasymachus himself said that rulers may command what is not in their interest and that subjects obeying these commands are doing justice.

You are right, Polemarchus. Thrasymachus said that justice for subjects is obedience to rulers.

Yes, Cleitophon, but he also said justice is the interest of the stronger, that sometimes the strong mistake their interest, but that   b
the subjects must nevertheless carry out what the stronger mistakenly order them to do. The inference is unavoidable that justice may equally be to the advantage or disadvantage of the ruler.

What Thrasymachus meant, said Cleitophon, is that justice is what the stronger believes to be in his interest. Obedience to this belief, in turn, is the just duty of the subject.

But he didn't say that, objected Polemarchus.

It doesn't matter, Polemarchus, said I. If that is the position Thra-   c
symachus now wants to take, let us accept it. Is that what you want

to say, Thrasymachus? Is justice what the stronger thinks is his interest, whether it really is or not?

Of course not. Do you think I would call someone stronger at the very moment he is making a mistake?

d Your admission that rulers are sometimes fallible led me to that inference.

That's because you are addicted to quibbling, Socrates. Would you call a man a doctor at the very moment he errs in diagnosing his patient? Does his error confirm his status as a doctor? Do we apply the same measure to mathematicians or grammarians, calling them by these names even when they make mistakes? True, it is customary to say that the doctor or mathematician or grammarian makes a mistake. But this is a loose way of speaking. I contend that
e none of these ever makes a mistake so long as his conduct accords with professional standards. When he does err, his skill has deserted him, and his professional status is in default. To be precise, then— and I know you are a great lover of precision—any craftsman ceases to be a craftsman when he makes mistakes. Just so with rulers. The moment the ruler makes a mistake, he nullifies his status as a ruler.
341 But so long as he is a proper ruler he never makes mistakes and always decrees what is in his own interest, and his subjects are always required to obey. Thus we return to what I said at the outset: justice is the interest of the stronger.

My dear Thrasymachus, do you really think me a quibbler?

Of course I do.

And do you imagine that I design my questions in order to trick you and sabotage your arguments?

It's not a question of imagination. I know very well that's what you
b do. But your tactics will fail. Whether you choose open debate or resort to cunning, you won't get the better of me.

I wouldn't dream of trying. But let us try to put misunderstandings behind us. Tell me, when we speak of the ruler, should we now understand the term in what you called its customary, or loose, sense? Or should we define the ruler more precisely in the way you advocated a moment ago?

I speak of a ruler in the most precise sense. Now go ahead and
c quibble and set out your snares. I am not afraid of you for the simple reason that you are no match for me.

But of course. Do you think I should be so mad as to imagine I could outwit a Thrasymachus? I might as well try to trim a lion's beard.

You tried it just now, but you botched it.

Let us leave off this exchange of compliments. Tell me, is the doctor, in your strict sense of the word, one whose first business is to make money? Or is it to heal the sick?

The doctor is a healer of the sick.

In the same strict sense, what of the ship's captain? Is he an ordinary sailor or is he commander of the crew?

He commands the crew.   d

Then his mere presence on board does not define his status. He is called captain not because he sails but because of his skill in commanding the crew.

True.

Therefore, specific professions or arts seek to discover something useful for other men.

Yes.

Yet is it not also true that the general purpose of every profession or art is to achieve its own perfection?

What do you mean?   e

Let me illustrate. Suppose you ask me whether the body is self-sufficient or whether it has needs that must be met from outside itself. I would certainly answer that it cannot be sufficient to itself because it is not always healthy; it sometimes suffers from infirmities. It follows that the body has interests or needs to which the art or profession of medicine ministers. Attending to the needs of the diseased body is, in fact, the origin and purpose of medicine, is it not?

It is.

Now consider the art of medicine itself—or any other art or profession. Would the art itself exhibit defects or infirmities analogous to those of the body? Would it be imperfect in the same way the eye would be imperfect if it lacked vision, or the ear if it had not the ability to hear? In every case of physical disability an art is required that will diagnose the defect and prescribe a remedy. Do medicine and the other arts and professions also require external prescriptions and remedies? Do the arts, in other words, need supplementary arts to heal their defects and promote their interests? Will these supplementary arts require, in turn, still other arts for the same purpose— and so on indefinitely?

Or are each of the arts autonomous, each one serving and guard-   b
ing its own interests? Or perhaps the arts suffer no defects at all. Then there is no necessity for self-treatment nor for remedies dispensed by others. If this latter formulation is correct, then the arts and professions are free to devote themselves exclusively to a single interest: to serve the subjects of their practice. If they are true to this purpose, seeking no advantage for themselves, their integrity is certain.

In the strictest sense of the word, will you tell me whether that is true?

Yes, it is true.

c Medicine pays no heed to its own interest but only to that of the diseased body?

That's right.

And the horse trainer attends not to himself but to the horse? Is it not then the same with all the arts? They have no needs; they care only for their subjects.

I agree.

Then we must conclude, Thrasymachus, that the arts are superior to their subjects and have authority over them.

Thrasymachus conceded as much, but with great reluctance.

Another conclusion: none of the arts, professions, or sciences serves the interest of the stronger; instead, all promote the advantage of the weaker.

d After much hesitation and inward struggle Thrasymachus also agreed to this.

So the true doctor concerns himself with the patient's interest and not his own. The true doctor is like a ruler whose subject is the human body; he is not a mere money maker. Are we agreed?

Agreed.

And a captain, in the exact sense of the word, is a ruler of sailors.

e He is not himself a sailor.

That has already been granted.

As captain and ruler he will prescribe and provide for the interests of the sailors under his command and not for his own interests.

Thrasymachus resisted but finally conceded this point, too.

So too with government. The governor—or ruler—insofar as he is true to his calling, will never consider what is to his own interest. He will take into account only the interest of his subjects and the requirements connected with the art of governing. These are the sole criteria by which he plans and governs.

343 By now it was clear that Thrasymachus's definition of justice had been stood on its head. But instead of replying, Thrasymachus asked whether I had a nurse.

Why ask such a question? You owe an answer to a question of mine.

Because your nurse evidently neglects to wipe your nose and leaves you sniveling. What's more, she leaves you ignorant of the difference between shepherd and sheep.

Why do you say that?

b Because you fancy that the shepherd or cowherd has the interests of his charges at heart, grooming and fattening them for their own sakes and not to serve the master's profit or his own. You carry this illusion into politics with the consequence that you fail to see how rulers really behave. The actual ruler or governor thinks of his subjects as sheep, all right, but his chief occupation, day and night, is how he can best fleece them to his own benefit. You have strayed so far from reality that you cannot even understand that what is just is simply something that is good for someone else. He who behaves justly does not benefit himself. It follows that a just subject properly serves the interests of the ruler but does so to his own injury. The dynamics of justice, then, consistently operate to advantage the ruler but never the subjects. The result is that injustice lords it over those who are truly simple and truly just. Because the unjust ruler is stronger, his subjects serve his interests and his happiness at the expense of their own.

The just man is always a loser, my naïve Socrates. He always loses out to the unjust. Consider private business. If a just man takes an unjust man for a partner and the partnership is later dissolved, it is invariably the unjust man who walks away with the lion's share of the assets. Consider their dealings with government. When taxes fall due, the just man will pay more and the unjust less on the same amount of property. Or, if the government is letting out contracts or disbursing money for some other purpose, those who are unjust will get it all, and the just will get nothing.

The just man in public office will reap no rewards. In the first place, as he conscientiously attends to the affairs of state, he must necessarily have little time left to attend to his own affairs. His principles forbid him to embezzle on his own account. They will also prevent him from handing out unlawful favors from the public treasury to others. In consequence, he will earn the enmity of his disappointed friends and acquaintances.

The unjust man is in exactly the opposite situation. I mean the same man as the one I spoke of before, the man of injustice who exploits others on a grand scale. I speak, namely, of the tyrant and of tyranny, the highest form of injustice. If you want to see how unjust acts benefit the tyrant, watch how he makes his crimes pay off. Watch how his own happiness and prosperity impoverish his subjects. Watch how he persecutes those who reject injustice and continue to act justly.

Force and fraud are the tyrant's chosen instruments. He uses them to deprive others of their property, not little by little but in wholesale lots. He makes no nice distinctions among his victims; private citizens, the public treasury, and sacred orders are all fair game.

Any one of these acts perpetrated by a private individual would be condemned and punished. The guilty one would be branded a thief, swindler, housebreaker, cheat, or robber of temples. But if a man not only steals from his fellows but also uses the powers of government to enslave them, one hears no such unfriendly epithets. All the world applauds every instance of triumphant injustice; all the world calls the unjust ruler happy and blessed.

The reason for this is that people censure injustice only because they fear to be its victims and not because they have scruples about being unjust themselves. So it is, Socrates, that injustice, when practiced on a large enough scale, is stronger and freer and more successful than justice. What I said at the outset, then, remains true. Justice is whatever serves the interest of the stronger; injustice, on the other hand, is whatever serves the personal advantage of any man.

Like a bath attendant pouring buckets of water on our heads, Thrasymachus had nearly drowned us with his oratory. Now he wanted to leave. But we all demanded that he stay and defend his position. I was particularly urgent in my plea that he remain: Thrasymachus, after unloading all those ideas surely you won't run off before ascertaining whether they are true or not. Have you so little concern for the real question before us, the question, that is, how each of us may live the best life?

You think that I don't care?

Evidently not. At least, you seem not to care about us. You don't seem to care whether our ignorance of what you claim to understand will make our lives better or worse. Please, Thrasymachus, share your knowledge with us. There are quite a number of us here. Any benefit you confer will surely be rewarded.

I should add that for my own part I am not convinced by your argument. I do not believe that injustice, even if it operates free of all restraint, is more profitable than justice. I grant that there might be an unjust man who uses force and fraud and gets away without a reckoning. Even so, I remain unconvinced that injustice has the advantage over justice, and there may be others who agree with me. But we may also be wrong; so let us benefit from your wisdom, and show us where we are mistaken.

How should I do that if you are not convinced by what I have just said? What else can I do? Are you asking to be spoon-fed?

God forbid. But I do ask you to be consistent. A while ago you offered an exact definition of the doctor, but you were not nearly so exact when subsequently you defined the shepherd. You said that the shepherd's purpose was to fatten sheep, not to benefit the sheep but to satisfy the banqueter who loves the pleasures of the table. Or else you wanted the shepherd to play the businessman whose aim is to sell the sheep profitably in the market. But shepherding is an art in itself and so requires nothing beyond fidelity to its own rules. Hence the shepherd, properly defined, is concerned with nothing else than the welfare of his charges.

Drawing on these observations I concluded that the same holds true for all kinds of authority, whether public or private. To the e extent that the ruler conforms to the strict definition of his function, he is concerned solely with the good of those he rules.

By the way, Thrasymachus, do you think rulers enjoy their power?

I don't just think so, Socrates; I know they do.

Is it not curious, then, that men holding lesser offices will serve only if they are paid? Apparently they think themselves entitled to due compensation since all benefits accrue to their subjects and none to the rulers. Except, perhaps, if they are imbued with the idea that 346 the very purpose of authority is to serve the subjects and not the rulers.

Now let me ask you a question, my friend. Are not the several arts differentiated by the specific functions each performs? Do say what you really think so that we may make some progress with the argument.

Yes, I agree that function explains their differentiation.

And each art benefits us in a particular way? Medicine restores b our health, navigation secures our safety at sea?

Yes.

And earning a living brings us wages; that is its specific function. Therefore, earning a living ought not to be confused with other functions any more than navigation ought to be confused with medicine simply because the sea captain has improved his health during a voyage. Given your zeal for exactitude, you would certainly not confuse medicine and navigation.

Certainly not.   c

No more can we assert that wage earning is the equivalent of medicine simply because someone stays healthy while working for a living. We must make the same judgment concerning the doctor himself. The fact that he takes fees for healing the sick does not mean that medicine is the same as money-making.

I agree.

And we are also agreed that each art, profession, or skill produces d its own distinctive benefit. At the same time, all who practice these diverse arts also receive a common benefit called wages. Thus all must share a common quality different from the diverse qualities of their specialized skills. That is, they each provide distinctive benefits in their capacity as members of a specific profession, and they all receive wages in their common role of wage earners.

Possibly.

So wages benefit the wage earner's account and do not derive directly from his art. In his professional role the doctor nurtures health; in

his wage-earning role he collects his pay. The same with the archi-
tect who builds a house, and the same with all the others. Each art
performs the functions proper to it and benefits its proper objects.

e   Now, if the person who performs professional services is not paid,
can he be said to benefit from his labors?

Apparently not.

But don't those same services constitute a benefit, whether they
are paid or not?

Clearly they do.

Then, Thrasymachus, we must return to an earlier proposition.
No art, craft, skill, or profession is designed to serve itself or its practitioners. Instead, its proper function is to serve its clients. In the
case of politics this means that governors should serve the governed
and not the other way round. That is, the stronger ought to seek the
advantage of the weaker and not their own.

This is why I said a moment ago, my good Thrasymachus, that
no one wants to hold office without recompense. No one wants to
cope with other people's troubles and try to resolve them without
347   being paid for it. Every officeholder expects pay in accordance with
the principle that the proper governor will never do what is best for
himself but only what is best for his subjects. Thus a man must be
induced to take office by wages in the guise of money, honors, or—
in case he still resists—by threat of a penalty for refusing to serve.

Money and honors as inducements to enter public life I can
understand, said Glaucon. But what do you have in mind when you
propose a penalty as a third kind of inducement?

b   This is the only inducement that will bring the best men into
government. After all, it is common to reproach those who covet
money and honors. Good men take that reproach seriously; hence
they are unwilling to govern in exchange for rewards they disdain.
They do not wish to accept the role of hirelings by contracting to
perform public duties in exchange for money. Nor do they wish to
be thieves, using their official position to pilfer public funds for private purposes. Further, they will not govern for the sake of honors
c   because they do not covet honors. The only way they can be persuaded to hold office is if some compulsion or penalty is imposed if
they refuse to serve.

I suppose considerations like these explain why it is thought
unseemly to seek public office instead of letting the office seek you.
In any case, it should be clear that the most severe penalty a man
can suffer who refuses to govern is to be governed by someone worse
than himself. I think it is the fear of such an eventuality that makes
the better men agree to take office. They do not anticipate either
benefits or enjoyment; rather, they assume political power as a nec-

essary evil, for the reason that they can find neither better men nor equals to govern in their stead.

In a city populated only by good men it is probable that as much d effort would be expended in avoiding public office as men now waste in striving for it. In such a city we could clinch the argument that the truly good ruler does not seek his own advantage but rather the advantage of those he rules. We could also demonstrate that the wise man would prefer to be governed and benefited by someone else rather than be burdened by having to attend to the interests of others.

For this reason alone I would not assent to Thrasymachus's argu- e ment that justice is the interest of the stronger. But let us return to that question later. More important is Thrasymachus's most recent statement that the unjust live better lives than the just. What do you think, Glaucon? Which life would you choose?

I would say that it is better to be just.

But did you hear Thrasymachus enumerating all the good things 348 that come to the unjust man?

Yes, I heard. But I am not convinced.

Should we try to find a way to convince Thrasymachus that he is wrong?

I am eager to do so.

Well, then, shall we counter Thrasymachus with a set speech of our own? He will then contradict us; we, in turn, will rebut him. Then we shall have to count and weigh the merits of the two sides of the argument. Finally, there will be a call for judges to make the b definitive decision for one side or the other. On the other hand, we could continue the pattern of our discussion so far, simply seeking to identify areas of agreement and disagreement. Then we could be our own advocates and judges. How do you wish to proceed, Glaucon?

Let us stay with the pattern you have been following.

Very well. Thrasymachus, can we return to the beginning of the argument? Your initial position was that perfect injustice is more profitable than perfect justice.

That's right. And I have already told you my reasons for taking c that position.

Then may I ask this question about justice and unjustice? Would you consider one of them to be a virtue and the other a vice?

Of course.

You would call justice virtue and injustice vice?

How charmingly you play the innocent. Would it be reasonable for me to agree when I have just said that injustice is profitable and justice is not?

But what do you say, then?

The opposite.

What? Do you really intend to equate justice to vice?

d   No. I would call justice a naïve simplicity or goodness of heart.

Then injustice is badness of heart?

No. Injustice is goodness of judgment: I should call it good policy.

It follows, I suppose, that you consider unjust men to be wise and good.

Yes, if they are capable of pushing injustice to its logical limits by conquering tribes and cities and imposing their wills on those they conquer and govern. If you imagine that I am talking about ordinary purse snatchers, I am ready to assert that even the lowest form of thievery is profitable if the thief is not caught. But I am not concerned with such petty activities; they do not compare with the kind of injustice on the grand scale to which I refer.

e   I understand, Thrasymachus. But still I am astonished that you would actually associate injustice with virtue and wisdom and consign justice to the realm of vice and folly.

That is my position.

It is a bold position, and it is not so easy to refute. Were you to assert, as many do, that injustice is profitable but at the same time morally odious, we could then argue the matter along more conven-

349 tional lines. But having equated injustice to wisdom and virtue and justice to their opposites, you will want to say that unjust behavior is honorable and a source of strength.

Spoken like a prophet.

Well, as long as I am convinced that you are speaking your mind, I am bound to pursue the argument. And it does seem to me, Thrasymachus, that now you are not mocking us but saying what you really think.

Why don't you just address yourself to my argument? What difference does it make whether or not I believe what I say?

b   It makes no difference. But I have another question for you. Would a just man ever seek to do wrong to other just men?

Of course not. Otherwise he would not be the simpleton he is.

Do you think he would ever overreach himself to the point where he might violate standards of just behavior?

No.

But how about his behavior toward unjust men? Would he consider it proper to get the better of one who is unjust?

Certainly he would, but he wouldn't have the nerve to do it.

c   That is not my question. What I am asking is whether the just man will try to get the better of another just man or only of an unjust man.

Only of the unjust man.

And what of the unjust man? Does he seek to get the better of the just man? Will he flout the rules of justice?

Of course. He will ignore all standards of justice; he is out to get the better of everyone.

Then the unjust man is one who will wrong both the just and the unjust. His chief object will be to get everything for himself.

Right.

Would you accept this formulation: the just man will not try to take advantage of his counterpart but only of his opposite; the unjust man, however, is ready to injure both.

Agreed.   d

We must now recall your earlier position: the unjust man is intelligent and good, and the just man is neither.

Well put.

Hence the unjust man may be numbered among the wise and good, and the just man among their opposites.

Obviously. Each must be likened to those who are like him.

Good. Then one can describe a man in terms of what he resembles.

How should it be otherwise?

So be it. Now, Thrasymachus, you know that some men are   e
musicians and others not. In respect to music, which ones would be called knowledgeable?

I presume we would say the musician is knowledgeable and the unmusical man not.

So a man is a good musician insofar as he is intelligent about music and a bad musician if he is not.

Yes.

Could one apply the same measure to the physician and the knowledge of medicine?

Yes.

Now, when a musician tunes his lyre by tightening and loosening the strings, is he trying to outdo other musicians or is he simply trying to meet the requirements for correct tuning?

The latter, Socrates.

But he does wish and expect to do better than the unmusical man?

Necessarily.

And how about the doctor? Are his prescriptions designed to beat   350
the competition from other doctors or simply to meet the standards of proper medical procedures?

The latter.

But he tries to do better than the layman?

Yes.

Let us now consider knowledge and ignorance in general. Would not the man of knowledge necessarily want to adhere to those standards of behavior common to men of knowledge?

He might feel the necessity.

b   What about the ignorant man? Being ignorant, would he not make indiscriminate claims to superiority over the intelligent and unintelligent alike?

No doubt.

But the man of knowledge is wise?

Yes.

And to be wise is to be good?

Yes.

c   Then the good and wise will not try to outdo their peers but only those lacking in goodness and wisdom?

Apparently.

But those who are bad and unwise will try to devise ways of getting the better of all men?

Apparently.

And does not the unjust man of your description, Thrasymachus, seek to use all men to his own advantage?

Those were my words.

While the just man will do the same only to the unjust?

Yes.

Then the necessary conclusion is that just men are like the wise and the good, while the unjust are like the ignorant and the evil.

Apparently.

Add to this our agreement that those things which are like are also virtually indistinguishable.

We made that agreement.

So it finally turns out that the just man is good and wise after all, and the unjust man is bad and ignorant.

d   Thrasymachus did not make these concessions as readily as I have recorded them. On the contrary, his discourse was marked by great reluctance and frequent backsliding. Indeed, as it was a summer day, he was also sweating prodigiously. I then beheld what I had never yet seen: Thrasymachus blushing. In any case, our agreement that justice is virtue and wisdom, and injustice vice and ignorance, permitted me to proceed to another point.

You remember, Thrasymachus, that we also agreed earlier that injustice is a very powerful force.

Yes, I remember. But I want to say with regard to the conclusion you have just now drawn that I continue to disagree with you. I

e   could reply, but you would be sure to accuse me of demagoguery. Now, either you allow me to speak as long as I see fit or, if you insist, continue with your questioning. In the latter case, I shall confine my response to nodding yes or no or muttering something noncommittal, the way one does when listening to old women gossip.

Surely you wouldn't agree to anything against your own convictions?

Anything to please you, since you won't let me speak my mind in any case. What more do you want from me?

Nothing. I shall then continue to ask questions, and you respond as you wish.

Go ahead.

I believe you made a statement earlier in the discussion that injustice is stronger than justice. But the contrary must follow if we hold   351
to our agreement that justice is wisdom and virtue. For this means that injustice is ignorance. Since ignorance is inferior to wisdom, injustice must then be weaker than justice. This point now seems unassailable. But I would like to consider it from another perspective. I presume you would agree that a city or a state can be unjust,   b
that it may try to enslave other cities unjustly and hold them in subjection.

Of course. This is exactly what the best state will do, the state which most nearly achieves complete injustice.

I understand that this has been your position. But I should now like to ask whether the stronger state can wield its power without being just or whether it must combine power with justice.

If your equation of justice with wisdom is true, then the state must   c
combine power with justice. But if my arguments are correct, then the state must combine power with injustice.

Your answers gladden me, Thrasymachus. You are doing much better than merely nodding and muttering.

I am trying to please.

Very kind. Please me once more. Could a city, an army, a gang of bandits or thieves, or, for that matter, any group seeking to realize common purposes succeed if the group members were constantly trying to wrong each other?

No.   d

Would they be more likely to achieve their objectives if their members refrained from being unjust to one another?

Yes.

This is because injustices generate hatred, quarrels, and factions. Only justice can create unity and love. Is that not true?

If you insist. I don't want to contradict you.

How good of you. Tell me more. If injustice invariably implants hatred, whether among groups of free men or slaves, will it not cause them to hate and injure each other, making it impossible for them to cooperate in common enterprises?

e   Yes.

So will it be also with any two individuals. Injustice will make them hate each other and so divide them. They will be enemies to one another and to all just men as well.

Agreed.

The same will hold for a single individual. Injustice will once again manifest its divisive effects and will put a man at odds with himself.

Let it be as you say.

352   Then it becomes apparent that wherever injustice appears—in the city, in the family, or in the individual—it first spawns factions and disunion and then excites enmity among the divided parts. Finally, anything so at odds with itself must become its own enemy as well as the enemy of all who are just.

Yes.

And the gods are just?

b   Have it your way.

Then the gods will count the unjust man their enemy and the just man their friend.

You are evidently enjoying your own argument. I won't contradict you because I don't want to offend your partisan audience.

Continue to answer as you have been doing, and you will be offering us real entertainment. So far we have shown that just men are both wiser and more effective in action. Unjust men, on the other hand, are incapable of any coherent or cooperative action. If we

c   observe, nevertheless that unjust men sometimes cooperate successfully in some joint endeavor, our powers of observation are at fault. If such men had been completely unjust, nothing would have prevented them from wronging each other. So there must have been some element of justice in each which prevented them from treating one another the way they treated their victims. It is this element of justice which must have brought them that degree of success they were able to achieve. They must have been only half-corrupted when they initiated their misdeeds, since utter villains are completely unjust

d   and would therefore be totally incapable of effective joint action.

This is what I understand to be the truth, Thrasymachus, and not what you have asserted. But now we come to the question we postponed earlier: whether the just have a better and happier life than the unjust. From what we have said up to this point I think the answer is already clear that they do. Still, it bears closer examination, for we are considering no ordinary matter. We are, in fact, inquiring into the right rules for the conduct of life.

Inquire away.

Tell me, then—does a horse have a specific function?

Yes.   e

And would you define the function as something only a horse can do or, at least, as something a horse does best?

I don't understand.

Look at it this way. Do we see only with our eyes and hear only with our ears?

Yes.

So that we can properly say that seeing and hearing are the respective specific functions of the eyes and the ears?

Clearly.

Here is another illustration which may help to clarify my point.   353
You could use a chisel, a dagger, or a carving knife to trim vines, but would you not do the best job if you used a pruning hook made to perform that specific function?

Yes, the illustration is apt.

Then the specific function of anything is that which it alone can do or which it can do better than anything else.

I understand you now. You have explained the meaning of specific functions to my satisfaction.   b

Can we then agree that everything performing a function must be measured by the excellence or deficiencies of its performance? Can we not say that the eye will perform either well or deficiently?

Yes.

Is not the same true for the ear and other things?

Yes.

Then we may generalize to say that all things have a function which is measured in terms of the excellence or defectiveness of its performance.

Very well.

Can the eyes perform properly if they are defective?   c

How could they if they are blind and cannot see?

Sight, in other words, is the proper excellence of the eyes. But let us defer that point. Here I would like to ask whether you agree with the proposition that things function adequately because of the excellence of their own qualities or inadequately because these qualities are defective.

I agree.

And our agreement would apply to eyes, ears, and all other things?

Yes.   d

Well, then, has not the soul a specific function which cannot be performed by anything else, a function which would include such things as reasoning, willing, and governing? Are these not functions specific to the soul? Could they ever be performed by something other than the soul?

No.

Does the soul not govern the conduct of life?

Certainly.

And the soul is to be measured in terms of its excellence and defects?

Yes.

If the soul lacks excellence, it cannot perform well?

That follows.

Then a person with a bad soul will govern his life badly. The person with a good soul will govern his life well.

That follows.

Do you recall our agreement that justice is the peculiar excellence or virtue of the soul and injustice its defect?

e   Yes.

Can we now agree that the just will live well but that it will go ill with the unjust?

Your argument makes it appear so.

Can we go further? He who lives well is happy, and he who lives ill is not?

Yes.

Hence the just man is happy and the unjust man miserable.

So be it.

354   And happiness pays well, but misery pays poorly.

Yes.

At last, then, my worthy Thrasymachus, we have discovered that injustice can never be more profitable than justice.

Then consider your entertainment complete, Socrates, on this feast day of Bendis.

You are the one who provided the feast, Thrasymachus, after you ceased to be angry with me and began to speak gently. Nevertheless—and through no fault of yours—I have not dined well. It strikes

b   me that I have been like a glutton, snatching at one dish after another and eating in such haste that I had no time to savor the food. I am afraid this is the way I have gone about our inquiry. We had not finished defining justice before I was off to examine whether it was the same as wisdom and virtue or ignorance and vice. Then I was unable to resist pursuing another line of inquiry into the comparative profitability of justice and injustice. So I must confess that the outcome of the discussion is that I know nothing. After all, if justice still remains undefined, I can hardly know whether it is in fact a virtue or a vice. Nor can I know whether the just man is in fact happy or miserable.

Book II

All this having been said, I thought the discussion was at an end. But on the contrary, the end turned out to be the beginning. With his usual energy, Glaucon objected to Thrasymachus's withdrawal from the contest. He went on to ask: Socrates, do you really want to convince us that justice is preferable to injustice, or will you be content if we only seem to be persuaded?

I would really like to persuade you.

Well, so far you haven't succeeded. Consider this question. Is there some kind of good we ought to strive for, not because we expect it to bring about profitable results but simply because we value the good for its own sake? Joy might be an example, or those sorts of harmless pleasures that leave nothing behind except the memory of enjoyment.

These are good pleasures to savor.

And can we agree that there is a second and different kind of good, valuable not only for its own sake but also for the desirable effects it produces? I think of sight, of knowledge, of health.

Of course.

How about a third kind of good? Gymnastic, medicine, the art of making money—all these yield benefits but are tiresome in the doing. Hence we think of them not as goods in themselves but value them only for their effects.

Yes, this is certainly another kind of good. But what is your point?

I want to know in which of these three categories or classes of goods you locate justice.

Justice belongs in the most valuable category. It is the good that the happy man loves both for its own sake and for the effects it produces.

But the multitude does not think so. Most people consider the practice of justice a burdensome affair. They think it a task to be avoided, if possible, and performed only if necessary to maintain one's reputation for propriety—and to collect whatever rewards such a reputation may be worth.

You are right. I know that is the common opinion; it is the opinion just now expressed by Thrasymachus when he scorned justice and praised injustice. But I am too stupid to be convinced of it, Glaucon.

b   Well, then, Socrates, listen to what I have to say on the subject, too. I think Thrasymachus conceded the argument before he should have. He reminded me of a snake, too soon charmed by the sound of your voice. As for me, neither the nature of justice or injustice is yet clear. I want to consider both of them quite apart from their effects or the rewards they might bring. What are they in themselves? What power do they exert within the confines of a man's soul?

c   To begin with, Socrates, I should like to revive Thrasymachus's argument. So I will speak first of all of the common view of the nature and origin of justice. Second, I shall argue that all who practice justice do so against their own will. This is so because they regard just behavior as something necessary but not as something good. Third, I shall stress that the rationale for such attitudes is rooted in the common view that the life of the unjust man is far better and happier than the life of the just man.

I do not believe these things myself, Socrates. But I admit that I become perplexed when I listen to the arguments of Thrasymachus and all those who believe as he does. My uncertainty is all the greater d   when I reflect that I have never yet heard an unambiguous proof that justice is always superior to injustice.

What I desire most, Socrates, is to hear someone praise justice for its own sake, and you are the one most likely to do so. Thus my purpose in praising the unjust life is to provoke a response from you that will effectively repudiate injustice and vindicate justice. Does my proposal please you?

What else could please me more? This is the one subject, more than any other, that a man of sensibility will choose to discuss—and delight in returning to the discussion again and again.

e   Excellent. I shall begin by discussing the nature of justice and its origin. Most men say that to be unjust is good but to suffer injustice is bad. To this opinion they add another: the measure of evil suffered by one who is wronged is generally greater than the good enjoyed by one who does wrong. Now, once they have learned what it is to 359   wrong others—and also what it is to be wronged—men tend to arrive at this conclusion: justice is unattainable and injustice unavoidable.

Those so lacking in strength that they can neither inflict injustice nor defend themselves against it find it profitable to draw up a compact with one another. The purpose of the compact is to bind them all neither to suffer injustice nor to commit it. From there they proceed to promulgate further contracts and covenants. To all of these they attach the name of justice; indeed, they assert that the true origin and essence of justice is located in their own legislation.

Their lawmaking is clearly a compromise, Socrates. The compromise is between what they say is best of all—to do wrong without incurring punishment—and what is worst of all—to suffer wrong with no possibility of revenge. Hence they conceive of justice not as   b something good in itself but simply as a midway point between best and worst. Further, they assert that justice is praised only by those too weak to do injustice and that anyone who is a real man with power to do as he likes would never agree to refrain from doing injustice in order not to suffer it. He would be mad to make any such agreement.

As you very well know, Socrates, this is the orthodox account of the nature and origin of justice. Its corollary is that when people practice justice, they do so against their own wills. Only those are just who lack the power to be unjust. Let us test this proposition by altering the power distribution and assigning the just and the unjust equal power to do what they please. We shall then discover that the   c just man and the unjust man will follow precisely the same path. They will both do what all nature decrees to be good. They will pursue their own interests. Only if constrained by law will they be confined to the path of justice.

The test I propose makes the assumption that both the just and the unjust enjoy the peculiar liberty said to have been granted to Gyges, ancestor of Croesus the Lydian. Tradition has it that Gyges   d was a shepherd in the service of the king of Lydia. While he was feeding his flock one day, there was a great storm, after which an earthquake opened a chasm directly in front of the place where Gyges stood with his flock. Marveling at the sight, Gyges descended into the chasm. There he beheld many wonders, among them a hollow bronze horse fitted with doors. When he opened one of the doors and looked within, he saw the corpse of a huge man, nude except for a gold ring on his finger. Gyges removed the ring and made his way up and out of the chasm.

Now when the shepherds next met to prepare their customary   e monthly report to the king concerning their flocks, Gyges attended wearing the ring. While there, he chanced to turn the stone of the ring on his finger inward, toward the palm of his hand. Instantly he became invisible to all eyes. He was amazed to hear those who sat   360 near him speak of him as if he were absent. Fumbling with the ring again, he turned the stone outward, away from the palm, and became visible once more. Now he began to experiment, turning the ring this way and that and always with the same results—turning it inward he became invisible, turning it outward he became visible again.

Once he discovered the ring's power, he hastily managed to have himself appointed one of the messengers to the king's court. On arrival he seduced the queen and then, with her help, murdered the king. Thus it was that he became king of Lydia.

Supposing now there were two such rings, the just man wearing one and the unjust man the other. No man is so unyielding that he would remain obedient to justice and keep his hands off what does not belong to him if he could steal with impunity in the very midst of the public market itself. The same if he could enter into houses and lie with whom he chose, or if he could slay—or release from bondage—whom he would, behaving toward other men in these and all other things as if he were the equal of a god. The just man would act no differently from the unjust; both would pursue the same course.

One might argue that here is the great proof that no one is willingly just; men will be just only if constrained. This is because every man believes that justice is really not to his interest. If he has the power to do wrong, he will do wrong, for every man believes in his heart that injustice will profit him far more than justice.

These are the settled convictions of all those who choose to adopt them. They hold that anyone who acquires extraordinary power and then refuses to do wrong and plunder others is truly to be pitied (and a great fool as well). Publicly, however, they praise the fool's example, convinced that they must deny what they really think so that they will not encourage unjust acts against themselves. I think I have spoken sufficiently to this point.

Next, if we are to choose between the lives of justice and injustice, we must be precise in distinguishing the one from the other. Otherwise we cannot choose rightly. We can make the distinction only by treating the two as strictly separate. We must assume the just man to be entirely just and the unjust man entirely unjust. Each must possess all the qualities appropriate to his character and role as a just— or unjust—man.

First, the unjust man: his behavior must be like that of a clever craftsman. Like any good physician or pilot, he must practice his art with an intuitive sense for what is possible and what is impossible, holding fast to the first and shunning the latter. When he makes a mistake, he must be able to recover and correct himself. This means that the unjust man must pursue injustice in the proper way. If he is altogether unjust, he must possess an unerring capacity to escape detection; otherwise, if he fails and is caught, he shows himself to be a mere bungler. After all, the highest form of injustice is to appear just without being so.

Perfect injustice denotes the perfectly unjust man. Nothing belonging to injustice must be withheld from him. He must be allowed to enjoy the greatest reputation for justice all the while he is com-

mitting the greatest wrongs. If by mistake any of his misdeeds should   b
become known, he must be endowed with ample powers of persuasion so that he can cover them up. Should he need to use force, let
him do so with boldness and manly strength—and by mobilizing
friends and money.

Having constructed a model of the unjust man, we must now do
the same for the just man. He will be noble and pure—in Aeschylus's words, one who wants to be good rather than to seem good.
Accordingly, he must be deprived of the seeming. Should he retain
the appearance of being just, he would also enjoy an esteem that   c
brings with it honors and gifts. In that case we could not know whether
he serves justice for its own sake or because he covets the honors and
gifts. He must therefore be stripped of everything but justice; his
situation must be the opposite of his unjust counterpart. Though the
best of men, he must be thought the worst. Then let him be put to
the test to see whether he will continue resolute in the service of
justice, even though all the while he must suffer the opprobrium of
an evil reputation. Let him so persevere—just in actuality but unjust   d
in reputation—until death itself.

Here we have charted the full course for both the unjust and the
just man and should be in a better position to judge which of the
two is happier.

My compliments, Glaucon. You have given your characters high
finish and form. One might think you were modeling a pair of sculp-
tures intended to vie for first honors at the exhibition.

I have spoken of them to the best of my ability. And if I have also
spoken truly, I think it should be an easy matter to anticipate and
describe what life holds in store for each. If I now use language in   e
my description that is sometimes rude—and even brutal—please
remember, Socrates, that my words should be attributed not to me
but to those who value injustice more than justice.

They will tell you that every man who is just, but whose reputation stamps him as unjust, will learn what it is to feel the lash, the
rack, the chains, and the branding iron burning out his eyes. And   362
after suffering all the other agonies he will be impaled on spikes,
there finally to learn his lesson that it is better to seem just than to
be so.

They will say that those words of Aeschylus apply far better to the
unjust man. He who wills to be unjust but not to seem so is the real
man of truth. He is the one who does not allow himself to be governed by opinion; instead he orders his affairs in accord with the way
life really is:

> He plows deep the furrows of his intellect
> and brings home prudence as his harvest.   b

His reputation for justice will bring him high office. He can enter into marriage with whom he will and arrange the same for his children when their time comes. He will do business or not at his option. His contracts and partnerships will always be profitable for he does not hesitate to be unjust. When he becomes involved in law suits or other kinds of disputes, he bests all who stand against him. In gaining the decision in each contest he enters he also augments his wealth. Hence he is increasingly capable of benefiting friends and injuring

c enemies. He is able to make sacrifices and other gifts to the gods in such a way as will display his magnificence. Consequently, he pays court both to the men he favors and to the gods far more effectively than just men can; he may therefore reasonably expect that heaven will bestow its favors on him rather than on the just.

So do both men and gods favor the unjust man over the just. This is what the multitude believes.

d   I was about to respond to Glaucon when his brother, Adeimantus, intervened with a question. Surely, Socrates, you don't believe the statement of the case is now complete?

What else would you add?

The quintessential point. It has not yet even been mentioned.

Well, this is a good moment to heed the proverb that bids a brother help a brother. So if Glaucon has omitted any kind of evidence bearing on the case, come to his assistance. For my part, however, Glaucon has already said quite enough to destroy all my defenses and leave me powerless to respond on behalf of justice.

e   That's just more of your nonsense, Socrates. But do listen to this further point. Unless we go on to examine the reasoning and the language of the others—I mean those who extol justice and condemn injustice—Glaucon's case remains incomplete, at least in my

363 view. You know well how fathers lecture their sons (and guardians their charges) about a man's obligation and also how they use words that compliment not justice but the good repute that comes with it. They calculate that a reputation for justice will gain a man public office and fortunate alliances and all the good things that Glaucon already said would accrue to the unjust man who wears the cloak of righteousness. Expanding still further on the value of reputation, they summon up the gods themselves to certify in abundant detail the heavenly blessings in store for the pious.

b   They bring the worthy Hesiod as well as Homer into their testimony. They cite Hesiod's lines where the gods make the very oaks belonging to the just man

> Bear acorns upon their topmost branches
> and honey from beeswarms far below on the midtrunk.
> His sheep are weighted down by their own soft fleece.

Hesiod adds on many similar blessings, and Homer concurs:

> To the good king who governs in fear of the high gods
> and upholds justice and the right the black earth
> yields reward: barley and wheat and trees   c
> laden and weighted with fair fruits.
> His flocks increase, and the teeming seas bring him fish.

Musaeus and his son sing of more tantalizing gifts from the gods to the righteous. With song and story they lead them down into the house of Hades. There they join the chosen ones, lying down on couches and feasting, crowned with garlands and drunk for all time. Indeed, in that place the fairest reward of virtue and the just life is d an eternal drunk.

Other poets spin out the rewards from the gods to greater lengths. They will have it that the fair legacy of the just and faithful shall be handed down to the third and fourth generations. So much for this style in praise of justice. But the same poets sound a different note where the wicked are concerned. These they bury in the mud of Hades; some are also compelled to fetch water in a sieve. Still alive in death, the unjust are suffered to have infamy heaped upon them e and to endure the very same collection of evils Glaucon said would befall those who, though deemed unjust, are truly just. That is all they have to say; such is the way they praise justice and condemn 364 injustice.

But we must proceed still further, Socrates, and observe that both prose and poetry play with still other variations on our theme. All the world declares that justice and right living are honorable and fair but at the same time tedious and unpleasant. Vice and injustice, on the other hand, are easy to learn and offer a profusion of pleasures. Only law and conventional opinion condemn them. For the most part, the argument continues, injustice pays better than justice. All hail the rich and those with other kinds of power and hasten to do them indiscriminate honor in public and private. But the poor and the weak they despise, even though admitting that they are better b men than the mighty.

The most bizarre of all these variations has to do with the relationship between the gods and virtue. The gods are said to visit sorrow and evil on many good men while bestowing happiness on many a scoundrel. Then come the priests with begging cups and itinerant soothsayers to the doors of the rich, talking up the powers they claim to have acquired from the gods and their skills at sacrifice and incantation. They declare that if a man—or any of his ancestors—should have committed a misdeed, it can be atoned for by entirely pleasurable festivals. Or else, if a man have an enemy, whether justly or not, he need pay only a small fee to cause his enemy to suffer injury— c all because these seedy characters claim knowledge of charms and enchantments that will constrain the very gods to do their bidding.

Finally, the poets are brought forward again, this time as witnesses to the allure and ubiquity of vice. Hesiod is recalled once more:

> Of evil there is plenty, easy for a man to find,
> and smooth is the path to its door.
> But the gods have decreed
> that toil, sweat, and a steep and weary road
> shall mark the quest for virtue.

On the other hand, Homer is called upon to testify that men are also able to lead these same gods astray:

> The will of gods can also be divorced from purpose.
> Having transgressed against them, erring men apologize
> with burning incense and libations.
> By prayers and sacrifice and vows of future temperance
> they would annul the heavenly wrath.

Next the sorcerers bring out a whole bushel of books by Musaeus and Orpheus, whom they call children of the moon and the Muses. These they use in their rituals, whose purpose is to persuade not only private individuals but whole societies that guilty deeds can be expiated and injustices forgiven. For the living, these objectives can be achieved by following a prescribed set of sacrifices interspersed with pleasant games. Nor do they neglect the dead. There are special rites for the defunct which they call functions, or mysteries. These promise us deliverance from the evils of the other world; if we disregard these liturgies, however, we shall suffer terrible things.

Now, Socrates, what are the young to think when they hear all this about virtue and vice among men and gods? In particular, what will be the effect on the quick-witted ones who are swift to sample a profusion of opinions and then to draw conclusions from the entire lot about the kind of life they ought to lead? Will they not ask with Pindar,

> Which way to climb a loftier tower
> where all my life shall be safe?
> By justice, or by unjust deceits?

They will say to be just without also seeming so can bring no profit; instead there is only pain and loss. But if a man chooses injustice and at the same time fabricates a contrary reputation for justice, he can expect to live like a god.

After all, the philosophers have proved that appearance is mightier than reality and hence the true lord of happiness. To appearance,

then, one must turn one's efforts without stint. A man must deceive.
He must don costumes and contrive stage effects that impart the
illusion of virtue even as he heeds the sage Archilochus and trails
behind him the wily and subtle fox.[1] If another objects that it is not
always easy to conceal wickedness, the answer can only be that noth-   d
ing great is easy. In any case, if one wants happiness, this is the way
to go. One can cover one's tracks by organizing political clubs and
secret brotherhoods and by relying on the professors of rhetoric who
teach the art of persuading courts and assemblies. And so, partly by
persuasion and partly by force, one can make illicit gains and yet go
unpunished.

It may be objected that neither force nor deception can prevail
against the gods. But what if there are no gods? Or what if they do
not concern themselves with the affairs of men? In either case, why
should we attempt to conceal our deeds from them? On the other
hand, even if the gods do exist and pay heed to our doings, we know   e
their ways only from old stories about them and from the poets who
trace their lineages. And these very people assure us that the gods
can be swayed and made to change their minds by sacrifices, vows,
and gifts.

Now we may believe in gods that will both punish and connive at
human misbehavior. Or we may believe that they have no power to
do either one or the other. But we cannot consistently hold both
beliefs at the same time. If the poets are right, we had best choose
injustice and then sacrifice to the gods some of the profits gained by
our wrongdoing. It may be true that if we are just we shall escape
heaven's vengeance, but we shall also be deprived of the fruits of   366
injustice. Choosing injustice, on the other hand, its fruits will be
ours, and then, in the old sequence of pride, transgression, and fer-
vent prayers for forgiveness, we shall escape once more by persuading the gods to set us free.

The final objection will be that there is a world awaiting us below
where we or even our children's children will suffer for our misdeeds
here on earth. And then the final rejoinder of the artful: But my dear
fellow, in the hands of the gods and in the rites for the dead there
are great powers of amnesty. This is what we hear from the greatest
cities, and the sons of gods, who became our prophets and poets,   b
assure us it is true.

What further argument could persuade us to prefer justice to the
most base injustice? Let us choose the latter, but when in the public
eye let us counterfeit the former. Then shall we prosper mightily
with both men and gods, in life and death, as both the multitude

---

1. Archilochus seems to have established the fox as the animal of cleverness and cunning.

c   and highest authorities have testified. Socrates, after all these consid-
    erations could any man who commands resources of mind, body,
    money, or family agree to honor justice? Would he not rather laugh
    whenever he hears justice praised?

        If there is a convincing rebuttal to these arguments, it could come
    only from a man with enough trust in the superiority of justice to be
    gentle with the unjust. He will not be angry, for he knows that a
    man can lead a just life only if the divine element in human nature
d   has consecrated him to a hatred of injustice. Or else, a person is won
    to justice through the attainment of wisdom. No others are willingly
    just. Knowing these things, he also knows that many condemn injus-
    tice only because they are cowards or too old or too weak to be unjust
    and that whenever any of these come to power they promptly resort
    to injustice themselves, so far as they are able.

        Socrates, there is a single cause that impels the flow of all these
    words from me and from my brother, Glaucon. We are astonished
    at all your self-professed advocates of justice—from the heroes of
e   ancient times and their surviving discourses down to the present day.
    None has ever awarded blame to injustice or praise to justice except
    in terms of the gifts, honors, or reputation each of them attracts.
    Both verse and prose have failed to convey their intrinsic qualities.
    They do not tell us how justice and injustice do their work within
    the human soul, out of the sight of both gods and men. No one has
    ever provided proof that the one is the greatest of goods and the other
367 the greatest of evils. Why did all of you not do this from the begin-
    ning and convince us from our youth up? Had you done so, we
    would not now be guarding against one another's injustices. Instead,
    each would first of all guard himself; each would banish injustice
    from his own conduct, so that his own soul might be safeguarded
    from the taint of evil.

        Thrasymachus and perhaps others might well have said all this in
    debating justice and injustice (and, in my opinion, grossly reversing
    their roles). But I have no reason to hide anything from you, Socra-
    tes. My only purpose in setting forth this argument with some
    vehemence and with all the intellectual force I could muster is that
b   I want to hear you refute me. Do not only teach us to understand
    the superiority of justice to injustice, but show us the effect each has
    on the well-being of the soul, and why the one effect is good and the
    other evil.

        But do also heed what Glaucon said and leave out all references
    to reputation. For unless you steal from both justice and injustice
    the reputation proper to each—and make each masquerade in the
    reputation contrary to its true nature—we shall say that you are not
    praising the reality of justice but are only dealing with appearances

and that you are preoccupied with censuring what injustice is reputed to be and not with what it really is. We shall think that you are actually urging us to be both unjust and hypocritical. In that case there would be nothing to distinguish your arguments from Thrasy- c machus's opinion that to be just is to serve another's good and to be unjust serves one's own—that justice is the interest of the stronger and so must harm the interest of the weaker.

You have said that justice belongs to that highest class of good things which not only produce good effects but which are, above all, valuable in themselves. Some of these are sight, hearing, health, and d intelligence, things whose value is innate and not a matter of opinion. So tell us how justice benefits a man intrinsically, and in the same way how injustice harms him. Let others praise or blame the respective rewards and reputations. I don't say I wouldn't listen to others debate these issues, including the matter of reputation. But you have spent all your life studying the question, and I expect better fare from you, Socrates, unless you tell me in your own words that you are unable to offer it. I repeat, then, disregard outward appear- e ances, and prove to us that justice is better than injustice by showing us the effects each has on a man's soul and how and why each effect can properly be called either good or evil.

I have always admired the brilliance of Glaucon and Adeimantus, but on this occasion their words gave me special pleasure. So I said to them: Sons of a noble father—Glaucon's friend put it well in the 368 elegy he wrote to honor you both for your heroic deeds in the battle of Megara:

> Sons of Ariston, you honor the godlike
> heritage of a famous father.

There must indeed be some divine spark at work in your natures that you should be able to make such formidable arguments on behalf of injustice and yet resist being convinced by your own reasoning. And I believe that you are really not convinced. I infer this, however, from my knowledge of your characters; if I had to deal with your b words alone, I would be suspicious of you.

But the greater my trust in you, the more difficult becomes my task. What can I say when I doubt my ability to offer you satisfactory answers to your questions? And my doubt is well founded, for you have refused to accept the arguments I used against Thrasymachus and which I thought had amply proved the superiority of justice to injustice. Yet I cannot remain silent; that would be a shameful course c to take when justice is under attack. As long as there is voice and breath in me, then, I think it is best to give to justice all the help that I can offer.

Glaucon and the others urged me to come to the rescue. They were unwilling to have the argument cut short and insisted on completing the investigation into justice and injustice, including an assessment of the advantages and disadvantages of each.

d   Well, I think all of you are pressing for an inquiry that is by no means an easy undertaking. We must keep our wits about us. And since our wits are not always sharp, we should do well to adopt a method of examination similar to that used when people without very keen vision are required to read small letters from a distance. This method would draw their attention to the same letters writ large, and I think they would count it a godsend if they could read the larger letters first then check the smaller letters against them to see if they correspond.

Agreed, said Adeimantus, but what kind of analogy are you trying
e   to draw with justice?

I will tell you. We sometimes speak, do we not, of a just man and also of a just city?

Of course.

And the city is larger than the man?

Yes.

Perhaps, then, there would be more of justice in the city; it might also be easier to observe it there. So if it is agreeable to you, let us
369   first inquire into the nature of justice and injustice in the city, and only after that in the individual. In this way we could begin with the larger and then return to the smaller, making comparisons between the two.

A good suggestion.

If we begin our inquiry by examining the beginning of a city, would that not aid us also in identifying the origins of justice and injustice?

Perhaps it would.

So that when our analysis is complete, we should be in a better position to find what we are seeking?
b   Much better.

Shall we try it, then? But before we do you may want to reconsider. I don't think it will be an easy task.

We have thought about it enough, said Adeimantus. Go ahead. Don't stop now.

Very well. A city—or a state—is a response to human needs. No human being is self-sufficient, and all of us have many wants. Can we discover the origins of the state in any other explanation?

I can imagine no other.
c   Since each person has many wants, many partners and purveyors will be required to furnish them. One person will turn to another to

supply a particular want, and for a different want or need he will seek out still another. Owing to this interchange of services, a multitude of persons will gather and dwell together in what we have come to call the city or the state.

Right.

And so one man trades with another, each assuming he benefits therefrom.

Right.

Come, then, let us construct a city beginning with its origins, keeping in mind that the origin of every real city is human necessity.

That is evident.

Now the first and greatest necessity, on which our very life depends,   d
is food.

Certainly.

Next is a place in which to live; third, clothing and the like.

Yes.

Then we must ask how our city will provide these things. A farmer will be needed, and a builder and a weaver as well. I suppose we should add a shoemaker and still another who can care for the needs of the body.

I agree.

Hence the simplest city or state would count at least four or five people?

Evidently.   e

Then how should they proceed? Should what each produces be made available to all? I mean, should the individual farmer produce food for himself and also for the rest? That would require him to produce, say, four times as much food as he could use himself. Correspondingly, he would invest four times as much labor in the land than if he were supplying only himself. Or should he decline to concern himself with the others? Should he produce food for his own needs alone, devoting only a fourth of his total effort to that   370 kind of work? Then he could allot the other three-fourths of his time to building a house, making clothes, and cobbling shoes. Choosing the latter, he wouldn't have to bother about associating with others; he could supply his own wants and be his own man.

I don't think he should try to do everything, said Adeimantus. He should concentrate on producing food.

I agree that this would probably be the better way. Your words remind me that we are not all alike. There is a diversity of talents among men; consequently, one man is best suited to one particular   b occupation and another to another. What do you think?

I think you are right.

Then a man would do better working at one task rather than many?

I think so.

It should also be obvious that work must be done at the proper time; otherwise it will not be work well done.

True.

The reason, I assume, is that commerce will not wait upon the pleasure of the workman. Instead, he must attend first of all to his work and not consider it a pastime.

Of course.

We can conclude, then, that production in our city will be more abundant and the products more easily produced and of better quality if each does the work nature has equipped him to do, at the appropriate time, and is not required to spend time on other occupations.

A sound conclusion.

Then, Adeimantus, we shall need more than our four original citizens to produce all that will be required. If the farmer's plow and hoe and other implements are to be of good quality, he will not be able to make them himself. The builder will also need equipment and supplies, and so will the shoemaker and the weaver.

True.

With carpenters, smiths, and other craftsmen joining our city, it will begin to grow considerably.

Yes.

Still, it wouldn't be a very big city, even if we added cowherds, shepherds, and other kinds of herdsmen in order to furnish oxen to the farmers for plowing and to the builders for hauling, as well as to supply fleece and hides to the weavers and the shoemakers.

But with so many occupations represented it would not be a very small city either.

True. And we must also note that it would be very difficult to establish a city that would not require imports. That means there must be still another class of citizens who import goods from other cities.

Clearly.

It follows that we must have goods to export. If our traders go forth empty-handed, with nothing to exchange for what they want from other cities, they must come home empty-handed.

Inevitably.

Then domestic production must exceed domestic demand, so that there will be a surplus of quality products to exchange with traders from abroad.

True.

Then we shall need more farmers and artisans. There must also be importers and exporters, those whom we call merchants.

We shall certainly need all these.

And if our trade is by sea, there must be sufficient numbers of   b
skilled sailors.

Yes.

Now, if we return to a consideration of the city itself, we must ask
how the inhabitants will trade the products of their labor. You will
remember that we founded our city in order to facilitate an exchange
of production.

Yes. They will trade by buying and selling.

Then there will be a market place and money as a medium of
exchange.

Surely.

Supposing the farmer or other craftsman brings his produce to   c
market but does not arrive at the same time as those who would buy
from him. Would he sit idly in the market place, wasting time he
could otherwise devote to productive work?

Not at all. There will be men at the market who will offer their
services to remedy the situation by acting as salesmen. In well-ordered
cities they will be those who are generally weakest in physical strength
and therefore of little use for any other kind of work. They will take
up their place in the agora, offering to exchange money for the goods   d
that sellers bring to market and then, in turn, selling to those who
want to buy.

So the need for money in the exchange of goods produces the class
we know as tradesmen. Is this not the name we give to those who
buy and sell in the agora, just as we give the name merchants to
those who perform the same function in trade between cities?

Yes.

Then there is still another class of workers whose intellects are   e
perhaps too weak to count them as full partners in the city but whose
bodily strength enables them to perform hard physical labor. They
sell their strength for a price, and the price is called wages. Hence
they are called wage earners, and they, too, will be part of our city.

True.

Well, Adeimantus, has our city now reached its full growth? Could
we call it complete?

Perhaps.

Where, then, do we find justice and injustice? How do they gain
entry into the city? Are they brought in by one or more of the groups
we have just included among the city's constituents?

I don't know, Socrates. Perhaps they have their origins in the   372
mutual needs of the city's inhabitants.

You may well be right. We must pursue the matter further and
not let up now. First, then, let us consider the way of life of the

people in the city we have just described. Won't they make bread, wine, clothes, shoes, and houses, too? They will work in the summer for the most part without clothes or shoes, but in the winter they will
b want to wear both. They will grind meal from barley and flour from wheat; then they will knead and bake cakes and loaves of fine quality and serve them on mats of reeds or on clean leaves. When they eat, they will recline on beds fashioned of yew or myrtle, they and their children feasting together and drinking their wine. All will wear garlands, singing hymns to the gods and enjoying one another's com-
c pany. But they will take care not to produce too many children in order not to run the risks of poverty or war.

Here Glaucon broke in: But you have provided no relish for the feast.

True, I had forgotten. Relish there must be: salt, of course, and olives and cheese, and there must be boiled roots and herbs of the sort that country people prepare. For a dessert they shall have figs, chick-peas and beans. They will roast myrtle berries and acorns in
d the fire, all the while drinking in moderation. Living this way in peace and health, they all can probably expect to reach old age and pass on the same life to their children.

But this is fare for a city of pigs, Socrates. Would you provide nothing else?

What do you suggest, Glaucon?

The usual things. If the people are not to be uncomfortable, they must be able to recline on couches and dine from tables. They ought
e to have sauces and sweetmeats the way we do.

Now I understand what you mean. We are to consider the origins not simply of a city as such but of a luxurious city. Your suggestion is probably a good one because it is in the luxurious city that we are more likely to discover the roots of justice and injustice.

I believe the city I have just described is well founded and that it will prove to be robust. But if you also want to examine a city in a state of fever, we can do that, too. It is in any case evident that many will not be content with simple fare and simple ways. They will want
373 couches and tables and other types of furniture. Sweets and perfumes, incense, courtesans, and cakes—all must be furnished in quantity and variety. And we must go beyond clothing, shoes, houses, and the other necessities I spoke of at first. There will be painting and embroidery, and gold and ivory will be sought after as ornamentation.

True.
b Then we must further enlarge our city. The well-founded city we started with will no longer be big enough. It must be extended and filled up with superfluities. There will, for example, be hunters in

plenty. There will be crowds of imitators—those who paint and sculpt. Others will make music: there will be poets and their attendants, rhapsodizers, players, dancers, and impresarios. There will be a market for a greater variety of goods, and stylish women will want dressmakers and more servants. Will not tutors be in demand as well, along with wet nurses and dry nurses, barbers and beauticians, cooks and bakers? We shall also require swineherds. There was no need for them in our original city, for there were no pigs there. Now, however, we shall need pigs, as well as other kinds of animals for those who wish to eat them.

You are right.

And this way of life will require many more doctors than were needed before.

That is certain.

Must we also assume that the territory which was at one time sufficient to feed the city will no longer be adequate?

Yes.

So we shall covet some of our neighbor's land in order to expand our pasture and tillage. And if our neighbor has also disregarded the limits set by necessity and has given himself over to the unlimited acquisition of wealth, he will, in turn, covet what belongs to us.

Inevitably.

Then the next step will be war, Glaucon. Or do you see some other outcome?

There can be no other, Socrates.

This is not the time to speak of the good or ill effects of war. What we can say is that we find war originating from the same causes that generate most of the private and public evils in the city.

Agreed.

So our city must be enlarged once more, this time by nothing less than a whole army. We must have it march out to fight our enemies in defense of all the wealth and luxury we have just described.

Does this necessarily follow? Cannot the people defend themselves?

Not if our initial assumptions about constructing the city still hold. Surely you remember our agreement that no man can perform many tasks well?

Yes.

And don't you think that war is an art and fighting a profession?

Yes.

Surely these are matters requiring as much attention as shoemaking.

You are surely right.

And do you recall our reasons for barring the shoemaker from the

other crafts such as farming, weaving, or building? Our objective was
that he should excel at making shoes. Our purpose was the same
with regard to all the other occupations. Each man was assigned an
occupation best suited to his nature and was expected to pursue that
c occupation all his days. He was to be free of all necessity to engage
in other pursuits; at the same time, he was not to let opportunities
slip in the practice of his own occupation so that he would become
a good workman.

Now it is obviously of the first importance that soldiers should do
their work well. But is the art of war so easily learned that a soldier
can at the same time be a farmer, a shoemaker, or active in some
other employment? After all, no one in all the world could become
expert at playing dice or checkers if he played only in his spare time,
instead of practicing from his earliest childhood to the exclusion of
d everything else. Is it credible that a man who takes up a shield or any
other instrument of war for the first time should forthwith become a
competent soldier, ready to fight on line where heavy armor is used
or in other forms of warfare? Neither can any kind of instrument or
tool by itself turn a man into an artist or an athlete; only learning
and practice can do that.

Could we find tools that would teach their own use, we should
have discovered something truly beyond price.

But now we approach the most important business in the city, the
task of the guardians. Accordingly, a guardian would have to spend
e more time than any other in education—in learning and practice.
By the same token, he would have to be freer than any other from
tasks extraneous to his work.

I should think so.

And he would also have to have a nature suited to his calling?

Of course.

Then, if we can manage it, we must evidently accept responsibility for selecting the persons whose natures make them suitable to
become guardians of the city.

Yes, the responsibility is ours.

And that is no light burden. So far as our strength allows, however, we ought to be willing to bear it.

Let us not be shirkers.

If we think of an aptitude for guarding, could we imagine there
would be any difference between the nature of a noble young man
375 and the nature of a young thoroughbred dog?

What is your point?

I mean that each must be keen in perceiving an enemy, swift in
pursuit and capture, and strong if he must then subdue him.

Yes, those are certainly necessary qualities.

And in order to fight well each must be brave as well as strong.

Of course.

And essential to bravery is spirit. Neither a horse, a dog, nor anything else is brave without being high-spirited. Surely you have
observed the indomitable and invincible qualities of spirit, how spirit
imbues every soul with ardor and fearlessness in all kinds of adver- b
sity.

I have.

So now we know what the physical qualities of the guardian's nature
must be.

Yes.

And we also know something of his quality of soul. He must be
spirited.

Yes.

But, Glaucon, will not these high-spirited natures be likely to be
quick-tempered and savage with one another, and with everyone else
as well?

That is undeniably a difficulty.

The difficulty is compounded by the requirement that they be c
fierce to their enemies but gentle to their friends. If they fail in this
respect they will destroy one another before their enemies ever get at
them.

Right.

What next, then? How shall we discover a nature which is at once
gentle and high-spirited if, as it seems, the two qualities contradict
one another? A good guardian must have both; but since that is an d
apparent impossibility, a good guardian must also be an impossibility.

Apparently.

Having arrived at an impasse, I took some time to reconsider.
Then I said: My friend, no wonder we are perplexed. We lost sight
of the subjects of our comparison; if we return to them we shall find
that their natures do in fact combine those opposite qualities we
thought irreconcilable.

How so?

In fact, combinations of opposites are a universal phenomenon,
but it is especially evident in the natures of those we chose to compare. Consider our thoroughbred hounds again: they are gentle to e
their friends and those they recognize but not to strangers.

That is true.

Then that which we thought impossible before proves now to be
perfectly possible. And so the standards we set for the guardian's
nature turn out to be perfectly reasonable.

It seems so.

Does it also seem to you that the guardian should have another quality in addition to that of spirit? Should he not be a philosopher?

What are you trying to tell me?

376   About something which is also to be found in dogs, and a remarkable characteristic it is, too.

What is it?

The fact that a dog will be fierce with a stranger, though the stranger has never harmed him, while he will be gentle with one he knows, whether he has received any kindnesses from him or not. Has that never struck you as quite marvelous?

I must say, I never thought much about it, but it is evident that dogs do behave in this way.

b   Surely this is an admirable trait in the dog's nature. Indeed, it is this trait that makes the dog a philosopher.

A what?

A lover of wisdom. Do you not see that knowing and not knowing are the sole criteria the dog uses to distinguish friend from enemy? Does it not follow that any animal that verifies his likes and dislikes by the test of knowledge and ignorance must be a lover of learning?

Oh, indeed.

And is not the love of learning the same as the love of wisdom which, in turn, is philosophy?

All are identical.

c   Then let us be bold. Having made the case for the dog, let us make the case for man as well: he who is gentle to friends and to those he knows must by nature be a philosopher.

Let us assume so.

Then we may conclude that the true guardian of city or state is one who is strong, swift, high-spirited, and a lover of wisdom.

Without doubt.

So much for the basic character of our guardian. But now comes the question of his upbringing and education. How shall we manage them? Is this question not germane to the principal objective of our inquiry, namely, the origin and role of justice and injustice in the

d   city? Of course, we do not want to be tedious by prolonging the argument beyond a reasonable length. Neither, however, do we want to omit anything essential to our discussion.

The question of education is clearly relevant to our inquiry.

In that case, my dear Adeimantus, we must not give up on it even though it should detain us for some time.

Let us face the question.

I suggest we proceed with our guardians' education in a spirit of leisure. We shall tell tales and recount fables that will serve to educate them.

Good.

And what better education than that which has been for so long e
part of our own heritage? That would mean, I suppose, gymnastic
for the body and music for the soul.

Yes.

And education in music should begin earlier than gymnastic?

It should.

And we understand music to include poetry and stories, do we
not?

Of course.

And these, in turn, are of two kinds. They are either true or false.

Yes.

And our students will have to be educated to understand both,   377
beginning with the false?

I don't understand.

But surely you realize that we always begin by telling children
fables. Of course, the fables contain some elements of truth, but by
and large they are false. And so the child is exposed to fable before
he is old enough to learn gymnastic. That is what I meant by saying
that we must start with music before taking up gymnastic.

I understand now.

Then you will also understand that the most important part of any
work is its beginning. This is especially true for the education of   b
young children. At this tender age they are the most impressionable
and therefore most likely to adopt any and all models set before them.

True.

Then we can hardly afford to let the children listen to just any
tales or fables recounted by just any teachers who happen along. We
surely don't want the children to adopt opinions and beliefs that
might be largely contrary to the kinds of values we deem desirable
for them to have when they become adults.

Certainly not.

Then our program of education must begin with censorship. The
censors will approve the fables and stories they deem good and ban   c
those they consider to be harmful. We shall persuade mothers and
nurses to tell the children stories from the approved list, assuring
them that the training of the soul is far more important than the
training of the body. If we apply this criterion, most of the stories
they tell now will have to be discarded.

Which stories?

Let us consider the greatest stories; that will help us to understand
the less renowned stories as well. The spirit and pattern will be the
same in both. Don't you think so?

It is likely. But I have yet to understand what you mean by the   d
greatest stories.

Those that have come down to us from Hesiod and Homer and

the other poets. Men have heard these stories again and again. We still hear them, and I believe that they are false.

Which stories do you mean? What fault do you find in them?

The most serious fault of all. They tell lies. Still worse, the lies they tell are malevolent.

How can we tell when they are lying?

e Whenever they tell a tale that plays false with the true nature of gods[2] and heroes. Then they are like painters whose portraits bear no resemblance to their models.

Such things are surely blameworthy. But be specific. What do you mean in particular?

First of all, I mean the greatest and most malevolent lies about matters of the greatest concern: what Hesiod said Uranus did to his
378 son Cronos and how Cronos revenged himself on his father. Then there is the tale of Cronos's further doings and how he suffered in his turn at the hands of his own son, Zeus.[3] Even were these stories true, they ought not to be told indiscriminately to young and thoughtless persons. It would be best if they could be buried in silence. If they absolutely must be retold, it should be only to a chosen few under conditions of total secrecy. And this only after performing a sacrifice not of an ordinary pig but of some huge and usually unprocurable victim. That should help cut down the number of listeners.

I must admit that the stories you cite are extremely objectionable.

b Yes, they are, Adeimantus, and they are not to be told in our city. No young man should be given to understand that even in the most outrageous crimes there is nothing outrageous. Nor should the child be taught to believe that in abandoning all restraint in order to punish the misdeeds of his father he will only be following the example of the first and greatest gods.

By Zeus, I agree. These stories are not fit to be told.

Nor can we permit it to be said that gods plot against gods and make war upon each other—which is in any case false—if we want our future guardians to abhor even the thought of quarreling among
c themselves. Still less shall we make up stories of battles among gods or giants; nor shall we permit the various episodes of their wars to be embroidered on our garments. We shall follow the same policy con-

2. Because of the basic polytheism of Greek religion, the word for god occurs commonly in both singular and plural. We have consistently spelled the word without capitalization. A reader should be aware that differing conceptions of divinity underlie the ensuing discussion.
3. Hesiod tells the story of the cosmic battle among members of three successive generations of gods in which the sons overthrew their fathers. First, Cronos castrated his father Uranus. Cronos then swallowed each of his children as Rhea gave birth to them. But Zeus she bore secretly and gave him to others to raise. To Cronos she gave a stone wrapped in swaddling clothes to swallow in place of the baby. When fully grown, Zeus forced Cronos to vomit up the stone and his other offspring, who joined with their liberator Zeus to form the final generation of ruling gods (Hesiod, *Theogony* 154–210 and 453–506).

cerning all the other endless quarrels of gods and heroes with their friends and relatives. If we could get them to believe us, we would tell our future guardians that quarreling is a blasphemy, and we would say that to this day there has never been a quarrel among citizens.

Now this is the sort of thing that the old men and the old women d ought to be telling the children right from the start. As the children grow older, the poets must be compelled to write for them in a similar vein. But the story of Hera put in chains by her own son Hephaestus is inadmissible.[4] So is the story of these two on another occasion when Zeus hurled Hephaestus down from heaven for taking his mother's part when she was being beaten. Once again, the battles of the gods in Homer's verse have no place in our city, whether they purport to be allegories or not. Young minds are not able to discriminate between what is allegorical and what is literal. At that age, whatever their minds absorb is likely to become fixed and unalterable. This may be the most important reason why tales for the e very young should epitomize the fairest thoughts of virtue.

I agree with you there. But were someone to ask where we should find these desirable kinds of stories or themes, how should we reply?

Adeimantus, at this particular moment we are not poets but foun- 379 ders of a state. Now it is proper that founders of states should be cognizant of the norms governing the general content of poetic compositions and the limits beyond which the poets must not go. But it is not the business of founders to compose the fables themselves.

Yes, but that's the whole point. What are the norms that should govern the telling of tales about the gods?

Well, they should be something like this. Whether portrayed in epic, lyric, or tragic form, deity should always be depicted as it truly is.

Agreed.

And is god not always good? Should he not always be represented b as such?

Yes.

Further, no good thing is harmful?

No.

And what is not harmful cannot harm?

Of course not.

And that which does no harm also does no evil?

It does no evil.

Can that which does no evil itself cause evil?

Impossible.

Then good produces good and is the source of happiness.

4. Hera was bound to a throne containing concealed chains given to her by her son Hephaestus.

Yes.

It follows that the good is not the cause of all things but only of good things. It cannot be blamed for those things which are evil.

c   Quite right.

If god is good, then, he cannot be the source of all things, as the multitude is prone to say. In the affairs of men god acts as cause but rarely; of most things he is not the cause. This must be true because in human life good things are few and evils are many. The good we receive we must attribute to god alone; for the causes of evil we must look elsewhere.

I think what you say is true.

d   Then we cannot countenance the follies and errors in the poets' descriptions of the gods. Homer, for instance, says:

> Two urns stand on the palace floor of Zeus
> filled with destinies he allots,
> one containing good things and the other evil.

He who receives from Zeus both kinds

> chances upon evil one day and good the next.

But when Zeus does not blend the lots and instead gives a man unmixed evil,

> Hunger drives him, a wanderer everywhere on earth.

So we must not have it said that

> good and evil are alike bestowed by Zeus.

e

Nor shall we approve if anyone tries to saddle Zeus or Athena[5] with blame for the broken oaths and treaties that were really Pandarus's own doing. Further, it is inadmissible to assert that Zeus and Themis fomented discord and strife among the gods. And our young people must not be permitted to hear these words of Aeschylus:

380

> When a god would utterly destroy a house
> he implants in men the guilty cause.

Such verse the poet uses in writing of the sorrows of Niobe.[6] But if he or any poet must concern himself with these and similar themes when recalling the house of Pelops[7] or the Trojan War, we must

5. During a truce in the Trojan War, Athena, disguised as Laodocus, appeared to Pandarus, a Trojan warrior, and persuaded him to shoot an arrow at Menelaus—an action that broke the truce and re-ignited the war (*Iliad* Book 4.86–103).
6. Niobe had boasted that she, with her twelve children, was the equal of Leto, who had only two divine children, Apollo and Artemis. The two gods killed all twelve of Niobe's children and left her sorrowing for her lost family.
7. The curse on the house of Pelops was applied to successive generations. Myrtilus, Hermes' son, cursed Pelops as he threw him into the sea, and this curse was carried out first upon Pelops's

make him conform to one of two requirements. Either he agrees not to ascribe the woes of men to the acts of gods, or he must provide some such explanation as we now are looking for ourselves. That is, what the gods did was just and righteous punishment, and those   b mortals upon whom it was inflicted benefited from it. But if instead they are portrayed as having been made miserable by the penalty and the gods declared to be the authors of their misery, this is something no poet will be allowed to say. On the other hand, if a poet should say that the wicked are miserable because they need to be punished and that the gods benefit them by providing the penalty, that we shall allow.

The proposition that a god, who is good, should cause evil to anyone is something we must strenuously deny. In a well-governed city it is something neither young nor old will assert or listen to. It must not be said or sung in verse or prose. It is a contradictory,   c profitless, and impious fiction.

I agree. I would vote to make your words law.

Then let this be one of the laws and principles in our city concerning the gods to which our speakers and poets must conform: a god is not the author of all things but only of good things.

Good.

We must consider a further proposition. Do you think that god is a wizard? Do you think he would play insidious games with us,   d assuming one shape at one time and another at another? Would he actually change himself and pass from his own form into many forms? Or would he deceive us by sometimes only feigning such transformations? Or is god simple? In that case, he would be less likely than any other being to depart from his own true form.

I shall need to think about that.

But what do you say to this? If something changes its form, it must either have changed itself or else there must have been some external   e cause.

Necessarily.

And is it not also true that things in their best condition are least likely to be affected or changed by external causes? The healthy human body, for example, is least likely to suffer adverse effects from food or drink or exertion. With plants it is the same. Those in full vigor will be the last to be damaged by high winds or the heat of the sun or any other cause.

sons, Atreus and Thyestes. Thyestes seduced Atreus's wife, but Atreus chopped up several of Thyestes' children and served them to their father in a stew. Atreus's children are Menelaus, whose wife Helen is given to Paris by Aphrodite, the extramarital gift that provoked the Trojan War; and Agamemnon, who is slain by his wife Clytemnestra and her lover Aegisthus (a surviving son of Thyestes). The children of Agamemnon and Clytemnestra are Orestes and Electra, who must arrange the murder of their mother at the command of Apollo.

I agree.

381   Then we can adduce that the soul that is bravest and wisest will be least vulnerable to confusion or disorders originating from external sources?

Yes.

By analogy, I suppose, the same principle applies to men's artifacts—furniture, clothing, and houses. Those that are well made are least liable to be changed by time and other influences.

True.

b   Then we ought to be able to assert a universal truth: everything that is well made in nature or in art is best able to withstand change from without.

Apparently.

Now, could we agree that god, and everything that belongs to him, is in every way perfect?

Of course.

It follows that it would be the least of all possibilities that god should be compelled by external pressures to take on many forms.

Least indeed.

Still, he could will to change and transform himself?

Of course.

Will he change himself into something better and more beautiful or will the change be in the direction of the bad and the ugly?

c   If god changes, it must necessarily be for the worse, for we cannot suppose him to be initially deficient in any way in either goodness or beauty.

Well said, Adeimantus. Now another question: would anyone, whether god or man, willingly make himself worse?

Impossible.

Then it is impossible for a god even to wish to change himself. Intrinsically good and beautiful, a god abides simply and forever in his own form.

I think that is an unavoidable conclusion.

d   Then, my good friend, we must not suffer any poet to tell us that

The gods appear as strangers from far lands
and roam men's cities in many guises.

Let no one fabricate falsehoods about Proteus and Thetis.[8] Neither let anyone in tragic or other kind of verse introduce Hera disguised
e   as a priestess appealing for alms for the life-giving sons of Inachos,

8. Proteus, the old man of the sea, is able to change into a variety of shapes. In the *Odyssey* (Book 4.455–459) he turns into a lion, a snake, a leopard, a boar, flowing water, a tree, and finally back into a man. Thetis turned into a fire, a lion, and several more elusive forms in order to escape the embrace of Peleus (Pindar, *Nemean Ode* IV.62 ff., and Ovid, *Metamorphoses* XI.238–246).

the river of Argos. Many other such lies must also be suppressed. Further, we must not permit mothers under the influence of poets to frighten their children with wrong versions of myths that say certain gods masquerade as strangers from strange lands and haunt the night. Instead, we will make them take heed lest they speak evil of the gods and make cowards of their children.

There can be no sanction for any such behavior.

Well, then, another question. If we are agreed that the gods are unchanging and do not will to change, could it nonetheless be true that by witchcraft and sorcery they could make us believe the illusion that they do indeed appear in many forms?

Perhaps.

But do you really believe that a god would lie in word or deed or would seek to victimize us with illusions?

I don't know.

Don't you know that the true lie, if one can use such an expression, is hated by men and gods alike?

What do you mean?

I mean the lie that finds lodging in the inmost part of men's souls and remains there to deceive them about all the things most important to their lives. This is the lie that has no friends. Men hate and fear it above all others.

I still don't understand.

That is because you think I am trying to say something profound. All I mean is that every man loathes the thought that he might be taken captive by a lie which would prevent him from distinguishing between reality and unreality. That his soul should be possessed by a lie whereby he is continually deceived and irrevocably ignorant is something no man wants to accept.

Now I understand, and I agree.

Then it must be correct to say that what I have called the true lie is ignorance in the soul of the man deceived. The lie in words, on the other hand, does no more than imitate what the true lie does to the soul. It bears only a somewhat shadowy resemblance to the true lie and is not altogether false. Is that not right?

Quite right.

We have said, then, that the true lie is hated by both gods and men.

I agree.

Now what about the lie in words? Could it sometimes be useful to some people and therefore not be considered hateful? Would it be advantageous in dealing with enemies? And how about those we call friends? Should any of these be bent on doing wrong by some act of folly or madness, might not the lie in words be helpful as a sort of medicine, as a means by which we try to divert them and prevent the deed from being done? Consider also the fables and stories from d the past that we have just been discussing. Because of our ignorance of the truth about the ancient times, our only recourse is to tell fables, patterning the false on the true as best we can so that our stories may have some use.

Yes, we men do all these things.

But would god find these kinds of lies useful? Would he lie about the past, for example, because he does not know the truth about it?

Such a notion would be absurd.

Then in god there is no lying poet.

No.

Well, then, would he lie because he fears his enemies?

e Inconceivable.

But he may have friends who are mad or given over to folly?

Fools and madmen are not friends of god.

Then god has no motive for lying?

None.

May we conclude that in all things deity and the divine are entirely free from falsehood?

Yes.

Then god is simple and true in deed and word. He is unchanging and unchangeable. He doesn't lie. Whether men wake or whether men dream, god never deceives them with visions or with words or by signs.

383 This is also what I think, when I hear you say it.

You would also concur, I assume, in a second law or principle to govern representations of the gods in poetry and prose. That is, the gods are neither wizards who confound us by transformations, nor do they deceive us by word or deed.

I concur.

Despite our esteem for Homer, then, we cannot admire the dream of lies that Zeus imparts to the sleeping Agamemnon.[9] Nor can we commend the verse of Aeschylus wherein Thetis alleged that Apollo b sang at her wedding,

> Foretelling the fair fortunes of her progeny:
> Long would be their days and free from pain and ills.
> He made complete the tale of heaven's blessings,
> singing a joyous hymn and gladdening my heart.
> I believed that Phoebus would not lie,
> that a prophet would utter only truth.

9. The dream deceiving Agamemnon tells him to muster the Greeks for battle because the gods have now agreed that Troy can be taken (*Iliad* Book 2.1–15).

But he himself who sang that wedding night,
he himself who feasted with us,
he himself who promised these fair things,
himself is now the slayer of my son.

We shall be angry with a poet who writes such lines about the   c
gods and shall forbid their presentation in public. Nor can we permit
teachers to make use of such poets in instructing the young if our
guardians are to become god-fearing men, and indeed godlike, insofar as that is possible for men.

I agree. I accept these laws and principles.

Book III

386 From childhood onward, then, these are the kinds of things we shall permit or forbid our guardians to hear about the gods, so that they will honor the gods and their mothers and fathers, and be true friends to each other.

I think these are good principles.

What next? If they are to be courageous they must learn still other lessons. They must learn not to fear death—or do you think anyone could be brave who is afraid of death?

No, I don't.

What about any man who believes the underworld is real and terrible? Will he be likely to be fearless? In battle, will he prefer death to defeat and slavery?

He will not.

Then we must expand our supervision to those who write and tell stories about these matters, too. We must ask them to speak better of Hades rather than worse, for what they tell us now is not true, nor is it edifying for those who are going to be warriors.

You are right.

Let us begin, then, by expunging the verse that follows and all other writings and sayings of the same ilk:

> I would rather be a poor serf
> on the land of one himself penurious,
> than be monarch of all who ever died.

and this:

> Lest to mortals and immortals
> the houses of the dead be conjured up,
> dark, hideous, dank,
> and abhorrent to the gods themselves.

and this:

> Ah, woe! So it is true:
> in Hades' house are souls and apparitions,
> but all intelligence is gone.

and:

> He was alone with his wisdom and wit.
> All the others were shadows and wraiths.

and:

> Unwillingly his soul went forth from his body
> to bewail its doom in Hades
> and lament lost manliness and youth.

and: 387

> Shrilling and gibbering,
> the soul slipped down like a vapor
> and vanished underneath the earth.

and:

> Like bats hanging in a darkened cave
> will cling to a rock together and shriek
> for the one that falls from the cluster,
> so their souls will screech and falter.

We shall beg Homer and the other poets not to be angry if we ban   b
these and all similar passages. Our objection is not that they are not
poetic; nor is it that they do not please most hearers. Rather it is
because the more poetic they are, the less they are suited to the ears
of boys and men being schooled to be free and so to fear slavery more
than death.

Further, we must suppress the entire vocabulary of terror and fear
customarily used to describe the world below. Styx, the tide of hate,   c
Cocytus, the river of lamentation, charnel house, withered shades—
all such terms that make men tremble will have to go. Horror stories
may be all right for other purposes, but our purpose is to prevent our
guardians becoming hot-headed from such stories or else degenerate
in nerves and heart.

Your concern is well taken.

Then let us do away with them.

Agreed.

And we must require the contrary sentiments in poetry and prose?

Clearly.

Surely we should expunge the wailing and laments of famous men?   d

They must go with the rest.

Consider, however, whether we shall indeed do right in getting
rid of them. Our purpose is to affirm that a good man will not think
death a terrible thing even should it befall another good man and
comrade.

That is our purpose.

Then he would not lament his friend as if something terrible had happened to him.

No.

Further, we would say of him that of all men he is most sufficient to himself in leading the good life. He has least need of anybody else.

True.

So he finds it less terrible than others to endure the loss of a son, a brother, a fortune, or anything else?

That follows.

And when misfortune overtakes him, he will lament but little and bear his sorrow in moderation?

Yes.

Then we shall do well to delete the lamentations of famous men. We can attribute them to women—and not to the better sort of women either—and to men of lesser account. We do this so that those we educate to be guardians of the city will disdain such behavior.

We shall be right in doing so.

Then we must turn once again to Homer and the other poets and ask them not to portray Achilles, himself the son of a goddess,

> lying on his side, then on his back,
> and again face down,
> then rising up distraught and quivering
> on a beach of the waste and barren sea,

nor scooping up ashes with both hands and pouring them on his head, nor giving way to grief and tears in Homer's various descriptions. Neither should Priam, close kin to the gods, be described in supplication,

> calling aloud and rolling in the dung,
> entreating each man by name.

Most particularly shall we entreat Homer and the others at least to spare us from those descriptions that have the gods themselves given over to lamentation and wailing:

> Alas! Ah, woe is me, unhappy mother,
> who gave birth to the bravest, and now to my sorrow.

If they insist on characterizing the gods in this way, they should at least not dare to misrepresent Zeus, greatest of the gods, by putting such words as these into his mouth:

> Oh, woe! My heart is afflicted
> that I should behold a man most dear to me
> being chased around the city of Troy.

or these:

> Oh, Sarpedon, dearest of men to me.
> Oh, sorrow, he is fated to be slain
> by Patroclus, Menoetius's son.   d

Now, my dear Adeimantus, supposing our youth should take seriously such nonsense about the gods instead of laughing at it? Would any of them in that case be likely to think such conduct unworthy of themselves? Would they not reflect that they are only men and therefore have no cause to rebuke themselves for behaving in the way the gods themselves behave? Would they not be likely to abandon shame and self-control, starting to wail and chant dirges at the slightest provocation?

Without doubt.   e

But our previous reasoning has shown that this is the sort of thing we ought not to permit. And I think we better stick to this position until somebody shows us a better one.

I agree.

Nor must our young men be too fond of laughter. Anyone who gives way to excessive laughter almost always provokes a violent reaction.

So it seems.

It follows that persons of importance ought not to be described as overcome by laughter. Still less should we sanction similar representations of the gods.

Just as you say: such representations of the gods are still less   389
acceptable.

Then these sayings of Homer about the gods are also unacceptable:

> Irrepressible laughter spread among the blessed gods
> as they saw their Hephaestus bustling about the palace.

No, we cannot accept them, according to your view.

If you choose to call it my view. At any rate, we must repudiate   b
them.

Further: we must prize truth. We said before that gods have no use for lies. If that is right, and if it is also right that lies are useful to men only as a kind of medicine or remedy, then only doctors should be permitted to use them. Lay persons have no business lying.

Obviously.

Only the rulers of the city—and no others—may tell lies. And their lies, whether directed to enemies or citizens, will be legitimate only if their purpose is to serve the public interest. But no private   c
person may tell lies to rulers. To do so would be a great transgres-

sion—greater even than if a patient were to deceive his doctor about the true condition of his body, or if an athlete were to practice a like deception with his trainer. Or, to draw a further analogy, we may liken it to a case where a man conceals from the captain the true conditions prevailing aboard the ship and lies about how he and his fellow sailors fare.

I agree.

d   Now if the ruler of a city catches anybody lying—besides himself—any of the craftsmen,

whether priest, carpenter, or doctor of medicine,

he will punish them for subversive practice, as damaging to a city as to a ship.

He will, if words are as good as deeds.

Next, our young people must learn moderation.

Certainly.

And would you agree that the main issues for the multitude con-
e   cerning moderation are obedience to the rulers and self-rule in regard to the bodily appetites?

I think so.

Then we shall commend what Homer has Diomedes say:

Friend, be quiet and obey my word,

and also what follows:

The Greeks marched forward with valor,
silent, in fear of their captains,

and all similar passages.

Yes, these are well said.

390   But what of these lines and those following them?

Oh, you, heavy with wine, timorous as a deer,
cringing like a dog—[1]

Are these and similar impertinences addressed to rulers by private citizens well said or ill?

They are ill said.

Certainly they are ill suited to prepare the young for the practice of moderation and self-control. But, on the other hand, if listening to such things provides some pleasure, we ought not to be surprised. Or what is your opinion?

The same as yours.

1. These words of insult are spoken by Achilles to Agamemnon, the leader of the Greeks at Troy (*Iliad* Book 1.225).

And here we have the wisest of men saying what he thinks the
fairest thing in all the world:

> Tables laden with bread and meat,   b
> the cup bearer drawing wine from the bowl
> and filling our goblets.

Will these words be conducive to temperance in a young man? Or
these?

> Hunger is the worst of destinies and deaths.

The same question applies to the tale of Zeus, alone and awake,
devising plans while men and the other gods slept, only to forget
them in a moment when roused by his lust for Hera. So overcome   c
was he by the sight of her that he did not even want to go to the
house, and they made love right there upon the ground. Zeus said
to Hera he had not felt so fierce a passion even during their courting
days when "deceiving their dear parents."

Nor will self-control among our youth be strengthened if they hear
the same theme recounted in the story of Hephaestus fastening together
the bodies of Ares and Aphrodite.[2]

By Zeus, I think you are right.

But, ah, the words and deeds of famous men enduring against   d
great odds—these are the kinds of things suitable for our young people to see and hear. Consider this example:

> He smote his breast and admonished thus his heart:
> Endure, my heart; far worse hast thou endured.

Excellent.   e

Next, our men ought not to covet gifts or money.

Certainly not.

Then they must not hear it sung that

> Gifts persuade the gods, gifts persuade dread kings.

Neither can we endorse the counsel Phoenix urged upon his pupil
Achilles: that he should accept gifts from the Greeks and help them,
but if they offered no gifts, he should continue to show them his
anger. Neither shall we say or believe of Achilles himself that he was
so greedy as to accept gifts from Agamemnon or that he demanded
payment to yield up a corpse and would otherwise refuse to do so.[3]

---

2. The story of Hephaestus's magical bed which entrapped Ares and Aphrodite in the act of
adultery is told in Book 8 of Homer's *Odyssey*.
3. The incident alluded to is Achilles' agreement to release the body of Hector to his father Priam,
a story told in Book 24 of the *Iliad*. It should be noted, however, that Achilles does not demand
gifts; he is prepared to return the body in response to the command of the gods.

391   Such conduct must not be condoned.

My regard for Homer makes me hesitate to charge him with outright impiety when he imputes such deeds and sentiments to Achilles. But he does not persuade me. Nor do others who say the same things. I cannot believe, for example, that Achilles would say to Apollo:

> You have impeded me, O most malignant of the gods.
> King of the bowmen, I would take revenge upon you,
> had I the power.

b   Neither do I trust those stories of his disobedience to the river god and his readiness to fight with him.[4] Nor will I credit the allegation that he promised and consecrated the locks of his hair to the other river god, Spercheus, and then offered them up instead to the dead Patroclus.[5]

That Achilles actually did all these things is something we must not believe. We shall reject the charges that he dragged Hector's body around the tomb of Patroclus and slew living victims on the funeral pyre. We must not suffer our youth to suppose that Achilles, pupil of the most wise Chiron—Achilles, son of a goddess and of Peleus, the most chaste of men and grandson of Zeus—could be so at odds with himself as to suffer from two contradictory maladies: greed such as becomes no free man and a brazen arrogance toward both gods and men.

No. These sorts of things we shall neither sanction nor believe.

Let us also adopt the same posture concerning those dreadful stories of rape that are told about Theseus, son of Poseidon, and Pirithous, the son of Zeus himself.[6] Let us refuse to believe that any other child of a god—or any hero—would dare to do such wicked deeds as people tell us nowadays. What we must do is either to require our poets to deny that such deeds were ever done or else to deny that children of the gods did them. They may speak of the deeds or of the doers, but must not join one to the other. We will not have poets attempting to persuade our youth that the gods beget evil and that heroes are no better than men. As we said earlier, such views are both sacrilegious and false. Or am I not right in saying we have already proved that gods cannot possibly cause evil?

You are right.

Furthermore, these views are harmful to those who hear them. A

c

d

e

---

4. Homer relates that Achilles ignored the urging of the Scamander River to stop bloodying its waters by the slaughter of so many Trojans (*Iliad* Book 21.214 ff.).

5. Achilles' father Peleus had vowed to offer locks of hair from his son's head when Achilles returned from Troy safely. Instead Achilles placed them on the pyre of his fallen friend Patroclus because he knew that he would never return home (*Iliad* Book 23.138–151).

6. Theseus and Pirithous joined to carry off Helen, Menelaus's wife, and Persephone, the queen of the underworld.

person will not fail to be lenient with himself and his own trespasses
if he believes that the kinds of shameful deeds we have just been
discussing are acts of

> the gods' own kin, the relatives of Zeus,
> of those whose ancestral altar
> flames high atop Mount Ida
> and in whose blood line courses still
> the flame of immortality.

So let us put an end to all these stories lest our youth sink into moral
turpitude.   392
  Yes, let us do so.
  Well, then, what is there still to talk about in the matter of cen-
sorship and storytelling? Have we omitted anything? We have already
considered gods, daemons, heroes, and the netherworld.
  We have.
  Then what we have still to discuss are the stories about men.
  Right.
  But, my friend, this is something we cannot possibly do at this
point.
  Why not?
  Because I suppose we shall again be saying that writers of both
poetry and prose speak falsely of men, and in matters of the greatest   b
moment. They will offer numerous examples of unjust men who are
happy and just men who are wretched. They will assert that there is
profit in injustice if it can be concealed, while justice is invariably
your loss and another man's gain. I presume that we shall forbid
them to say these things and then compel them to say and sing to
the contrary. Do you concur?
  I am sure of it.
  Your assent implies that we now agree on the basic principles
governing our whole procedure of inquiry.
  You are right.
  That means we must first discover the nature of justice, and we
must then prove that justice profits its possessor, whether or not he   c
has a reputation for justice. Only after that could we reach agreement about the kinds of stories that ought to be told about men.
  True.
  In any case, we have now said enough about the thematic content
of stories and poetry. Next, I suppose, we must consider style; then
we shall have completed our examination of both form and content
in literature.
  I do not understand what you mean.
  Then I must try to make you understand. Maybe you can get my

d   meaning more easily if I first put a question. Is not everything in
poems or stories a narration of either past, present, or future events?
    What else should it be?
    And narration takes the form of simple narration, or of imitation,
or of a combination of both?
    Here again I am unclear as to your meaning.
    I fear I must be making myself ridiculous as a teacher if I have so
much difficulty in being understood. Perhaps I can show you my
meaning more easily if I follow the example of men who are not able
to express themselves very well. Instead of trying to encompass the
whole of the subject I shall separate out a part and see if I can discuss
that in such a way as to illustrate my point.
e   You recall the opening episode in the *Iliad* in which Homer says
that Chryses begged Agamemnon to set his daughter free? Agamem-
393 non angrily refused, and then Chryses, in his turn, called down the
anger of the gods upon the Achaeans. These were some of the verses:

    He appealed to all the Greeks, especially to the sons of Atreus,
    twin commanders of the army.

Now from his opening words until he completes these lines Homer
, speaks in his own person. He does not attempt to suggest that anyone
but himself is speaking. But after this point he turns to impersona-
b   tion, writing as if he were himself Chryses, as if we were actually
listening to the old priest's words and not to Homer. He then goes
on to use this two-tiered narrative style in describing all that occurred
in Troy and Ithaca and in the entire *Odyssey*.
    True.
    Now, narration includes both dialogue and the descriptive writing
that links the dialogues, does it not?
    Of course.
c   But when a poet impersonates one of his characters in dialogue
does he not as far as possible assimilate his own style to that of the
character he is depicting?
    He does.
    And if one likens oneself to someone else in voice or gesture, is
that not imitation?
    Certainly.
    It seems, then, that in such cases Homer and the other poets carry
forward their narrative by means of imitation.
    Evidently.
    If, however, the poet always writes in his own person, composing
all his verse and narrative without attempting to conceal himself,
then he could not be accused of imitation. Lest you once again have
d   difficulty understanding, I shall explain how the poet might go about

doing this. Supposing Homer had said that Chryses came to beseech the Achaeans, and in particular their rulers, to accept payment of ransom and restore his daughter, and that Homer had then continued to speak in his own person instead of impersonating Chryses? That would be narration, pure and simple, and the passage would have looked like this (not being gifted in poetry, I won't try to put this to meter):

> The old priest came to the Achaeans and prayed before them that the gods would grant them victory over Troy and a safe journey home. But he also begged them to honor the gods by accepting the ransom and releasing his daughter. Upon hearing his words, his audience was moved and ready to assent, but Agamemnon grew angry and ordered him to leave and not to return lest next time he find that his priestly garments might prove insufficient to guarantee his protection. Chryses' daughter would not be released, Agamemnon said; he would instead keep her and she would grow old with him in Argos. Then Agamemnon commanded Chryses to depart and not vex him if he wished to get home safely. On hearing this the old man was frightened and departed in silence. Once away from the Greeks' camp he prayed at length to Apollo, invoking the god with all his titles, reminding him of all that he had done to please him, and asking for recompense for any of his gifts, whether temples built or sacrifices offered, that might have found favor. He prayed that in return for these gifts the god should smite the Achaeans and make them suffer for his tears.

e

394

Now this, my friend, is simple narration. No imitation intrudes.   b
I understand.

Or one may imagine the opposite case in which there is only dialogue and the intervening narrative passages in the person of the poet are omitted.

Yes, I understand that, too. That is the style in which plays are written.

You are right. Now I think I can clarify what I was unable to explain earlier. There are the kinds of poems and stories which are told entirely by means of imitation: tragic and comic plays among   c
them, as you pointed out. There is another and contrary kind in which the poet recites in his own person, best exemplified, I should think, by lyric narrative. There is still a third kind that employs both techniques: epic poetry, for example, and a number of other poetic forms, if you follow me.

I now understand what you have been saying.

You understand, then, what I meant when I said we had done with content and could go on to consider form?

Yes.

What I meant to say is that we must come to an understanding   d
concerning imitation, concerning the mimetic art. We must decide

whether to permit our poets to be imitators, or whether they should be imitators sometimes and sometimes not—and in each case what sorts of things they ought to imitate. Still another matter to decide is whether we should forbid imitation altogether.

I infer that you are raising the question whether we should admit tragedy and comedy into our city or not.

Perhaps, and perhaps still more than that. I do not yet know myself. But just let the wind blow; it will set the course for the argument.

e   Well said.

The point is this, Adeimantus. Do we want our guardians to be good mimics or not? Or is what we are saying here also related to what we said before: each person can perform only one occupation well, and by dabbling in many he will excel in none?

The relationship is obvious.

Then the rule governing actual behavior is also applicable to the imitation of behavior: a man will do better imitating only one thing rather than many.

That is right.

It appears, then, that a man skilled in mimicry and able to imitate many things will hardly be suited to the pursuit of some serious
395   occupation. I say this because even when two varieties of imitation are very closely related, like comedy and tragedy, a writer cannot succeed in both. You did say just now, didn't you, that comedy and tragedy are both imitations?

I did. And I also agree that no one can successfully write both comedies and tragedies.

Just like no one person can be good at both reciting epics and acting in plays?

I also agree to that.

b   Nor can anyone be both a comic and a tragic actor—and all of these limitations appear in the realm of imitation, don't they?

Yes.

Adeimantus, I think that human faculties are fragmented into even smaller particles than these examples would suggest. It is this fragmentation that prevents people from imitating—or even doing—many things well.

I agree.

Then we must adhere to our original principle: those who are to become guardians should be released from all other duties in order
c   to become experts in guarding the freedom of the city and should do nothing but what serves that freedom. They should neither do nor imitate other things. If they must imitate, let them imitate what is appropriate to their vocation. From childhood on, let them pattern themselves after men who are—among other things—courageous,

temperate, reverent, and free. But they should never do anything that is unseemly for a free man to do. Nor should they seek to become clever at pretending to do unseemly or shameful acts, lest from imitation they develop a taste for the reality. Or haven't you noticed   d
how pretenses that persist from youth far into adulthood harden into habits and become second nature to a person's mind and body, as well as to the words he speaks?

I have noticed.

Then those we are educating to become good men ought not—since they are men—to play the parts of women, young or old. They should not imitate a woman quarreling with her husband, blaspheming against heaven, boasting and swollen in her own conceit, or grieving and wailing over misfortunes. Still less should they   e
impersonate a woman who is sick or who is in love or in labor.

Certainly not.

Nor may they play the roles of either female or male slaves nor perform any slavish act.

Right.

Neither should they impersonate a coward nor any other kind of bad man whose behavior is repugnant to the standards we have just now been prescribing. They ought not to act like those who mock or scold each other, who use foul words whether drunk or sober, or   396
who sin against themselves or their fellows in any of the ways such men know how to do. And they should not learn to imitate madness in word or deed. Lunatic and evil behavior in men and women they must come to know, but they themselves must neither practice nor imitate such behavior.

You are right.

But how about this? Should they be permitted to impersonate smiths or men in other crafts, or oarsmen or those who call time for them on triremes, or anything else connected with these things?

How could they do so, anyway? They have not been permitted to   b
observe these things in the first place.

Well, then, shall they imitate neighing horses or bellowing bulls, the rush of the river or the ocean's roar, thunder, or anything else of this kind?

Impossible. They have already been forbidden to be or play the madman.

If I understand you rightly, you want to say that any good and true   c
man will tell stories in a particular style, one contrary to the habitual style of a man who is bad and false.

What are these styles?

I think that when a good man narrates the words or deeds of another good man, he will want to impersonate him and will not be ashamed d of this kind of mimicry. He will, of course, prefer to imitate the good man when he is acting firmly and wisely; less so if his model is languishing because of illness, love, drunkenness, or some other infirmity. When he comes to speak of a bad man, however, he will not wish to imitate a base and inferior person, except in those few instances where his subject is behaving properly. Even the attempt to do so would embarrass him, not simply because he is unrehearsed

e in mimicking such characters, but also because he finds it distasteful to adopt baseness as a pattern for his own behavior. All these things he disdains unless he does them in jest.

I expect you are right.

The style of his narrative, then, will be like that we just now illustrated with Homer's verses. It will employ both imitation and simple narration, but imitation will be only a small part of the longer discourse. Or am I talking nonsense?

397 Indeed not. This is certainly the style of speaking that such a man must employ.

But the other kind of man will be undisciplined when he speaks. The more debased he is, the more readily he will imitate anything and everything. He will regard nothing as unworthy and will attempt to regale his audience with all kinds of imitations, including those we mentioned just a moment ago—rolling thunder, noise made by

b wind or hail, or by axles and pulleys. Or sounds made by pipes, trumpets, flutes, or other sorts of instruments. He will bark like a dog and imitate sheep or birds. Thus his style in speech and action will depend entirely on imitation; at best, it will include a minimum of pure narration.

Yes, that's the way he will behave.

Well, then, these are the two kinds of style I had in mind.

I see.

The first style is one that displays little variation. If it is combined with an appropriate intonation and rhythm, a proficient speaker will

c have little difficulty conforming to the style. The regularity of rhythm conduces to the same end: simplicity and directness in the mode of expression.

I agree.

But how about the second of the two styles? Will it not be contrary to the first? It is crowded with variations: accordingly, must it not find expression in a multitude of melodies and rhythms?

It must.

Is it not also true that the two styles separately and together comprise all poetry and, indeed, all verbal expression?

Necessarily.

d What are we to do then? Shall we welcome all these styles into

our city? Or should we admit only one of the first two? Or the combination of the two?

My preference would be to admit only the one style which unam-
biguously expresses the good.

Ah, but the combination of the two styles is also very charming,
Adeimantus. The man who speaks in this style is the most pleasing
of all to boys and their teachers, and to the mob as well. He is the
opposite of your choice.

I know.

Even so, I suppose you would agree that the mixed style is not
appropriate for our city since our inhabitants are single-minded people, each doing one thing only.   e

I do agree.

And it is this kind of city only in which a cobbler will stick to his
cobbling and not try to be a pilot as well. The farmer will be a farmer
and not also a judge, and the soldier will stick to soldiering and not
try to be a businessman on the side. And so it will be with the rest of
the occupations, will it not?

Yes.

Then what if someone should arrive in our city who is clever   398
enough to play all sorts of roles and to imitate anything? If he pro-
poses to put on a performance and recite the poetry he has brought
with him, we shall certainly bow to him and pay him homage, calling him sweet, blessed, and wonderful, and say that there is none
like him in the city. But we shall also say that the law forbids his
kind to remain in the city. Then we shall anoint him with myrrh,
garland his head with wool, and send him away to some other place.
For our part, and for the good health of our souls, we shall continue
to employ poets and storytellers who are less amusing and more aus-
tere. They will speak in the style of the good man and will tell their   b
stories in accordance with the rules we laid down at the beginning
when we first began to describe the education of our soldiers.

If we had the power, that is what we would do.

Now, my friend, may we say that we have completed our discussion of that part of music and literary education comprising stories
and myths? We have considered both content and form.

Agreed.

Then only song and melody remain to be discussed?   c

Clearly.

What we ought to say about them should be clear to anyone in
light of what we have said already.

Glaucon laughed. I fear the word *anyone* doesn't fit me. Offhand,
I don't know what we ought to say, though I might be able to guess.

I presume that you certainly know this much: all songs have three d   parts—words, melody, and rhythm?

That much you may safely presume.

As far as the words are concerned, it doesn't matter whether they are sung or said: they should conform to the rules we have already laid down.

Right.

And melody and rhythm must be compatible with the words?

Of course.

But, remember, we said earlier that we had no need for dirges or songs of sorrow.

We did.

e   Tell me, you are a musician. What are the modes of music appropriate to dirges?[7]

The mixed or tenor Lydian, the tensed or bass Lydian, and some others.

They must be prohibited. They are of no service even to women—especially to those who would make the best of themselves—let alone to men.

You are right.

Further, drunkenness and softness are unbecoming to guardians.

So is indolence.

Wholly unbecoming.

And what modes of music are associated with drinking and laxity?

Certain Ionian modes, but some Lydian modes as well—those that are called "relaxed."

399   Would you want warriors to become acquainted with these modes?

Certainly not. But you have not yet mentioned the Dorian and Phrygian modes.

Well, I really know nothing of the modes of music. But I do know that we should have a model appropriate for the words of a brave man at war or in some other situation of violence. Such a situation might be one in which he has lost the struggle and faces pain or

b   death or some other mishap but nonetheless confronts fate steadfastly and with endurance and sets about countering her blows.

There should be another mode for the same man when he is engaged in works of peace, matters having to do not with force or necessity but marked by free will. These should be works of prayer, if addressed to a god; if meant for men, they should persuade by teaching and admonition. This same mode should also fit the contrary case in

---

7. This whole discussion concerns musical modes, which would be most easily understood as different scales formed by varying intervals between the tones. Modes were used for set types of songs—e.g., Lydian for dirges, Ionian for drinking songs and music at more relaxed moments. Dorian and Phrygian modes accompany songs whose subjects are courage, tranquility, and sobriety.

which a man is willing to yield to the persuasion of another, who is in turn teaching him and admonishing him to change his opinions. It should express his rejection of arrogance and his readiness to learn, his qualities of moderation and modesty, and his willingness to perceive the merits of another's lesson.

These are the modes we shall want—the modes of necessity and   c
freedom. Let us retain these modes which best convey the spirit of men who are temperate and brave in both success and failure.

Indeed, these are the Dorian and Phrygian modes I just now recalled to you.

Well, then, our melodies and songs won't require instruments with many strings or those able to span all the harmonies.   d

I wouldn't think so.

So there will be no place for anyone who manufactures lutes and harps or any other kinds of multistringed and panharmonic instruments.

Evidently not.

How about flute makers and flutists? Shall we admit them to our city? Or is it not true that the flute's range makes it the very model after which all multistringed instruments and panharmonic music are patterned?

It is true.

What is left is the lyre and cithara. These we shall use in our city; in the countryside the shepherds could play on some sort of pipe.

Well, this conclusion apparently follows upon our premises.

Surely no one could suggest that we are proposing innovations if   e
we prefer the instruments of Apollo to the instruments of Marsyas?[8]

God forbid!

But, by the Dog of Egypt, there is something we have done—and without even noticing it. We have been purging away those things we discussed earlier that transformed our city into a city of luxury.

And so we have behaved with temperance and moderation.

Then let us complete the purge. After harmony it is appropriate to consider rhythm. We won't require complexity or great diversity in the basic beats. We should instead seek to discover rhythms that express the qualities of a brave and orderly life. After observing a   400
man of such qualities we should let his style of speaking set the pattern for meter and melody instead of requiring him to conform to some externally imposed rhythm. Glaucon, you told us about the modes of music. Now teach us what rhythms to choose.

I really can't do it. There are three basic kinds of rhythm that

8. Traditionally the lyre is the instrument of Apollo; the aulos, similar to a modern flute, that of Marsyas. Marsyas was bold enough to challenge Apollo to a contest with each using his instrument. Marsyas lost and was skinned alive.

provide the framework for the systems of meter, just as there are four basic notes from which all melodies are produced. That much I have observed and can tell you. But which kinds of systems and combinations reflect which sorts of lives is something I do not know.

b   We might seek counsel from Damon, our master of music. We could ask him which kinds of meter express slavishness, insolence, madness, and the other evils, and which give expression to the contrary qualities in a man. I think I once heard him speak rather obscurely of a complex Cretan rhythm and of another he called dactylic or heroic. He arranged all this, I know not how, matching the rhythms to the rise and fall of the foot and to the interaction of long and short. Unless I am mistaken, he referred to iambic and trochaic rhythms to which he assigned long and short notes. Also, in some of these

c   arrangements he seemed either to praise or disparage the meter as much as the rhythm—or perhaps both combined. I am just not sure: so let us reserve the matter for Damon's consideration. A thorough analysis of these matters would require a long discussion. Or do you disagree?

On the contrary, I very much agree.

But we should have no difficulty in seeing that grace or its absence in human conduct is connected with the effects of good or bad rhythm.

We can certainly say that much.

d   And we said before that rhythm and harmony should conform to the words and not the other way around. If this requirement is met, then good words will result in good and appropriate rhythms while evil words will have the opposite effect.

Yes, the words must come first and set the tone.

Now what about the words and the style in which the soul is governed?

Of course.

And everything else follows from words and style?

Yes.

Then we can say that good words, good harmony, good grace, and

e   good rhythm follow from the good order and disposition of the soul. By "good disposition" we don't mean "good-natured," a term so often used as indulgent description of someone who is simple-minded. We mean to describe instead a soul in which reason has been educated to govern in goodness and truth.

I agree.

Are these not the things our youth must strive for if they are to fulfill their own true purposes?

This is what they must do.

401   And are not many of these things to be found in painting and in all similar arts—weaving, embroidery, furniture making, and archi-

tecture? So too in the natural world of animals and plants. In all of these we can find grace and gracelessness. Gracelessness, disharmony, and discord are closely linked to evil words and an evil temper. The opposite qualities are bound together in the same way.

You are right.

Should we conclude, then, that our supervision should be confined only to poets, compelling them to summon up the image of goodness in their poems or else to forgo writing poetry among us? Or should we extend our guidance to those in the other arts and forbid representations of any kind of evil disposition—of what is licentious, illiberal, and graceless—whether in living creatures, in buildings, or in any other product of the arts of man? Here, too, we would penalize disobedience by excluding them from the practice of their art in our city. In this way we could protect our guardians from growing up in the presence of evil, in a veritable pasture of poisonous herbs where by grazing at will, little by little and day by day, they should unwittingly accumulate a huge mass of corruption in their souls.

By the same token, we should seek out artists and craftsmen whose natural gifts enable them to discern true beauty and grace. Then we shall have a salubrious climate in which our young may dwell and benefit from all their surroundings, where works of beauty are conveyed to eye and ear like breezes bringing health from wholesome places. In this way, from early childhood on, they would easily live in harmony and friendship with beauty and reason, coming finally to resemble them.

A truly noble concept of education.

That is why education in poetry and music is first in importance, Glaucon. Rhythm and harmonies have the greatest influence on the soul; they penetrate into its inmost regions and there hold fast. If the soul is rightly trained, they bring grace. If not, they bring the contrary. One who is properly educated in these matters would most quickly perceive and deplore the absence or perversion of beauty in art or nature. With true good taste he would instead delight in beautiful things, praising them and welcoming them into his soul. He would nourish them and would himself come to be beautiful and good. While still young and still unable to understand why, he will reject and hate what is ugly. Then, later, when reason comes to one so educated, his affinity for what is good and beautiful will lead him to recognize and welcome her.

You have given the best possible reasons for studying poetry and music.

Do you also see that this way of studying them resembles the way we learned to read? We could not become proficient in reading until we knew the individual letters of the alphabet and recognized each of them in all the various word combinations in which they appear. So we learned that it was necessary to pay attention to everything—great or small—and disregard nothing in our texts if we were ever to become letter-perfect and so fully literate.

True.

Supposing we had seen some letters reflected in a mirror or in water? We should never have known what they were unless we had previously come to know them in their original forms. But is it not also true that knowledge of both original and likeness is attained through one and the same kind of study and discipline?

Yes.

By the gods, then, I am right. We can have no truly educated men—no true musicians whether we speak of ourselves or of those we want to train to be guardians—unless we can understand the nature of such things as courage, temperance, generosity, or nobility, both in their original essential forms and in the resemblances of the forms. We must understand their opposites as well, also in form and image. We must understand them in all the combinations in which they appear—great or small—paying attention to everything and disregarding nothing. And once again we must recognize that we attain this kind of understanding through one and the same kind of study and discipline.

You make a compelling case.

Then wherever there is a correspondence between beauty in the soul and in the body, both reflecting beauty in its original form, will that not be the fairest sight of all for those who can see?

Surely the fairest.

And the fairest is the most beloved?

Of course.

Then the well-educated man, the true musician, would love this kind of person. But where there is disharmony, there he would not love.

He would not love if the defect were in the soul. But if it were a defect of the body, he would not turn away; he would love nonetheless.

I understand. You know whereof you speak, and I agree. But let me put another question: can there be any connection between temperance and the extremes of pleasure?

How could there be? After all, we know that extreme pleasure drives a man out of his mind no less than extreme pain.

And his bonds with virtue are severed?

Yes.

But there are links between pleasure, insolence, and license?

Yes.

Do you know of any pleasure more exciting and sensuous than sex?

No. Nor any more likely to drive a man mad.

But is not true love temperate and harmonious, a love of beauty and order?

Indeed.

So nothing of madness or license must be allowed to intrude upon true love?

No.

Then mad or intemperate pleasure cannot be sanctioned. Lover b and beloved who love rightly must not have anything to do with it.

No, Socrates, they must not.

I assume, then, that in the city we are founding you would propose a law whereby a lover is permitted to kiss and touch his beloved with honorable purpose like a father would his son, if the beloved consents thereto. But he would be allowed to go no further; otherwise, by manifesting a want of taste and culture, he would court c disgrace.

Quite right.

Would you also agree that our discussion of music is now finished? What could be more fitting than to complete our analysis by showing that the purpose of poetry and music is to cultivate the love of beauty?

It is a fitting conclusion.

After education in music, then, comes gymnastic?

Yes.

Here, too, our youth must be trained beginning in early child- d hood and then throughout their lives. You should think about these matters yourself, but this is what I believe: contrary to the doctrine that soundness of body produces soundness of soul, I think that goodness of soul develops excellence in the body's capabilities. What do you think?

I agree.

After properly training the mind, would it also be proper to place it in charge of all the details concerning care of the body? If so, we can avoid prolonged discussion of these matters and confine our- e selves to a consideration of general guidelines.

A good procedure.

Well, we have already said that our charges must abstain from drunkenness. Surely a guardian is the last person who should be permitted to get so drunk that he has no idea where he is.

You are right. It would be absurd to have to appoint a guardian to guard another guardian.

What next? How about their food? Our athletes will be participating in the toughest contests, will they not?

Yes.

404   Do the athletes we see around us now train in such a way as to prepare themselves for these kinds of contests?

Perhaps.

I am dubious. Their regimen is a rather drowsy one and perilous to the health as well. Have you not observed how they sleep away their lives? Moreover, if they deviate in the slightest from their prescribed routine they become vulnerable to potent and dangerous diseases.

I know.

Then we need some better kind of training for our athletes who must prepare for the contest of war itself. They must become like sleepless hounds, keen in sight and hearing. They must prepare for b   campaigns in which they will face many changes in food and drinking water, and they must be able to endure both sun and storms without succumbing to illness.

I agree.

May we not conclude, then, that the best training in gymnastic would resemble the training in music we have just finished describing?

In what respect?

It would be simple and good, particularly that part of the training which prepares men for war.

How do you mean?

One can learn in this respect from Homer himself. You remember that when the heroes are banqueting in the field, Homer allows them no fish even if they dine on the shores of the Hellespont. Nor c   are they permitted boiled meats; roast is the prescribed fare. After all, roast is the food most convenient for soldiers. There is no need for them to carry along pots and pans. All they have to do is light a fire.

True.

Further, I believe Homer never makes mention of sweets. Now that is something that all men in training can appreciate. Anyone who wants to get his body in shape must abstain from sweets altogether.

They do well to learn and practice such a regimen.

d   But if this is your opinion you could hardly commend the rich foods served in Syracuse or the spiced cuisine of all of Sicily?

I guess not.

Nor, I suppose, would you approve a little Corinthian wench for any man trying to keep in shape?

Definitely not.

And such delicacies as Attic pastries are not to be thought of?
No.

I take it, then, that these latter varieties of food and love resemble the kinds of indiscriminate excess we found a while ago in the pan-harmonic way of composing poetry and song, and also in the resort e to all kinds of rhythm.

That is a fair comparison.

Then we see that variety and complexity in music produce licentiousness; in gymnastic they produce disease. Simplicity in music, however, begets temperance in the soul; in gymnastic it brings health to the body.

Yes.

It follows that when disease and licentiousness start to spread in a   405 city, they will give rise to increased numbers of hospitals and courts of law. Those who practice medicine and law, in turn, will give themselves airs when they see how seriously they are taken by great numbers of free men.

No doubt about it.

And there is no surer sign of corrupt education in a city than when a multitude of its citizens run to consult the most skillful doctors and lawyers, and when the patients and clients include not only the lower classes of working people but also those who claim to have been educated as free men. Or would you not agree that a man shows himself to be base and ill educated if he feels compelled to surrender b the care and custody of his own body and soul to others, who then become his masters and judges because he is unable to master and judge himself?

I agree. That is the most shameful thing of all.

But perhaps you would agree it is still more shameful if a man fritters away all his days in courts of law, sometimes as defendant and sometimes as plaintiff. Moreover, because he knows nothing better, he continually congratulates himself on being so shrewd that he can do injustice with impunity because he knows every dodge, every eva- c sion, and every trick of the trade to wriggle out of the consequences of his acts. To top it all, he does these things for ends that are trivial and worthless. He has no idea that there is a better and nobler way to live than one which depends on constantly trying to persuade dozing judges.

You are right, this is still more shameful.

Shameful again to resort to medicine not because of some wound or one of those illnesses that come with the seasons but because of sloth and the kind of dissipated life we spoke of earlier. Shameful d that the body should come to emit waters and winds like a marsh and that the doctors, the sons of Asclepius, should respond with a

104 · THE REPUBLIC

104   THE REPUBLIC

display of ingenuity by dreaming up new names for new diseases, like flatulence and flux.

It is true. The doctors are certainly giving diseases some novel and exotic names.

I don't believe there were any such diseases at the time of Asclepius. I infer this from the fact that at Troy his sons did not rebuke the woman who gave the wounded Eurypylus an inflammatory compound of Pramnian wine liberally mixed with barley and cheese gratings. Nor did they censure Patroclus, who had charge of the case.[9]

A strange potion for anyone in that condition.

Not so strange when you recall that before the time of Herodicus doctors had no notion of current medical practices, which deserve to be regarded as a veritable education for illness. Herodicus was a trainer of athletes. Then he became sickly, and so he sought to combine medicine and gymnastic. The result was that he discovered how to torment himself and, after him, many others.

How?

By inventing lingering death. Since his malady was incurable, there was no hope of recovery. But he was obsessed with tending to it—and tormented if he deviated in any way from the regimen he had prescribed for himself. Thus his struggle against death left him no time for the business of life. The reward for his skill was that he managed to prolong such a life until old age.

A noble reward for his efforts!

But appropriate enough for one who didn't know that Asclepius chose not to instruct his successors in this kind of medicine. Asclepius omitted it not from ignorance or inexperience but because he knew that in all well-governed cities each man has a task to perform that precludes perpetual illness and constant doctoring. It is absurd that we take this for granted in the case of a craftsman but not in the case of those who are rich and reputedly happy.

What do you mean?

This. When a carpenter falls ill, he expects his doctor to give him a medication that will cause him to vomit up his illness or cause it to be purged from below, or else to resort to cauterization or surgery. Should the doctor prescribe instead a prolonged course of treatment with bandages about the head and all that goes with it, the carpenter will make haste to say that he has no time to be sick and that a life without work and preoccupied with illness isn't worth living. Then he will bid farewell to such a doctor and resume his customary way

---

9. This mixture was given by a serving woman to Nestor and the wounded Machaon in the *Iliad* Book 11.624–644. Eurypylus was wounded and cared for in the same book, but Plato seems to have mixed the two scenes here. In addition, Patroclus was not even present while the potion was being mixed.

of life, attending to his business—or, if his body cannot take the strain, he dies and is thus freed from all his troubles.

Such a man evidently understands the right use of medicine.

And is that not because he has a task to perform, and because for him life without work is unacceptable?

Obviously.

But do we not say that the rich man has no particular task he could not manage to neglect if circumstance compelled him?

That is the common opinion.

How about Phocylides' maxim that after a man gets rich he ought to practice virtue?

Before, too, I should think.

Well, let's not quarrel with him about that point. The thing we need to do is to find out whether or not virtue is something the rich man ought to practice lest he find life intolerable otherwise. Or are we to suppose that obsession with bodily ills interferes with the practice of carpentry and the other arts but is no obstacle when it comes to practicing what Phocylides preaches?

We can make no such supposition. Care for the body that goes beyond simple gymnastic is excessive and among the greatest of all such obstacles.

Yes. It causes trouble both in the household and in military service as well as in more sedentary administrative offices in the city. Above all, it impedes teaching, learning, or any kind of meditation if one is always imagining headaches and dizziness and then complaining that philosophy is their cause. A man who always supposes that he is being made ill and is constantly anxious about his bodily functions will never find his way to virtue.

Clearly not.

Then shall we be right in saying that Asclepius knew this? Can we say that he introduced the art of medicine to benefit those whose nature and way of life gave them sound bodies but who suffered from some distinct and identifiable disease? For these he prescribed drugs or surgery and then counseled them to continue their customary activities so as not to deprive the city of their services. But for those whose bodies were riddled by disease he did not try to prolong a wretched existence with diet or infusions or evacuations and so increase the likelihood that such patients would beget similarly wretched offspring. He did not think it worthwhile to treat a man incapable of living a normal life since such a one is of no use to himself or to the state.

Your Asclepius is a real politician.

Indeed. And just because of this his sons and successors proved to be good fighting men at Troy and practiced medicine in the manner

407

b

c

d

e

408

I described. Remember the wound that Pandarus inflicted upon Menelaus:

> They sucked the blood from it and applied a soothing poultice.

But they did not prescribe what he should eat or drink thereafter any more than they did for Eurypylus. They took for granted that their remedies would heal any wounded man who was previously healthy and regular in his habits, even if he should chance to drink that b Pramnian wine punch. But they thought a man constitutionally sickly and intemperate was of no use to himself or anyone else. They believed that the art of medicine ought not to be squandered on his ilk and that he should not receive treatment even if he were richer than Midas.

And your sons of Asclepius are ingenious.

Indeed. Yet Pindar and the tragic poets pay no attention to these truths. To the contrary, they will have it that Asclepius, despite the fact that he was the son of Apollo, took a bribe of gold to cure a rich man who was already at the point of death and for this reason he was c struck by a thunderbolt. But we shall adhere to the principles we set forth earlier. We shall not believe their two-part libel. Instead we shall say that Asclepius was either the son of a god but not greedy, or greedy but not the son of a god.

That's all very well, Socrates. But what do you say to this point? We must have good physicians in our city, and those most likely to be good will have treated the greatest number of people, the healthy d as well as the sick. Similarly, the best judges would be those who have had the most experience with all manner of men.

I certainly want our doctors and judges to be good. But do you know which ones I consider to be good?

I'll know if you tell me.

I'll try. But you have put a case which compares things that aren't comparable.

How so?

It is true that the best doctors would be those who began as youths not only to learn the principles of their art but also to become familiar with as many diseased bodies as possible. It would be well if they themselves were not robust and had experienced all diseases in their e own bodies. But you understand that this would not hold true if doctors used their bodies rather than their minds to cure their patients. Then it could be allowed that their bodies should experience all these evils. But since it is the mind that cures the body, it is the doctor's mind which must be kept free from evils; a diseased mind is not competent to cure anything.

True.

But it is different with a judge, my friend. He uses his mind to 409
judge other minds. It is impermissible that he should grow up and
be on familiar terms with those whose minds are evil. And it would
be specious to say that he should himself have practiced every kind
of evil so that he might more readily diagnose evil in others. Instead,
he must shun evil natures during his growing years, and remain
untainted by them, if he is to be a good and fair judge and if his
judgments are to accord with justice. These observations should explain
why good men often appear to be somewhat simple-minded in their
youth. They are easily deceived by the wicked because they lack   b
models of evil behavior in their own minds.

That is exactly what happens.

It follows that a judge must be old and not young. He must be late
to learn about injustice. And he must learn about it not as something
inhabiting his own soul but as something he has trained himself to
understand through long observation as an alien presence in alien
souls. He must learn to understand the measure of evil not by way   c
of experience but by dint of knowledge.

A man like this would surely be the noblest of judges.

He would also be a good judge—and that was the nub of your
question. The man who has a good soul is good. But someone who
is cunning and quick to suspect evil, someone who counts himself
an expert in trickery, someone who keeps his guard up because he
always expects to encounter patterns of behavior similar to his own—
such a man does appear to be clever when he is with his own kind.
But when he is among his elders and in the company of good people
he seems instead to be stupid. There his suspicions seem incon-   d
gruous, and he cannot recognize people of good character because
he has within himself no criteria to determine what is good. Still, he
consorts more often with bad people than with good; hence he seems
both to himself and others wise rather than foolish.

Very true.

Then we cannot look to this man to be our wise and good judge;
the man we described previously must be our candidate. For vice
will never understand virtue nor, for that matter, will it ever understand itself. But the virtuous nature, having become educated over
time, will ultimately be able to understand itself and vice as well. I
believe that the man with a virtuous nature—and not the evil man—
will prove to be the one who is wise.   e

I concur.

Very well. Does it now follow that we should prescribe the kind
of medicine and the kind of law we want to see practiced in our city?
Those who practice these arts will minister to people who are truly   410
well mannered in body and soul. As for the rest, those with bodily

defects they will let die, and those with incurable evil in their souls they will kill.

This would surely be the best way both for the state and for the individuals who suffer these ills.

And then the youth of our city, educated to that simple music that engenders temperance, will want to avoid behavior that might require them to appear in court.

Yes.

b   And so too with the musician: if he observes the same rule of simplicity in practicing gymnastic, he will avoid having to appear at the doctor's office except in case of extreme emergency.

Right.

And he will go through the exercises and drudgeries of gymnastic primarily in order to bring greater vitality to the spirited element in his nature and not simply to increase his physical strength. He will not be like the common-run athletes who diet and exercise only for the purpose of building muscle.

You are right.

Well, then, Glaucon, should we conclude that those who origi-
c   nated an educational system based on music and gymnastic had a different purpose in mind than that which is so often attributed to them? Did they intend something other than that the one should train the soul and the other the body?

What do you mean?

I mean their most likely purpose was that both should be concerned chiefly with the education of the soul.

How so?

Have you never noticed what happens to a person's mind when he concentrates exclusively on gymnastic and totally neglects music? Or to one who does the contrary?

What does happen?

d   The first kind of behavior results in a temperament of harshness and savagery. The second produces softness and effeminacy.

Yes. I have observed how those who turn exclusively to athletics become fiercer than they should be, while those who care only for music become softer than is good for them.

It should be evident that ferocity is a product of the spirited part of our nature. Properly educated and disciplined, it becomes courage. But if given too much stress it will find expression in harshness and cruelty.

I think you are right.

e   Whereas the philosopher is gentle. But if indulged too much, this quality of gentleness will produce laxity and softness. It must be trained so that it will remain both gentle and disciplined.

I agree.

Now have we not stipulated that our guardians must combine high spirit and philosophy?

That is true.

And these qualities must harmonize with one another?

Of course.

And where this kind of harmony prevails in a man's soul, he will be marked by temperance as well as courage?   411

Certainly.

But where the soul lacks this harmony, a man will be both barbarous and cowardly?

He will.

Now consider a man who gives himself over to music, letting his ears serve to funnel the music into his inner being, and there lets it play upon his soul. Assume that he listens to those soft, sweet, and mournful airs of which we spoke just a while ago and that he spends his entire time with the delights of singing and being sung to. The initial result would be that whatever high spirit he possessed would become malleable as iron does; it would become useful instead of brittle and useless. But if he persists and becomes music's captive,   b
the softening process will then result in melting and thaw, and the spirited element in his soul will finally dissolve. It will be as if the sinews of his soul were cut, and he will have become a "feeble warrior."

True.

If a man's nature is weak in spirit to begin with, he will reach the end result quickly. But if initially he is endowed with high spirit, weakening it makes for instability: trifles will quickly irritate and just as quickly soothe him. With men of this sort, high spirit will be transformed into anger and hot temper, and they will be irritable and   c
discontent.

Precisely.

On the other hand, if a man works hard at gymnastic and is vigorous at mealtime, but shuns music and philosophy, will he not become very fit? Will he not at first show high spirit and be filled with pride over the condition of his body? Will he not be braver than he was before?

Indeed he will.

But suppose he does nothing else. Suppose he never comes to know the Muse. Even if we assume some love of learning in his   d
soul, he remains a stranger to inquiry and instruction. Participation in discussion is foreign to him, and so is every other form of culture. Because his mind never wakes up, because it never receives nourishment, because his sense perceptions remain untutored, his soul

becomes blind, deaf, and powerless.

That is true.

Such a man ends up a stranger to the Muses and an enemy of philosophy. He ceases to use the language of persuasion. Instead he becomes like a beast, always intent upon achieving his purposes by means of violence and savagery. Thus he lives out his life in brutish incomprehension and ignorance, without harmony and without grace.

That is also true.

It seems to me, then, that some god conveyed to men the two arts of music and gymnastic, one to instruct a man in his quest for knowledge and one to tutor his high spirits. These arts pertain to the categories of body and soul only indirectly; they have to do first of all with philosophy and spirit and with the ebb and flow of tension and relaxation that brings about their harmonious adjustment.

So it appears.

Then we must conclude that one who achieves the fairest blend of music and gymnastic in the instruction of his soul will be a greater musician by far than one who simply tunes the strings of an instrument.

That is likely.

Shall we not need this kind of man to rule our city if its constitution is to be safeguarded and perpetuated?

That we shall.

Then these will be the guidelines for educational policy. There is no reason to encumber our understanding of them by appending inventories of dance fashions and of styles in hunting, athletic matches, and horse races in the city. It is pretty clear that we have in hand the principles which ought to govern such activities, and so there should no longer be any difficulty in comprehending them.

Maybe.

Very good. What should we consider next? Must we not decide who shall rule and who shall be ruled?

Clearly.

Well, it should be obvious that the older should rule the younger.

Yes.

And the rulers must be the best of the elders?

Yes.

And are not the best farmers those most skilled in farming?

Yes.

So if we want the best guardians we must choose those most skilled in guarding the city.

Yes.

So they must first of all be intelligent and prudent in managing the affairs of state, and they must be concerned for interests of the city.

Yes.   d

And will not a man be most concerned for that which he most loves?

He will.

Further, will a man not be likely to love whatever appears to have interests coinciding with his own, whose fortunes for better or worse will affect his own accordingly?

That is the way it is.

It follows that we must set apart from the other guardians those men whose lives convince us that they are the ones most likely to be   e zealous for the interests of the state and least likely to contravene them.

A suitable selection.

Then I should think that we must keep them under observation at every stage of their lives. We must see whether they are steady in their resolve to guard and serve the state. We must see whether their minds hold fast to the principle of public duty, never permitting either force or deception to make them give up the conviction that they must do what is best for the state.

What do you mean by "give up"?

I will tell you. It seems to me that whenever a man's mind relinquishes a belief, the cause is either voluntary or involuntary. It is voluntary when a false conviction yields to a better understanding. It   413 is involuntary when a man gives up a conviction that is true.

I understand the voluntary part, but I need to learn about the involuntary loss.

But don't you see that men part willingly with evil but unwillingly with good? Is it not good for a man to possess truth but bad if falsehood possesses him? And don't you think that holding fast to truth is what enables men to see things as they really are?

I see. I agree that men will not willingly renounce true opinion.

But what if they do so anyway? They must be victims of theft or   b force or witchery.

Once again, I fail to understand.

Then I must be talking like the tragedians. I mean that some whose opinions are stolen from them are overcome by persuasion. Others forget. In the one case their convictions are annulled by argument, in the other case by time. Surely you understand me now?

Yes.

Next, I mean by the victims of force those who are compelled by violence and pain to change their minds.

I understand. You are right.

I am sure you would also agree that those deceived into abandon-   c ing their convictions because they have been seduced by pleasure or terrified by fear are victims of witchery.

Yes. It seems that every kind of deception bewitches the mind.

Then recall what I said just a moment ago. We must seek out those who will best guard their own inner convictions of duty to serve the interests of the state at all times. We must mind their behavior from childhood on and require them to perform the kinds of tasks most likely to make a man fall victim to deception or otherwise forget his convictions. We shall choose those who will remember and will

d   not be deceived. The rest we shall reject. Do you agree?

Yes.

We shall continue to test for the traits we are seeking in them by requiring that they engage in hard labor, suffer pain, and endure combat.

Agreed.

Then we must devise still further tests that will show us how they cope with the cunning of witchery. Just as horse trainers expose their colts to sudden noise and commotion to see whether they will take

e   alarm, so we must confront our charges while they still are youths with the lures of pleasure and the terrors of fear. And we shall test them with far more care than men test for gold in fire. Then we shall see who maintains his composure and proves invulnerable to witchcraft. We shall see who effectively guards his heritage and himself. We shall see who preserves his inner harmony and rhythm through every trial, who prizes the characteristics that will serve the city best. Boy, youth, and man, he who triumphs in the time of testing and

414 comes out uncorrupted is the one we must choose as our ruler and guardian. During his lifetime we shall bestow awards upon him; in death he shall be buried with highest honors and suitable memorials. But the man who fails to meet these standards must be excluded from government. I think, Glaucon, that this can serve as a general notion of how our rulers and guardians should be selected and appointed; it is only an outline, of course, and I do not pretend to be exact.

My thinking is very much the same as yours.

Then it will be right to call these men guardians in the fullest

b   sense of the word. They will stand guard against enemies abroad and friends at home, so that the former won't have the power—nor the latter the will—to work injury to the city. The younger ones whom we have so far called guardians will from now on be called auxiliaries, and they will aid the rulers in upholding the principles of their government.

Agreed.

Now then, we spoke some time ago of useful lies. Could we contrive one now, a noble lie that might be believed by the rulers them-

c   selves, or at least by the rest of the city?

What kind of lie do you have in mind?

Nothing new. It is like one of those Phoenician tales telling of things that have happened before in many parts of the world—or so the poets assert and have induced men to believe. But it concerns something that is perhaps unlikely to happen in our own day, and it would certainly be difficult to persuade men to believe it.

You sound as if you find it hard to say what is on your mind.

With good reason, as you will discover when I say it.

Well, speak up. Don't be afraid.

All right, I shall speak, even though I hardly know where to find   d
the words or the audacity to utter them. I shall try to persuade first the rulers, then the soldiers, and then the rest of the people that all the training and education they have received from us are actually products of their own imaginations, just the way it is with a dream. In reality, they were the whole time deep within the earth being given form and feature, and the same with their weapons and all other accouterments. When the process was complete, they were all   e
delivered up to the surface by their mother earth, whence it comes that they care for their land as if it were mother and nurse and feel bound to defend it from any attack. Likewise do they regard their fellow citizens as brothers born of the same soil.

No wonder you hesitated so long before telling your lie.

Yes, I had good reason, didn't I? But hear the rest of the tale. We   415
shall tell them that although they are all brothers, god differentiated those qualified to rule by mixing in gold at their birth. Hence they are most to be honored. The auxiliaries he compounded with silver, and the craftsmen and farmers with iron and brass. So endowed, each will usually beget his own kind.

Nevertheless, they are all related to one another; therefore it may   b
sometimes happen that a silver child will be born of a golden parent, a golden child from a silver parent and so on. To govern rightly in these matters is the chief duty of the rulers. They are charged by the god to let nothing else play more important a role in their work as guardians than the concern and scrutiny they devote to the admixture of metals in the souls of their children. And should they themselves beget sons alloyed with brass or iron, they are forbidden to take   c
pity upon them in any way; they must assign to each one a status appropriate to his nature and not hesitate to thrust him out among the farmers and craftsmen. By the same token, should these produce any children bearing the stamp of gold or silver, they shall be honored and raised up, some to be guardians and some auxiliaries. And all this will be done and sanctioned by the rulers, who profess belief in a prophecy of ruin for the city if a brass or iron man should come to rule it.

Now, do you see any way we can persuade our citizens to believe this tale?

d   No. But there may be a way to persuade their sons and successors, and their posterity after that.

Well, even that much would have a good effect in making them care more for the city and for one another. In any case, I think I understand what you are trying to say, and I believe tradition will give direction to our tale.

Now we shall arm these sons of earth and let them come forth under the command of their rulers. Once they have arrived, let them
e   seek out the fairest place for a citadel that will best enable them to suppress internal rebellion against the laws and to repel any foreign enemy who chooses to play wolf against the flock. And after they have made camp and offered sacrifices to the proper gods, let them build their dwellings. Or should it be otherwise?

It is well so.

And these must prove to be adequate shelters in both summer and winter?

Agreed, since I assume you are speaking of their houses.

Yes, but they are the houses of soldiers and not of money-makers.
416   What kind of distinction have you in mind here?

I will try to explain. Surely shame and terror would ensue should shepherds train dogs to help them in guarding their flocks, and then indiscipline or hunger or some other ill should cause the dogs to attack and injure the sheep themselves, thus ceasing to be dogs and becoming like wolves.

Shame and terror indeed.

b   Then we must take every precaution to prevent our auxiliaries from behaving in similar fashion. They must never treat our citizens in this way. They must never be allowed to use their superior strength in such a way that will transform them from friends and allies into savage masters.

You are right.

And would not a good education provide the chief safeguard against such eventualities?

But that they already have.

We ought not to be too sure about that, Glaucon. What we can
c   be certain about, however, is that they ought to receive the right education, whatever it may be, if they are to be gentle to those they rule and to one another.

Right.

A thoughtful man would observe that such an education is not enough. The houses and other possessions provided the guardians
e   ought not to be such as will degrade their performance as guardians

and incite them to wrong their fellow citizens.

A thoughtful observation.

If this is to be the character of the guardians, then, does it not follow that their dwellings and life styles must be something like what I am about to describe? In the first place, none must possess private property, excepting only what is indispensable. Second, their habitations and storage places shall be open to all who care to enter. They will receive their food from the other citizens in quantities appropriate for warrior-athletes who are brave and temperate. An agreement will stipulate that their rations shall be provided by their fellow citizens as an annual stipend for the guardians' services. The amount of the stipend should be sufficient to meet their needs for the year but must not exceed them. Thus there will be neither superfluity nor want. And, like soldiers in the field, they will live together and eat their meals in common.

Gold and silver, we shall tell them, they have already in their souls in divine measure from the gods. They have no need of human metals nor is it meet that they should profane the divine gift by exposing it to the contamination that comes with coveting mortal currencies. Many are the evil deeds committed for the sake of the coin loved by the many, but the gold that dwells within remains untainted. Among all the citizens, however, only the guardians shall be forbidden to touch and handle gold and silver. They shall not enter houses where they are, they shall not hang them about their limbs as ornaments, nor shall they drink from gold or silver.

This way of life will make them saviors of the state and of themselves. But if they begin to acquire houses, lands, and money, they will become householders and farmers instead of guardians. They will cease to help their citizens and will instead become their masters and their enemies. They will hate and be hated. They will plot and be plotted against. Their days will be filled with a fear of their own citizens far greater than the fear of foreign enemies. Thus will they shift course in the direction of danger and shipwreck for the city and for themselves.

These, then, are the reasons for the provisions we have made for our guardians concerning their housing and other matters. And we shall want to make them into law, shall we not, Glaucon?

By all means.

Book IV

419   But now Adeimantus broke into the argument: how will you answer the criticism that you are not making your rulers particularly happy? Furthermore, you discredit them by saying it is their own fault. They are the masters of the city, but they get no advantage from it. Other men purchase lands and build large and beautiful houses. They collect suitable furniture, entertain guests, and build private shrines where they worship the gods. In sum, they possess what you would deny to your governors. They have stores of gold and silver and an abundance of everything coveted by those who expect to live the good life. Your rulers, on the other hand, seem to be mere mercenaries hired by the city to do nothing but sit still and stand guard.

420   Yes, and my rulers serve for nothing but board and lodging with no additional pay. They can't travel abroad or give presents to pretty girls or spend money on any of those things that other people, who assume they are having a good time, take for granted. All these prohibitions and more should be added to the counts in your indictment.

      Right.

b   But now let us answer the criticisms.

      Please.

      Well, then, we must proceed along the same familiar path. Then we shall find what to say.

      The first thing we will say is that we should not be surprised if the way of life we have sketched out for our rulers would actually turn out to be the source of their greatest happiness. But that is another issue. Our present concern in founding the city is not how to make

c   any one class happier than the rest but how to make the whole city as happy as possible. For we maintain that the contented city is where we are most likely to find justice. Injustice, on the other hand, is to be found in the unhappy and therefore worst-governed city. If we can demonstrate the truth of these statements, we might finally bring our inquiry to a close.

      So our first task is to construct the happy city. Later we shall examine its opposite. We are not trying to separate off a few of its inhabitants for their particular pleasure; instead, our task is to inquire into the needs of the city as a whole.

We might compare our procedures here to the coloring of a statue. Someone might come up and criticize us, objecting that we have failed to apply the most beautiful colors to the appropriate parts of the statue. The eyes, he might argue, are the very ornaments of a sculpture, but we have painted them in dull colors rather than bright ones. A reasonable reply to our critical friend would be to say that our business is not to paint the eyes to be so beautiful that they don't look like eyes nor to distort other parts of the statue. Instead, we want to make the whole beautiful by assigning what is appropriate to each part.

Now we should be able to understand that we mustn't indulge the guardians with so much happiness that they will forsake their roles as guardians. We could as well order the farmers to dress in purple and fine linen and hang golden chains about their necks, encouraging them to till their land only when they pleased. Or we could have the potters put away their wheels so that they might instead recline on couches to feast and engage in drinking bouts around the fire, throwing their pots only when they felt so inclined. We could follow similar policies toward all the others in the city; then everyone would live in bliss, and the whole city would be happy.

But this is obviously bad policy. Under such conditions there will be neither farmers nor potters nor any other class in proper condition to serve the city's needs.

Actually, the other classes are not that important. Cobblers who make or repair shoes badly and nonetheless praise their own shoddy handiwork aren't going to do much damage to the city. But if the guardians should betray their mandate to serve the city and its laws, the city will surely be destroyed. Conversely, only the guardians have it in their power to make the city content and well managed.

We want no scoundrels governing us. Our purpose is to create true guardians of our liberties, men least likely to do the city harm. Anyone who conjures up elegantly dressed farmers giving themselves over to feasting and reveling is certainly not thinking of a real city but of something quite different.

All these things we must keep in mind when we face the question of whether to arrange for the greatest happiness for the guardians or for the city as a whole. These must be our guiding convictions as we persuade and compel both the guardians and the auxiliaries to do as I have said in order that they may be the best possible craftsmen in their roles as governors. We must do the same with all other kinds of craftsmen; in this way the entire city will be well governed and will prosper accordingly. Then we can leave it to each class to achieve the kind of happiness that nature confers upon it.

I think you are right.

I wonder if you will agree to a related proposition.

What is it?

d   That craftsmen and their crafts are ruined by two basic causes.

What are they?

Wealth and poverty.

How so?

Well, suppose a potter becomes wealthy—do you think he will continue to care about his craft?

Of course not.

Then he will become idle and careless, more than he was before? That is, he will become a worse potter?

Much worse.

On the other hand, if he is too poor to provide himself with tools
e   or anything else needed for his trade, he will turn out shoddier products. Moreover, his sons and apprentices will find him a poor teacher. Accordingly, they will be still worse craftsmen than he.

No doubt about it.

It follows that wealth and poverty alike injure both the craftsman and his wares.

So it seems.

Then these are still other things the guardians must at all costs
422   prevent from infiltrating into the city. Wealth spawns luxury and indolence; poverty makes for meanness and incompetence. Both foster discontent.

But, Socrates, how will our city make war without having wealth, especially if it must fight a city with plenty in the treasury?

b   There are difficulties in fighting against one rich city, but it is easier to fight against two.

How can you say that?

Remember that the men from our city will be athletes of war, and they will be matched against men of wealth. If we think of one well-trained boxer fighting two nonboxers who are wealthy and fat, don't you agree that the boxer would have an easy win?

Maybe he wouldn't if they both came on at once.

c   Suppose he could retreat and wait for the first man to appear and then strike him; after that he could deal with the second man in the same way. Suppose one boxer used this strategy not merely against two adversaries but against many. Could he not vanquish a lot of men like that, even in the very heat of the day?

Yes.

And do you agree that rich men are even less versed in the art of war than in the art of boxing?

I do.

Then it will undoubtedly be easy for our warrior-athletes to fight twice or three times their own number.

I won't dispute you.

There are also other strategies available. Supposing our city sends an embassy to one of the two rich cities. Once there, our ambassa- d dors will simply tell the truth: we have renounced gold and silver, and you will find none in our city. But in the neighboring city there are gold and silver in plenty. Let us conquer it together, and you may take and keep all the loot. We want none of it. Now there's an irresistible offer. Who would rather attack our city whose soldiers fight like tough and wiry dogs? Who would not prefer to ally with us instead and go after some really fat and tender sheep?

But, Socrates, supposing one city conquers all the wealth of the others. Wouldn't such an immensely rich city be a danger to a city e without any wealth at all?

Ah, but you are simple! You must understand that only the kind of city we have been describing deserves to be called a city. Other cities are mere aggregations of factions. Not one of them is a city in the true sense of the word. Each is divided into at least two cities, a 423 city of the rich and a city of the poor. The two cities are enemies to one another, and each of them is fragmented further into many smaller classes or factions. It would be a great mistake to treat with all these divisions as if they constituted a single unity.

You must recognize instead that you are really dealing with anarchy. This means that you must seek to play off one group against another. You must redistribute wealth and power and privileges, taking from some individuals and groups and giving to others. If you follow this policy you will always have many allies and few enemies.

As long as our city is governed by the rules of wisdom and temperance we set out a little while ago, it will be the greatest city, not in reputation, to be sure, but in reality. Even if it has only a thousand soldiers to defend it, it will be united in defense. This is what will set it apart from most of the other cities, whether Greek or barbarian, however large they may be and whatever their reputations b for greatness.

I agree.

But what should be the limits of the city? How shall we instruct our rulers concerning the city's proper size? What are the best geographical boundaries, beyond which the city ought not to expand? I think the answer is this: let the city grow so long as there is unity among its inhabitants and consent to its government. If we accept c this as a proper answer, we must hand down another instruction to our guardians: let our city be neither small nor large; let it be united and self-sufficient.

Surely a trifling requirement.

Ah, yes. Just like that innocuous requirement we laid down earlier: that any inferior children produced by the guardians must be
d   removed from the ruling class and relegated to a place among the lower groups. Conversely, superior children born among the lower groups should be elevated to the guardian class. Surely all this will be accepted as consonant with the general rule applicable to all citizens: one man, one job. That is, each man should perform the work that best suits his own nature. Then he would truly be going about his own business, at one with himself, and not distracted or divided. With contentment general among its inhabitants, the city, too, will be one and not divided.

We must declare, Adeimantus, that the rules we are prescribing
e   ought not to be seen as burdensome. Really, they are trifles if care is taken to safeguard the one great thing—or I should say the one thing sufficient to the purpose.

What is that?

Education. If our citizens are well educated and learn to be men of discernment, they will easily grasp these and many other matters
424 not yet discussed, like mating, marriage, and the procreation of children. They will see that all things in the city must be arranged to conform as closely as possible to the proverb that friends have all things in common.

Good.

Now, if the city gets a proper start, its growth will gather momentum like a turning wheel. For good education produces good natures,
b   and good natures develop increasing affinity for good education, so that both become better with each generation.

That is why I say that education must be the chief concern of the guardians. They must be constantly alert to ensure that no corruption creeps in. They must not permit any innovation in gymnastic, music, or poetry that might undermine the established order. They must be zealous. You know those lines in the *Odyssey* that "men most like to hear the latest tune that strikes the ear." Well, our guardians must realize that the poet is often involved in other things
c   than simply promoting new songs. They must examine whether he really means to praise a new style of singing. That we must never accept, much less praise. The foundations of music and poetry cannot be disturbed without danger to the state; any such disturbance must be prohibited. So says Damon the music master, and I believe him.

I do, too.

It follows, then, that the very citadel for the guardians' defense of
d   the city must be located in the realms of music and poetry. Certainly

here is where license and lawlessness infiltrate most easily. This is because their medium is art and amusement where their presence seems unlikely to do harm.

The harm is not immediately evident, said Adeimantus. But little by little it begins to settle in and find a home in people's attitudes. Unobtrusively it spreads into all forms of manners and behavior. Strengthening their hold, lawlessness and license invade and debase the rule of contract and other business practices. Then they flood into the realm of laws and constitutions until in the end all public e and private rights are destroyed.

Is that what really happens?

So it seems to me, Socrates.

Then our youth must be trained more strictly. If amusements become lawless and, in consequence, the youths themselves become 425 lawless, then it is impossible that they should grow up to be well-mannered and virtuous citizens. But if young people start off with appropriate kinds of play and amusements, and if music and poetry impart habits of good order, we can attain the opposite result. Then good order will accompany them in all things and help them grow. Good order is also a restorative that can heal all the ills with which the previous society was burdened. Seeing this, young people will go still further and rediscover those customs and rules that were deemed trivial and abolished by the previous rulers.

What customs and rules?

Things like the young observing a respectful silence in the pres- b ence of their elders; rising when older persons enter and making place for them; honoring their parents; comeliness in dress and deportment. Of course, it would be futile to try to legislate these standards for behavior. Just because they are written down is no guarantee that they will be adhered to.

True.

Like attracts like. A good beginning will lead to a good end, an c evil beginning to an evil end. But having said all this, we shall still have to concede that it is too difficult to legislate in such matters.

You are right.

By the gods—here is another issue to deal with. What do you think of all those transactions in the market, of contracts between merchants and laborers, and of contractual relations among men in d general? What about charges of slander and assault, or initiating lawsuits and summoning juries, or taxes imposed in markets and customs houses? Indeed, what should be said about the whole multitude of rules for land and sea that govern police, commerce, and harbors—must we legislate for these?

There is no need, said Adeimantus, to impose laws about these e   matters on good men. They will find out soon enough for themselves what kinds of administrative regulations are necessary.

Yes, my friend, if only god helps them to preserve the laws we have already given them.

It's true. Without god's help they will go on making and mending both their laws and their lives in search of perfection.

You make them sound like sick men who will not leave off their
426 intemperate habits. What a charming life they have: always doctoring themselves with the result that their ailments multiply and worsen. Then if anyone comes along peddling some nostrum, they are convinced that it will cure them.

But their most charming characteristic is this: the one who tells them the truth will be deemed their worst enemy. They do not want
b   to hear that nothing can help them—neither drugs, nor surgery, nor amulets, nor incantations, nor anything else—until they give up idling, gluttony, wenching, and drunkenness.

I must say I don't think there is much charm in being angry with someone who gives good advice.

Then, Adeimantus, if you will recall our earlier remarks, neither would you be likely to praise the collective behavior of cities that imitate the sick men we have just discussed. When cities are badly governed, they are just like these poor wretches. They forbid their
c   citizens under pain of death to meddle with the corrupted constitution. But whoever ingratiates himself with flattery and favors, anticipating and gratifying their humors, will be hailed as a great and benevolent statesman.

Now I suppose there are some grounds for admiring the bravado
d   and bluster of those who are willing and even eager to serve such cities.

Yes, but not in the case of those who are deluded by the mob's applause into thinking themselves statesmen.

Oh, come now. Can't you make some allowances for such wretched
e   specimens? If a man doesn't know how to measure and is told by a crowd equally ignorant that he is six feet tall, how can you expect him not to believe it?

You're right. He will believe it.

Then don't be so hard on these lightweights. Surely there is something pleasing about the way they go on making and amending laws, always imagining that they will find ways to put an end to dishonesty in business and in all the other transactions we just mentioned. They don't see that they are simply cutting off the Hydra's heads nor (as the myth tells us) that for each severed head two will take its place.
427 Yes, said Adeimantus, that's exactly their situation.

In any case, the fathers of the constitution ought not to have to bother with drawing up a long list of detailed statutes and ordi-nances. In a badly governed city no one would pay attention to them anyway. In a well-governed city, on the other hand, they would be superfluous. Some of the rules would merely elaborate on already accepted behavior. As for the rest, one could easily enough ascertain which rules should be formalized by legislation.

Then what else is there left for us to do in our role as constitution b makers?

For us, nothing else. But it remains for Apollo in Delphi to enact our basic and most important and precious laws.

What are those?

Laws concerning the founding of temples and forms of worship; all matters having to do with gods, spirits, and heroes; procedures for burying the dead and caring for the tombs of the departed in order to keep us in their grace. These are matters that we human beings cannot fully comprehend. Thus, if we are wise, we will not permit c any man to claim he can manage or legislate for them. Instead we must turn to the ancestral god for instruction, to the ancestral god of all human beings who sits at the center and navel of the earth and from there helps us understand.

You are right.

Then, son of Ariston, we have finished with founding the city. Next, you, your brother, and Polemarchus, and all the others must d find something that will illuminate the city. The light must be clear and strong so that we may discover where justice and injustice are located. We must be able to see what is the difference between them. We want to know whether it is justice or injustice that brings a man happiness. We want to know if justice and injustice are qualities that affect happiness differently according to whether they are practiced openly or in secret.

Socrates, said Glaucon, what is all this nonsense about our having to undertake this search? You promised to search for it yourself. You e said you would be ashamed if you failed to serve justice by every means in your power.

You are right to remind me. I will make the search, then, but you must all help.

We will.

I believe we can find what we are looking for by making the fol-lowing assumption: the city we have founded—if we have built rightly—will be good in the fullest sense of the word.

That is certain.

It means that the city is wise, courageous, temperate, and just.

Necessarily.

Now, if we find some of these qualities in the city, can we assume the ones not yet found will nonetheless be present?

428   Let us assume it.

Then we can proceed as we would if we were seeking any one element in a set of four. If we discover that one element before the others, we shall have accomplished our task. But if we find the other three first, the one we are looking for will necessarily be the remaining one in the set.

That seems right.

Then let us apply this method as we inquire into the four virtues in our city. Of these virtues, wisdom is evidently the first. But I must

b   add that there appears to be some peculiarity connected with it.

What?

Well, let us see. The city is certainly wise, for it abounds in good counsel. Good counsel, in turn, is a sort of skill or proficiency, something generated from knowledge and not from ignorance.

Of course.

c   But there are many and diverse skills in the city and many proficiencies. Consider those practiced by carpenters, smiths, and farmers. Are these the skills that produce wisdom and prudence in governing?

No. They could only serve to produce and teach excellence in cabinetry, ironworking, and agriculture.

All right, then. Is there any form of skill or knowledge possessed by some of the citizens of the city we recently founded that attends

d   not to particular interests but to the general interest, to the city as a whole in both its domestic and foreign policies?

Yes.

What is it, and where is it to be found?

It is the art of guardianship practiced by the city's rulers whom we recently described as guardians in the fullest sense.

What description will fit the city possessing this kind of knowledge?

A city that is prudent and truly wise.

e   Will there be more smiths or guardians in our city?

Far fewer guardians.

They will, in fact, be fewer than all the other groups who are known by the names given their professions. This means that the

429   city built in accordance with the principles we have discussed will be wise thanks to its smallest group, the ruling class. And this is the peculiarity to which I referred earlier: the class whose knowledge is the only knowledge that merits the term *wisdom* seems ordained by nature to be the smallest class of all.

True.

Apparently, then, our discussion of wisdom as one of the four virtues in the city has given us some understanding of its nature and where it is to be found.

If we follow the same approach, I think we can discover the nature of courage, where it is situated, and how it imparts its spirit to the entire city. Now whoever calls a city brave or cowardly will think b first about its armed forces. This is so because the character of the city is not determined by the bravery or cowardice of the citizenry as a whole. The city is brave because there is a part of it that is steadfast in its convictions about what is to be feared and what is not to be feared. These convictions constitute an integral part of the education c prescribed by the city's founder. They also define the meaning of courage.

Would you please say that again? I don't think I understand.

Courage is a preservative. Strengthened by education, it preserves convictions about the things that are legitimately to be feared and those that are not. Courage makes a man hold fast to these convictions no matter whether he is threatened by danger or lured by desire. Neither pain nor pleasure will move him. If you like, I shall try to d illustrate what I mean with a comparison.

I would like that.

Well, then, consider dyers. When they wish to dye wool so that it will hold fast the true sea-purple color, they begin by choosing a white wool. Then they prepare and dress the wool with great care so that the white may perfectly absorb the purple. Only then does the dyeing begin. What is dyed in this way is color-fast, and neither soap e nor lye can dull the color's brilliance. But if these procedures are neglected, you know what purple or any other color will look like.

Yes, it will be faded and ugly.

So we make this comparison with the dyers to illustrate the results we were trying to achieve in selecting our soldiers and educating them in music and gymnastic. We were contriving influences that 430 would lead them to take on the colors of our institutions like a dye. With the right temperament and the right education their convictions about danger would be indelibly fixed. They would resist all solvents: pleasure, for instance, which can corrode the will more effectively than any caustic agent. They would likewise refuse to yield their convictions because of sorrow, fear, or desire, the strongest of b the other solvents. The quality I call courage, then, is the strength to hold fast to the proper convictions about what is worth fearing and what is not. Or do you disagree?

No, I agree with you. And I assume your comparison meant to exclude the kind of uninstructed courage to be found in a slave or in an animal. This is an admirable quality, but it ought to be called something other than courage since it is not produced by education.

c   You are exactly right.

Well, then, I accept your definition of courage.

Good, but let us restrict the definition to the courage of citizens.
If you wish, we can return to this whole matter at another time. But
now we are in pursuit of justice. Given our priorities, I think we
have said enough about courage for the time being.

I concur.

Well, then, after wisdom and courage we wanted to search out
d   two further virtues in the city. One is temperance—or moderation.
The other is justice, the grand object of all our inquiries.

Agreed.

Now, do you think we could go ahead and move directly to a
consideration of justice without first inquiring into the nature of
temperance?

I don't know. What I do know is that I should regret turning
immediately to justice if that meant missing the opportunity for a
better understanding of temperance and self-control. So let us look
at these first.

e   It would be wrong of me to refuse.

Go ahead, then.

I will. To begin with, temperance seems more clearly related to
peace and harmony than to wisdom and courage.

How so?

It appears to me that temperance is the ordering or controlling of
certain pleasures and desires. This is what is implied when one says
that a man is master of himself. It is a curious expression because it
431 suggests that a man is both his own master and his own servant. But
I believe the proper meaning of the phrase is that there is both good
and bad in the soul of man. When the good part governs the bad, a
man is praised for being master of himself. But if bad education or
bad company subjects the good (and smaller part) of the soul to the
b   bad (and larger) part, a man will be blamed for being unprincipled
and a slave of self.

Now look at our newly founded city. If temperance and self-mastery are in charge, if the better part rules the worse, we may well say
that the city is master of itself.

I agree.

We may say that the mass of diverse appetites, pleasures, and pains
c   is to be found chiefly among children, women, slaves, and the many
so-called freemen from the lower classes. But the simple and temperate desires governed by reason, good sense, and true opinion are
to be found only in the few, those who are the best born and the best
educated.

Yes.

Both the few and the many have their place in the city. But the
meaner desires of the many will be held in check by the virtue and   d
wisdom of the ruling few. It follows that if any city may claim to be
master of its pleasures and desires—to be master of itself—it will be
ours. For all these reasons, we may properly call our city temperate.
I agree.
There is another point. In our city, if anywhere, rulers and subjects will share a common conviction as to who should rule. What   e
does this agreement suggest about the location of temperance? Will
we find it among the rulers or the subjects?
In both, I should think.
Then we were not wrong in detecting a similarity between temperance and some kind of harmony. Temperance is different from
wisdom and courage, each of which is associated with a particular
part of the city. Temperance, on the other hand, pervades the entire   432
city, producing a harmony of all its parts and inhabitants, from the
weakest to the strongest. And this holds true however you want to
measure strength and weakness: by force, or numbers, or wealth, or
wisdom. Hence we may properly conclude that temperance is a con-
sensual agreement between superior and inferior as to which should
rule. And we should note that our conclusion applies both to individuals and to societies.
Agreed.
Now we have inquired into three of the four chief qualities of our   b
city. The fourth and final quality is justice. But here we must take
care that it does not elude us. We must be like hunters who surround
a thicket to make sure that the quarry doesn't escape. Justice is clearly
somewhere hereabouts. Look sharp, and call me if you see it first.   c
I wish I could. But I am only your follower, with sight just keen
enough to see what you show me.
Well, say a prayer and follow me.
Show me the way.
The wood is dark and almost impenetrable. We will have a hard
time flushing out the quarry. Still, we must push on. . . . There, I   d
see something. Glaucon! I think we're on the track. Now it won't
escape us.
Good news.
But we have really been stupid.
How so?
Because a long time ago, at the beginning of our inquiry, justice
was right in front of us, and we never saw it. We were like people   e
who look in the distance for what they already have in their grasp.
We looked away from what we were seeking and trained our eyes
instead on distant objects. And that is why we did not find it.

What do you mean?

I mean that all this time we have been talking about justice without realizing that our discussion has already begun to disclose its substance.

I am getting weary of your lengthy preambles.

433   All right. Tell me now whether I am right or wrong. You remember the original principle we laid down at the founding of the city: each citizen should perform that work or function for which his nature best suits him. This is the principle, or some variation of it, that we may properly call justice.

We often said that.

We also said that justice was tending to one's own business and
b   not meddling in others'.

Yes.

So minding one's own business really appears, in one sense, at least, to be justice. Do you know how I reached this conclusion?

No.

You remember we were inquiring into the four cardinal virtues of a city. We examined temperance, courage, and wisdom; now justice remains the one still to be considered. What we will find is that
c   justice sustains and perfects the other three; justice is the ultimate cause and condition of their existence.

Now that we have wisdom, courage, temperance, and justice fairly before us, it would be hard to decide which of the four virtues effectually contributes most to the excellence of the city. Is it the harmony existing between rulers and subjects? Is it the soldier's fidelity to what he has learned about real and fictitious dangers? Or wisdom and watchfulness in the rulers? Or, finally, is it the virtue that is
d   found in everyone—children, women, slaves and freemen, craftsmen, rulers, and subjects—which leads them each to do his own work and not to interfere with others? These are questions not easily answered.

Yes. They are very perplexing.

But we can at least accept the conclusion that the fourth virtue of minding one's own business rivals the other three virtues in con-
e   tributing to the city's excellence. That is to say that justice is at least the equal of wisdom, courage, and temperance.

Here is something else that points to the same conclusion. You would assign the responsibility for judging lawsuits to the rulers of the city, would you not?

Certainly.

And are lawsuits decided on any other ground than the proposition that a man may neither take what is another's nor be deprived of what is his?

That is the proper principle.

And the just principle?

Yes.

Here, then, is another demonstration that justice commands a man to have and to hold only what is his own.   434

True.

But see if you agree with me on this point. I would argue that no great harm is done if, say, carpenters and cobblers would decide to exchange tools and occupations, leaving their own businesses and taking on the others'. I don't see much harm even if some attempted to practice both skills at once.

Neither do I.

Suppose, however, that a cobbler or any other man nature designed to be an artisan or tradesman becomes ambitious because he has   b become rich or because he is physically powerful or has attracted large numbers of followers. Suppose he then attempts to force his way into the warrior class. Or imagine that a warrior, unsuited for the task, seeks to occupy a seat among the guardians. Finally, imagine someone trying to combine into one the roles of artisan, soldier, and statesman. All this kind of behavior can only lead to the ruin of the city.

I agree.

So any person from one class who meddles in another does his city the greatest wrong. This flouting of the maxim to mind one's   c own business is the very definition of injustice. Conversely, when craftsmen, soldiers, and guardians tend to their own business, that is justice. The city will be just.

How could it be otherwise?   d

Nonetheless, we had better wait a bit before giving unqualified assent to these propositions. We can be certain about the nature of justice only if its role in the individual turns out to be identical to its role in the city. If we cannot establish the identity, we must make a fresh start. But let us first finish what we have already started.

Remember that we began with the proposition that if we first examined justice on a larger scale, it would be easier to understand   e justice in the individual. We used the city as our larger measure. We founded the best city we could because we were confident that in a good city we would find justice. Now let us apply our findings to the individual. If they hold for both city and citizen, we will rest our case. But if justice in the individual is shown to be different, we   435 must return to the city for further investigations. Perhaps if we adopted procedures to examine city and citizen simultaneously, we could rub them up against one another and generate enough friction to light the countenance of justice and fix it firmly and forever in our own minds.

The approach seems promising, said Glaucon. Let's try it.

All right. If we use the same name for two things, city and man, one large and one small, they will be alike in that quality to which their common name refers. It follows that as far as the quality of
b   justice is concerned there will be no difference between the just man and the just city.

I agree. The man will resemble the city.

But we must remember that we deemed the city just when each of its three classes attended to its own business. We also called the city temperate, brave, and wise because of the particular qualities and dispositions of the classes. If we now assess the individual in the same way, we must demonstrate that the same three elements from which they spring are actually present in the individual and have the
c   same effects and consequences. In order to do this, of course, we have to halt for a moment to deal with a minor question. Does the individual soul have these three elements or not?

Hardly a minor question, Socrates. But what is worth questioning is seldom easy.

d   You are right, Glaucon. I must say then that I don't think that our present procedures of inquiry will lead us to the truth of this matter. We need to follow another more difficult and much longer path. But perhaps we can reach at least some useful conclusions based on what we have said so far.

That will satisfy me.

It will satisfy me, too.

Then don't hold back.

Very well. Surely we must admit that the same qualities we observed
e   in the city are also to be found in the individual. Indeed, it is obvious that the individual transmits them to the city. Where else should they come from? Consider the quality of spirit or courage of those who inhabit the northern regions of the Thracians and Scythians. It would be ridiculous to suppose that this collective quality has any other source than the citizens who possess the same quality as individuals. The love of learning, which is a particular characteristic of
436 our society, also originates with individuals. So does the love of money in Egypt and Phoenicia.

So much is easy to see. But the next step is more difficult. Is our whole soul involved in whatever we do? Or is bravery, intellectual effort, and bodily appetite each the exclusive product of a distinct
b   and separate part of the soul? Is our nature an undivided entity, or is it a set of disconnected components?

This is a tricky question. But let's begin by trying to ascertain
c   whether the parts of the soul are identical to each other or different. An example may help. Can something be both at rest and in motion at the same time?

Never.

Then we can infer that nothing acts in opposite ways at the same time. Nor can anything exist simultaneously in two opposing states. If, then, we seem to perceive the soul behaving in contradictory ways or reflecting two opposing states at once, we must conclude that the soul is many and not one.

Now let us tighten up our agreement so that it won't become unraveled again as we go along. Assume a man is standing still but at the same time waving his arms. It would be clearly incorrect to assert that the man is in the same moment at rest and in motion. The correct observation would be that part of the man is moving and   d
part is motionless. Agreed, Glaucon?

Agreed.

If someone is fond of quibbling, however, he might try out some fancy variations on this theme. He might point out, for example, that a spinning top revolves and at the same time remains fixed to a single point. He could then try to dazzle us by concluding that the top as a whole and in all its parts is at once both moving and unmoved and that the same holds for any object circling around a fixed point. But we would refuse to accept the conclusion. A top has an axis and   e
a circumference; the axis, insofar as it remains vertical, stands still while the circumference spins. One part moves and one part does not. On the other hand, of course, should the axis tilt away from the perpendicular during the spin, then it will also be moving.

Right.

Then we won't be hoodwinked or disconcerted by those who argue   437
otherwise.

No.

Very well. Since we don't want to bother to review all the possible objections to our assumption nor take the time to refute them, let us go ahead and assume the correctness of our position. But if we ever come to think otherwise, then we must renounce the assumption and all the inferences we have drawn from it.

Agreed.

Then should we say that the following kinds of pairs are composed   b
of opposites: attraction and repulsion, desire and aversion, agreement and disagreement? And should we observe that any proper discussion of opposites applies to actions as well as emotions?

Yes.

Keeping in mind the pairs we just described, would we not say that thirst, hunger, willing and wishing, and desires in general are examples of the active element in the pairs? The one who desires   c
something actively searches for the object of his desire; he tries to draw to himself the thing he wants to possess. Seeking satisfaction,

he will put the question to himself and then answer yes.

That's the way it happens.

What about not wanting, not desiring, not willing? Shall we class them with the passive components of our pairs, along with rejection and repulsion?

d   Of course.

Then can we classify all desires as belonging to the same element in human nature? Can we also recognize that among the desires the most insistent are hunger and thirst?

Your conclusions seem reasonable.

Now if we consider thirst itself, does it desire anything else than simply to drink? Must the drink be warm or cold, much or little? Must it be a drink with some specific characteristic? Of course, if you

e   are hot, you might prefer a cold drink, and if you were cold you would want to drink something hot. Similarly, the intensity of your thirst will decide whether you drink much or little. But thirst itself desires nothing more than drink itself. The same can be said for the way hunger desires food.

I agree. Each desire is paired to the object attracting it. The simple desire is attracted to the simple object.

438   We need to be careful at this stage of our argument. Someone is likely to raise the objection that people don't desire simply to eat and drink; they want to eat and drink well. Then he will likely go on to say that we always desire what is good.

The objection carries some weight.

But remember we are dealing in complementary pairs. There must

b   be congruence and dependence between the two units in the pair. This requires, in turn, that the attributes of both units in the pair must be either general or particular in nature.

I don't understand.

c   I know you understand that something can be greater only in relation to something else. If it is much greater, the less must be much less. If it is only sometimes greater, it is only sometimes less. This principle of relativity applies to all complementary pairs: more and fewer; double and half; heavier and lighter; faster and slower; and to the other kinds of related pairs like hot and cold.

True.

If we turn to the sciences, we will find the same principle at work. The purpose of science is the general one of attaining knowledge. But if we focus on a particular area of knowledge, we get a particular form of science, an identifiable scientific speciality. As an example, when men learned to build houses, they developed the science of

d   architecture, a body of knowledge obviously distinct from others. Its unique character is due to the unique purpose it serves. The same specialization of purpose accounts for the emergence and differentiation of all other branches of specialized knowledge.

If these illustrations have clarified some of the issues, you may now be able to understand better my original proposition about how things relate to each other. If one unit in the relationship is universal e
and abstract, the other unit will also be universal and abstract. But if the content of one is particular and specific, it will be the same with the content of the other. I don't mean that each pair is alike in content. We couldn't say that the science of health and sickness is both healthy and sick, or that the knowledge of good is good and of evil is evil. I simply mean that the knowledge of any special thing—health and sickness, for example—is necessarily a special kind of knowledge. Hence it is not called knowledge or science in a general or unqualified sense. Instead it is known as the science of medicine.

I understand. Your argument seems sound.

Let us attempt to summarize by returning to thirst as one of the 439
related pairs we cited earlier. The general relationship in this pair is between thirst and drink. A certain kind of thirst, it is true, relates to a certain kind of drink. But thirst in itself wants neither much nor little, good nor bad, nor any particular kind of drink. It simply wants to drink.

Agreed.

Thus a thirsty man, insofar as he is only thirsty, desires only to drink. This is what he wants and seeks.   b

Clearly.

But if a thirsty man refrains from drinking, it must be due to a part of him different from the thirsty part that pulls every animal to water. This conclusion is in accord with our earlier finding that nothing can behave in opposite ways at the same time. We can illustrate the principle with still another example: we do not say that an archer's hands pull and push the bow at the same time. We say rather that one hand pulls and the other pushes.

Of course.   c

Very well. Have you ever observed people who are thirsty and yet unwilling to drink?

Yes, often.

What are we to conclude in such cases? There must be something in these people that urges them to drink and something else that bids them abstain, something that overpowers and inhibits the initial urge.

Yes.

And what is the inhibiting agent? Is it not reason and reflection? And does not the agent that urges and attracts find its source in pas- d
sion and sometimes in disease?

Evidently.

Then it would be reasonable to conclude that the soul is composed of at least two distinct parts. One is the reasoning part. The other is appetite or desire, where hunger, thirst, and sexual passion have their abode along with other irrational drives.

e   The conclusion is reasonable.

Then we are agreed about these two parts of the soul. But is there a third? What about the spirited part which enables us to feel anger or indignation? Is this something separate, or is it identical with one of the other two parts?

I should think it is akin to the desiring part.

A story I once heard may help us find an answer. One day Leontius, the son of Aglaion, was coming up from the Piraeus alongside the north wall when he saw some dead bodies fallen at the hand of the executioner. He felt the urge to look at them; at the same time he was disgusted with himself and his morbid curiosity, and he turned away. For a while he was in inner turmoil, resisting his craving to look and covering his eyes. But finally he was overcome by his desire

440   to see. He opened his eyes wide and ran up to the corpses, cursing his own vision: "Now have your way, damn you. Go ahead and feast at this banquet for sordid appetites."

I have heard that story, too.

Leontius's behavior shows clearly that desire and anger are two different things and sometimes go to war with one another.

Yes, the meaning of the story is obvious.

b   We often see this kind of behavior where a man's desires overmaster his reason. This results in his reproaching himself for tolerating the violence going on within himself. In this situation a man's soul can resemble a city riven by two warring factions. The spirited part, here in the guise of anger or indignation, will ally with reason against the passions. Indeed, every time reason rejects what the passions propose, neither anger nor indignation nor any other expression of spirit will desert to passion's cause. I don't believe you or anyone else could cite a single instance where spirit and the passions have united against a confident reason.

I could not.

c   Now think of the man who believes he has committed a wrong. If he is of noble nature, he will not resent it if he subsequently suffers hunger, cold, or other kinds of retribution. He would consider them just punishment. He will not even wish to be angry.

But ponder the opposite situation. A man believes he has been wronged. In response to hunger, cold, and other afflictions he fumes

d   and smarts, regarding himself as a victim of injustice. He grapples with his tormentor in the name of righteousness. He perseveres until victory or death—unless reason, like the shepherd, calls off the dog.

An apt illustration. It parallels the relationship we established between guardians and auxiliaries in our city. The guardians are the shepherds and the auxiliaries the dogs trained to obey their masters.

We understand each other well. But do you see how our position   e
has changed? Just minutes ago the spirited element of the soul appeared to be the ally of the appetites and desires. But now, when the soul is torn by internal divisions, we see spirit arrayed alongside reason.

Yes.

Hence we must now ask whether spirit is distinct from reason or only a function of reason? If the latter, the soul must consist of no more than the two elements of reason and appetite. Or does the soul   441 in fact resemble the city as we have described it, held together by the three classes of craftsmen, auxiliaries, and guardians? If the analogy holds between soul and city, then the spirited part is an authentic third element in the soul. And if it is not corrupted by bad education, spirit will enlist in the service of reason.

No question about it. The soul must be composed of three parts.

Right, but only if spirit, which has already been distinguished from appetite, can now be distinguished from reason.

That is easily proved. Even young children display spirit almost from birth—that is, they frequently display indignation or anger. On the other hand, many of them never seem to discover where it is that reason rules, and most manage it only late in life.   b

You observe truly. One can say the same thing of animals. Homer makes a similar point in the words we have cited earlier: "He smote his breast and chided his heart." Homer's intention was clearly to mark off the difference between reason and spirit: man's reasoning part judges between better and worse and rebukes that part which   c harbors unreasoning anger.

You are exactly right.

At last, then, strenuous effort has helped us to reach agreement that the structure of the city corresponds to the structure of the soul; both are composed of three basic elements.

Yes.

Wisdom is the same in the man and in the city. Courage in the city is the same as courage in the individual. Virtue is the same quality in both. A man and a city will be deemed just or unjust   d according to the same standards.

Yes.

Let us not forget that justice in the city is founded in the good order to which each citizen doing his own work contributes.

We have not forgotten.

Let us not forget either that justice in the individual depends on each of the various elements in his nature doing its own work. It is   e proper that the reasoning element should rule because it is wise and capable of foresight in planning for the whole. It is clearly appropriate that the spirited element should be the servant and ally of reason. The joint influence of music and gymnastic should be able to harmonize the two. Mental and physical training will cooperate to refine reason and moderate the wildness of the spirit. The reasoning part will be nourished by the study of noble literature; harmony and rhythm will tame the spirit.

442

Then, when reason and spirit have been trained to understand their proper functions, they must aid each other to govern the appetites that constitute in each of us the largest and most insatiate part of our nature. Here is where we must be watchful lest the appetites wax strong and overbearing by dint of constant indulgence and gratification to the point where they are tempted to defy all limits. Overrunning the territories of soul and city, desire will claim for itself the right to govern. With that the good order of soul and city will be undone and the capitulation to unreason will be complete.

b

A deplorable outcome.

Only the firm alliance of reason and spirit can prevent it. This alliance is also beautifully designed to guard against the external enemies of both body and soul. Reason would do the planning, and spirit would do the fighting, holding fast to the ruling strategy and courageously accomplishing the mission set by reason.

c

Note that this is what we have earlier called bravery in the individual, the virtue which permits neither pain nor pleasure to pry him away from the word of reason concerning what to fear and what not to fear.

Right.

And we said a man is wise if that small element in him called reason governs according to what is good for the soul's three elements, for their own sakes and in their mutual relations.

Then we concluded that the temperate man is one in whom the three elements are in harmony. There are no quarrels among the parts because there is agreement among them that the rational element should govern the whole.

d

That is exactly the nature of temperance in both the man and the city.

And, once again, justice. We have described again and again the qualities that make a man just. Is justice different or less evident in the individual than in the city?

I see no difference between the two, said Glaucon.

Good. But for any who may still doubt, let us see if we can convince them with some simple illustrations. Suppose, for example, a man deposited some money on trust with the government of a just city or with a just man. Would not his money be equally safe with both? Would either embezzle the money?

e

443

He need have no concern in either case.

Will the just person, as man or citizen, ever steal from other men or from the state? Would he commit treachery or sacrilege? Would he violate his oath or break agreements? Would he engage in adultery? Would he fail to honor his parents or neglect divine services? Never.

And are we agreed that the source of this behavior is a soul in   b which each part is doing its own work with the consequence that the functions of ruling and being ruled are properly allocated?

Yes.

Then justice is nothing else than the power that brings forth well-governed men and well-governed cities. Our dream has come true. We have made real what we only surmised at the outset of our inquiry when we suspected that some divine power was drawing our atten-   c tion to a basic pattern of justice.

I agree. This is what we have accomplished.

Yes, that first model of justice helped us greatly, Glaucon. We learned from it that justice is somehow related to a division of labor reflecting the natural talents of the city's inhabitants: it is just that he who is naturally a cobbler should stick to cobbling, and the same for carpenters and all the other occupations.

Evidently.

But the early model was analogy, not reality. The reality is that justice is not a matter of external behavior but the way a man pri-   d vately and truly governs his inner self. The just man does not permit the various parts of his soul to interfere with one another or usurp each other's functions. He has set his own life in order. He is his own master and his own law. He has become a friend to himself. He will have brought into tune the three parts of his soul: high, middle,   e and low, like the three major notes of a musical scale, and all the intervals between. When he has brought all this together in temperance and harmony, he will have made himself one man instead of many.

Only then will he be ready to do whatever he does in society: making money, training the body, involving himself in politics or in business transactions. In all the public activities in which he is engaged he will call just and beautiful only that conduct which harmonizes with and preserves his own inner order which we have just described. And the knowledge that understands the meaning and importance of such conduct he will call wisdom.

Conversely, behavior that subverts the inner order he will deem   444 unjust. The kind of intellect that sanctions such behavior he will condemn as ignorant and foolish.

Socrates, you have said the exact truth.

Then I believe we could defend the claim that we have discovered the just man and the just city and explained the nature of justice in each of them.

I believe so, too.

Let us stake our claim, then. Our next task is to examine injustice.

b   Here the soul's three parts become contending factions, meddling in one another's business to the point where civil war breaks out. Or one part of the soul rebels against the rest with the purpose of seizing the governing power, usurping the very authority to which it is properly subject. Such anarchy and dissension can only be the product of intemperance, cowardice, ignorance, and every kind of vice. All these evils together concoct the essence of injustice.

Exactly.

c   If we now understand justice and injustice, we ought to be able to understand the difference between just and unjust behavior.

How can we do that?

By means of an analogy. There are practices that bolster health in the body and practices that lead to illness. Health requires that the body be ordered and governed as intended by nature. Illness disrupts this natural order.

Yes.

d   So also with justice and injustice. Just behavior produces justice in the soul and unjust behavior injustice. Justice, like health, depends upon the presence of a natural order governing the soul in the relations of its parts and in the conduct of the whole. With injustice, as with illness, the natural order has vanished from the soul, giving place to its opposite.

Agreed.

e   Then we can agree that virtue is the very health, beauty, and strength of the soul, while vice makes the soul sick, ugly, and weak?

Yes.

What is beautiful, then, must lead to virtue and what is ugly to vice?

Yes.

445   Well, then, we have only one other matter to consider. Is it profitable to live one's life in the cause of justice and beauty, whether or not anyone takes notice? Or is it more profitable to be unjust, provided you can escape punishment and thus escape repentance, too?

But, Socrates, now you are really asking a ridiculous question. We all know that when our health is irreparably ruined, life is no longer worth living, no matter how much wealth, power, and luxury may

b   be ours. No more would one wish to cling to life if the soul's paramount principle were to be corrupted. With the principle of justice in ruins men are condemned to do whatever they like—except to banish evil and restore themselves to virtue.

Yes, the question is ridiculous. But it has helped us to reach the point where we may see truth clearly with our own eyes. We are close to proving our conclusions, and this is no time to slow up.

Certainly not.

Come up here, Glaucon, and observe all the various forms of $\qquad$ c evil—or, at least, the forms most worth considering.

I'm coming. Go ahead.

Look. Our argument has lifted us to such a great height that it almost seems we are at the top of a tower. From here we can see that virtue is a single and unmistakable quality. Vice, however, appears in countless guises. Four of these require our special attention.

What do you mean?

Well, to begin with, I believe there are as many different types of soul as there are types of government.

How many?

Five kinds of government, five kinds of soul. $\qquad$ d

What are they?

The first of the five types is the just and virtuous soul and city we have just described. In the case of the city, it has two names. The city is a monarchy if a single man of justice governs it. If government is in the hands of several just men, it is called an aristocracy.

I see.

I join the two forms together because there will be no difference between one or several governors in their fidelity to the city's laws, $\qquad$ e provided they have been educated in the manner we prescribed.

You are probably right.

Book V

So this is the kind of city and government—and the sort of man—
449   that I would call just and good. If I am right, anything deviating
from this standard must be mistaken and evil. There are such devious
forms. They are four in number, but they all harbor one and the
same evil, one that afflicts citizen and city alike.

What are the other forms?

Just as I was about to enumerate them and trace their evolution, I
b   noticed Polemarchus, who was sitting a little away from me, take
hold of Adeimantus's cloak, pulling him backward while he himself
leaned forward. He whispered something in Adeimantus's ear of which
I caught only a few words: Shall we let him go or not?

At this Adeimantus raised his voice: Certainly not.

May I ask who it is that you are not letting go?

You.

c   And why are you not letting me go?

We think you are being evasive. You are cheating us out of a
whole chunk of the argument, and not the least important either.
You don't want to bother with explanations; so you think you can
escape with some casual remark about how it is obvious in regard to
women and children that possessions among friends will be held in
common.

Well, Adeimantus, was that not right?

Yes, but *right* needs to be defined, like everything else, in terms
of the particular community under consideration. Communities have
many different characteristics; you ought not to slight those you have
d   in mind. We have long been waiting for this moment, anticipating
that you would discuss both the begetting of children and their education, and explain as well the entire matter of the community of
women and children. We think that the quality of management in
these matters will have great importance—indeed, decisive importance—for the constitution of the state. But now you already want to
discuss other kinds of constitutions before properly concluding an
450   examination of this one. Hence our complaint, and we shan't let

you go until you consider these matters as fully as you have the rest.

I agree, said Glaucon.

Consider it unanimous, Socrates, said Thrasymachus.

You confront me with a formidable challenge. Just a moment ago I was rejoicing in the assumption that we had completed the discussion of our city, and I was only too glad to leave things as they were. But now you want to reopen the whole debate, starting again from the beginning, as it were. You have no idea what a swarm of words your questions will provoke. I suspected some such trouble, and I did my best to avoid it, Thrasymachus.   b

Do you think we have come here looking for fool's gold or for genuine discourse?

Yes, but time must set limits to discourse.

That is true, Socrates, said Glaucon. But for wise men this kind of discussion ends only with life itself. So don't be so solicitous about us. Just see to it that you are not remiss in your own efforts. We want you to explain to us how this community of wives and children among the guardians is to be managed. What about the rearing of children from birth to their entry into school, a period thought to be the most difficult part of education? Try to tell us how these things will be.   c

You do not ask easy questions, my dear friend. My answers will raise even greater doubts than anything I have said so far. You may question whether the proposals I make are practical. And even if they appear to be practical, there may be doubt that they are also desirable. This is the reason I am so reluctant, my good comarade. I fear that our reasoning may turn out to be nothing but a dream.   d

Don't worry. We shall be neither apprehensive nor hostile. We shall be a judicious audience.

Best of friends, with that remark I suppose you intend to encourage me.

I do.

Well, you have managed to do just the contrary. True, it would be a great encouragement if I were confident that I would be speaking from knowledge. To speak the truth about things one loves and values to friends one loves and trusts strengthens both courage and conviction. But to be in doubt—as I am—to speak while one is still in search of answers, is a slippery and dangerous path. I say this not because I fear being laughed at—that would be childish. What I fear is that I may mistake the truth, foundering and dragging my friends with me into error, just at the point where a slip of this sort would do the most damage. So it is, Glaucon, that I must pray that Nemesis will not come to plague me for the things I am about to say. For I truly believe that killing a man involuntarily is a lesser crime than misleading men about the nature of law and its relation to beauty,   e

                                                                      451

b goodness, and justice. It is better to take such a risk in the company
of enemies than with friends. So now you see that your encouragement is no help to me.

Glaucon laughed. Well, Socrates, if we detect any jarring notes
in your argument and are injured by them, we shall acquit and release
you beforehand. Nor shall we accuse you of perjury. So take heart
and say on.

Well, in the eyes of the law a man who is acquitted and released
in such a case is guiltless. Perhaps it will be so in this case as well.

We understand each other. Speak.

Then I must retrace my steps. Perhaps it would have been better
c to speak earlier, but maybe we shall manage it this way, too. Since
we have discussed men at sufficient length, it is time to speak of
women. I broach the subject the more readily because you have
urged me on.

To men born and educated in the manner we have been describing I think there is only one way to relate the role and function of
women and children. We started our discussion, I believe, by ascrib-
ing to the men the duty of guarding a flock?

Yes.

d Then let us pursue the analogy. Let us assume that the birth and
education of women will be governed by the same guidelines we
prescribed for the men. We can decide later whether or not this
procedure seems appropriate.

What do you mean?

This. Do we separate off male and female dogs from one another,
or do we expect both to share equally in standing guard and in going
out to hunt? Should all activities be shared, or do we expect the
females to remain indoors on the grounds that bearing and nursing
the pups incapacitate them for anything else, leaving to the males
the exclusive care and guarding of the flocks?

e There should be no such differentiation. The only distinction
between them is that we consider males to be stronger and females
weaker.

Now then, can one get any animal to perform the same functions
as another without giving both the same guidance and training?

No.

452 Then if women are to do the same things as men, we must also
teach them the same things.

Yes.

The men were taught music and gymnastic, were they not?

Yes.

It follows that we must teach the women the same two arts, as well
as learning and practice in the art of war.

From what you have said I suppose it does follow.

Perhaps conventional wisdom would ridicule some of these proposals if we tried to put them into practice.

It surely would.

Well, what do you think would be the most obvious target for ridicule? Perhaps the idea of women attending the wrestling schools and exercising naked with the men, especially when they are no longer young? The whole scene would resemble the behavior of those   b
zealous old men who still persist in going off to exercise in the gymnasium despite all their wrinkles and ugliness.

Our present notions would call the whole thing absurd.

Yet we have vowed to speak our minds. Therefore we must not be daunted by all the wisecracks that will greet such innovations. Nor must we mind what the resident wits say about women studying music and gymnastic, about women bearing arms, nor, above all, what   c
they say about women riding astride horses.

You are right.

And having begun to set out our guidelines, we must deal openly with their harsher aspects. We may ask the wits to stop being witty and try to be serious. After all, we can remind them that until fairly recently the Greeks thought it shameful and absurd to behold a man naked, just as many barbarians still do today. And when the Cretans first built gymnasiums, and later the Spartans, I suppose the humor-   d
ists also had their day. Don't you think so?

I do.

But when experience showed it is better to strip down than to cover up, laughter vanished. Reason provided a new perspective, teaching the wise man to ridicule nothing but evil. On the other hand, any man who mocks anything other than folly and wrong is also the kind who will seriously suppose he is capable of setting up   e
some standard of beauty other than the good.

You are right.

These are the kinds of proposals, then, that we must first test out to see if they are possible or not. And we must open up the debate to anyone, whether in jest or earnest, who wants to take the negative.   453
The basic question concerns the nature of women: can a woman perform all or none of the tasks a man performs? Can she manage some but not others? Is she really capable of waging war? Would not these questions serve as the best point of departure for our inquiry and therefore lead us to the best conclusion?

Much the best.

Why not conduct the debate by taking the negative ourselves? If we present our opponents' case, then they won't be left defenseless when we attack.

b   Nothing can stop us.
      Let us then state the case of the speaker for the negative.

> Socrates and Glaucon, he will say, there is no need that others should
> dispute you in these issues. After all, when you founded your city you
> agreed that each person should mind his own business and do the one
> thing for which nature suited him.
>   Yes, I suppose we did agree. Yes. Certainly.
>   Can you deny that nature has made a great difference between men
> and women?
c
>   Certainly not.
>   Does not this natural difference require that each sex should perform
> a different function?
>   Certainly.
>   Are you not in error, then? Are you not contradicting yourselves by
> conceding the difference in the natures of men and women and then
> turning around to argue that they should perform the same functions?

      How about surprising me with an answer to that question?
      That's not easy at a moment's notice, Socrates. My only response
to such an onslaught is to invite and urge you to make our rebuttal
clear, whatever it may be.
d   Now, Glaucon, you see why I was so diffident about broaching
the role and education of women and children. I foresaw and feared
these and many other difficulties.
      By heaven, these are no easy matters. No, by Zeus, they are not.
      You are right. But whether one falls into a small pool or into the
great ocean itself, he will have to swim all the same.
      That's the truth.
      Then we must swim, too. Perhaps a dolphin will take us on his
back, or maybe some other deliverer will enable us to reach shore.
e   Maybe.
      Let's see if we can find a way out. Now, we agreed that different
natures should have different functions and that there is a difference
between the natures of men and women. But then we said that men
and women should perform the same functions. This is the inconsistency we are charged with, is it not?
      It is.
454   Ah, Glaucon, what glorious power there is in the art of contradiction!
      How so?
      Because so many seem to practice it even against their wills. They
imagine they are reasoning together when, in fact, they are only
picking quarrels. This happens because they are unable to define the
issue being considered nor are they able to analyze it into its logical
components. So instead of engaging in dialectic, they merely engage
in debate.

That often happens. Is it happening to us now?

Yes, it is. I fear we, too, have been verging on polemics without   b
being aware of it.

How so?

Well, all this time we have boldly and forcefully insisted that different natures ought to perform different functions. While making these assertions, however, we did not once pause to consider what in fact we mean by different functions and what actually distinguishes one nature from another.

No, we didn't.

Hence we might trip over some such question as to whether bald   c
men and men with long hair are by nature identical or different. If we agreed that they are different and that the bald ones are by nature cobblers, then we should have to forbid the longhairs from making shoes.

But that would be absurd.

Yes, absurd. And for no other reason than our failure to stipulate in the beginning that we are not concerned with every conceivable difference or similarity that exists between one nature and another but only with those relevant to a person's work. We can clarify our meaning by observing, for example, that a man and a woman who both have the qualifications to be a physician have the same nature.   d
Do you agree?

Yes.

But two men, one a physician and one a carpenter, have different natures?

Oh, entirely different.

So, then, those men and women who display distinct aptitudes for any given kind of work will be assigned to do that work. If a critic can do no more than bring up the one distinction between man and   e
woman—that the one begets and the other bears children—we shall say that for our purposes he has offered no proof of difference at all. We shall continue to affirm that our guardians and their wives should perform the same tasks.

And we shall be right in doing so.

As our next step, then, we should invite our critic to tell us precisely where a woman's nature differs from a man's when it comes   455
to conducting the affairs of state.

Fair enough.

Perhaps he will respond the way you did a little while ago and say that it is hard to find an appropriate answer right off, but that after a little reflection it becomes less difficult.

He might.

Should we ask the one who is raising objections to go along with

b   us if we can prove that none of the activities connected with governing the state is peculiarly the province of women?

By all means let us do so.

Then let us put this question to him: how do you distinguish between
the person naturally gifted for some particular task and one not so
gifted? Is it that the one learns easily and the other not? That is, does
one learn to pursue a subject on his own after very little instruction,
while the other, even after he has received a great deal of tutoring
and guidance, is unable to remember anything he has learned? Do
you differentiate between a person whose mind is adequately served
by his body and someone who finds his body a hindrance? Would
c   you use any other criteria to differentiate one who is well suited to
his work from one who is not?

No.

Now, then, can you think of any of the human arts in which men
do not generally excel women? Let's not make a long story out of it
by bringing up weaving and baking cakes and boiling vegetables,
matters in which women take pride and would be mortified should
d   a man best them in these skills.

You are surely correct in saying that the one sex excels the other
in every respect. But it is also true that individually many women
are more skilled than many men, even if your general proposition is
true.

Then we must conclude that sex cannot be the criterion in
appointments to government positions. No office should be reserved
for a man just because he is a man or for a woman just because she
is a woman. All the capabilities with which nature endows us are
e   distributed among men and women alike. Hence women will have
the rightful opportunity to share in every task, and so will men, even
though women are the weaker of the two sexes.

Agreed.

Could we then assign all the tasks to the men and none to the
women?

How could we propose such thing as that?

Well, then, we shall want to say instead that one woman has the
capacity to be a doctor and another not, that one woman is naturally
musical and another is unmusical.

Certainly.

456   Could we deny that there are some women who are warlike and
natural athletes while others love neither war nor gymnastic?

I don't think we can.

Again, are there not women who love wisdom and those who do
not? Are not some women high-spirited and some not?

There are all these kinds of women, too.

Hence it must also be true that one woman is fit to be a guardian and another unfit. For these are the same criteria we used when we were selecting men as guardians, are they not?

Yes.

As guardians of the state, then, women and men are naturally the same, except that one is weaker and the other stronger.

Apparently.

It follows that women with the requisite qualities must be chosen   b to live and guard together with men of like qualities since they have the necessary competence and are naturally kin.

By all means.

And the same natures ought to perform the same functions?

Yes.

So we have closed the circle. We agree that we do nothing against nature by educating the guardians' wives in music and gymnastic.

We are agreed.

Since we have legislated in harmony with nature, we have not   c proposed anything impractical or unattainable. On the contrary, we may say that if anything contradicts nature, it is the way things are done today.

So it appears.

Now we designed our inquiry to test whether our proposals would turn out to be both possible and desirable?

Yes.

Well, I take it we have just established that they are possible.

Yes.

Then we must see if we can agree that they are also desirable.

Clearly.

In preparing a woman to be a guardian, then, we won't prescribe one kind of education for women guardians and another for the men because their natures are the same.

No. There should be no differentiation.   d

Let me ask you a question.

About what?

About men. Do you think some are better and some worse, or are all alike?

They are certainly not all alike.

Then which do you think will become the better men in the city we are building: the guardians who are being educated in the manner we have prescribed or the cobblers who received instruction in the cobbler's art?

An absurd question.

I understand your answer. You mean that the guardians are the   e best of our citizens.

By far.

And will not the women guardians be the best of the women?

Yes.

And can we wish for the state anything better than that it should nurture the best possible men and women?

Nothing.

457   And the education we have prescribed in music and gymnastic will produce this outcome?

Without fail.

Therefore the institutions we have proposed for the state are not only possible, they are the best possible.

Quite so.

Then wearing virtue as a garment, the guardians' wives must go naked and take part alongside their men in war and the other functions of government, and no other duties will be required of them. Owing to the weakness of their gender, however, they shall perform b   the less burdensome tasks. When they are at their exercises for the body's benefit, any man who laughs at their nakedness will be "gathering unripe fruit," for he does not know what he ridicules nor where his laughter leads. He is ignorant of the fairest words ever spoken: what is beneficial must be beautiful; only the harmful is ugly.

You are right.

Having successfully reached this point in our legislation for women, c   we could compare ourselves with a swimmer who has surmounted a wave without being drowned by it. Our argument that men and women guardians should pursue all things in common turns out to be consistent in itself, since we have found our proposals to be both possible and beneficial.

That was no small wave, either.

You won't think it was so big when you see what the next one looks like.

Go ahead, then, and let me see.

Here it is. I think that everything we have said so far leads up to the following law.

What law?

d   That all the women shall belong to all the men and that none shall cohabit privately; that the children should also be raised in common and no child should know its parent nor the parent its child.

A far greater wave, indeed. Your proposal raises questions about both practicability and utility that will provoke the greatest misgivings.

I shouldn't think anyone would want to debate its utility. The desirability of having wives and children in common, were it possible, ought to be self-evident. But I suppose the main subject of dispute would be whether or not it would be possible to establish such a community.

I expect both aspects of the proposal will produce plenty of debate.   e

I see that you want to entangle me in both questions at once. I hoped for your consent in the matter of utility, so that I could escape from having to discuss it. Then I would only have to consider the question of feasibility.

Your escape efforts have been detected. You won't be allowed to run away, and you will be obliged to defend your case on both counts.

I will pay your penalty. But first, relent a little. Let me go on holiday, like men with lazy minds are wont to do, so that they may   458 entertain themselves with their own thoughts as they walk alone. These men pursue their desires without pausing to inquire how they might be achieved. All such considerations they dismiss in order to spare themselves the trouble of weighing the possible against the impossible. They assume that what they wish is already at hand, giving their imaginations free rein in concocting the details and relishing in advance what they will do when everything is in place. So do idle minds become more idle still. I now yield to this same   b weakness. I would like to postpone the feasibility issue for later consideration. With your permission, I shall assume the feasibility of my proposal and proceed to inquire how the rulers will arrange the particulars in practice. At the same time, I shall seek to demonstrate that nothing could be more beneficial to our city and its guardians than a successful implementation of our proposal. Let us consider this first, and then we can address the other issue.

Permission granted. Proceed as you suggest.

I suppose that worthy rulers will be prepared to command and worthy helpers ready to obey. In some of their commands the rulers   c will obey the laws. In those matters of detail that we have left to their discretion their commands will imitate the spirit of the laws.

Presumably they will.

As their lawgiver, you will have selected these men. You will apply the same criteria to select women whose natures are as similar as possible to those of the men. They will live in common houses and   d eat at common meals. There will be no private property. They will live together, learn together, and exercise together. The necessities of nature, I presume, would see to it that they will also mate with one another. Or is necessity too strong a word?

Not if you mean the necessities of love. They attract and compel most people with far greater force than all geometric necessities posited by the mathematicians.

You are right, Glaucon. But irregularity in sexual relations or in e any other matters has no place in a happy city; the rules will not tolerate it.

They would be right.

Then it is evident that we must make marriage a sacred relationship, so far as may be. And those marriages that attain the highest degree of sanctity will produce the best results.

Agreed.

459 What will produce the best results? You can help me, Glaucon, for I have seen hunting dogs and a number of pedigreed cocks at your house. Have you noticed something about how they mate and breed?

What?

Well, first of all, even though all of them are thoroughbreds, some prove out better than others?

True.

So are you indiscriminate in how you breed them, or do you breed from the best?

From the best.

b And which age do you select for the breeding? The young or the old or, so far as possible, those in their prime?

Those in their prime.

And if you failed to supervise the breeding in this way, you would have to expect that the quality of your stock of birds and hounds would deteriorate?

Certainly.

Would it be the same with horses and other animals?

Without doubt.

Well, then, old friend, if the same holds true for human beings, we can see how urgent is our need for rulers with the highest skills.

c It does hold true, but what of it?

I say this because the rulers will have to employ many of the kinds of drugs we spoke of earlier. Remember we said that those who can be healed by submitting their bodies to diet and regimen do not need drugs and can be attended by an ordinary doctor. But we know that where it is necessary to prescribe drugs, a physician with greater imagination and audacity will be indispensable.

True, but what is your point?

I mean that the rulers will probably have to resort to frequent doses
d of lies and mystifications for the benefit of their subjects. You will recall that we said these kinds of lies could be advantageous if used after the manner of medical remedies.

And we were right.

And the right use of this sort of medicine will very often be imperative in matters of marriage and the begetting of children.

How so?

It follows necessarily from the conclusion we reached a moment ago. The best of the men must mate with the best of the women as often as possible. Inferior should mate with inferior as seldom as possible. In order to safeguard the quality of the stock the children of the best unions must be retained for nurture by the rulers, but the others not. And how all this will be managed must be known to none but the rulers, so that the guardian flock will not be divided by dissension.

Quite right.

So we shall appoint certain times of festival and sacrifice when brides and bridegrooms will come together. For these occasions we shall have our poets compose appropriate marriage hymns. But how many marriages take place will be left to the discretion of the rulers. They will want to keep the number of citizens as nearly constant as possible (allowing for wars and plagues and like events) so that our city will become neither too great nor too small.

Right.

Then I suppose we shall have to invent some kind of ingenious lottery for use at each of the marriage festivals so that the inferior ones will blame their lot on bad luck and not on the rulers.

By all means.

Prizes and honors must be awarded to those of our young men who excel in war and in other employments, including the privilege of more frequent love-making with the women. These devices offer us a ready pretext to insure that they will be the ones begetting the most children.

True.

Children so born will be placed in the care of officials appointed for the purpose. These will be men or women or both, since both men and women will hold official positions, will they not?

Yes.

So the children of the superior parents will be led into a pen or paddock in a different quarter of the city where they will be given over to nurses living there. But it will be our policy to remove children of inferior parents and any who are born defective to some unknown and unseen place.

Yes. Your procedure is obviously a necessary condition for maintaining quality in the guardian stock.

The rulers will supervise the nursing of the children. They will lead the mothers to the pen when their breasts are full, but they must take every precaution to prevent any mother from recognizing her own infant. Should a mother have insufficient milk, they will provide a substitute to suckle the child. But they will see to it that the mothers themselves do not nurse too long, so that they will be spared getting up at night and other burdensome tasks. Both wet and dry nurses will be on hand to perform these duties.

Your guardian mothers are getting off easy.

They should. But let us address the next point in our proposal. We said that children should be born of parents in their prime.

We did.

e   Would it be fair to reckon that men are in their prime for about thirty years and women for twenty?

Between what ages?

Beginning at twenty, the women will bear children for the state until the age of forty. Men will enter their prime when they demonstrate swiftness in running and will beget children until they reach their fifty-fifth year.

461   I see. You mean that the prime years coincide with maturity in both body and mind.

Now if anyone older or younger than the ages we have indicated meddles in these matters of procreation, he shall be accused by the city of impiety and injustice. Even if his trespass goes unnoticed, his child will have been born unattended by the prayers and sacrifices of the priests and priestesses and of the entire city at the time the marriage ceremonies take place. These devotions are offered so that good sires may beget ever-better offspring, that fathers who render good service to the state may produce sons who will bring the state still

b   greater fortune. But the child of the circumstances we just mentioned shall be conceived in gross incontinence and born in darkness.

Right.

We shall apply the same rule to a man who is still within the age eligible for procreation but who mates with a woman with whom the rulers have not paired him. We shall charge him with foisting upon the state an unauthorized and unholy bastard.

Quite right.

These rules, I should think, will apply only to the age range we specified. We shall permit men past their prime to form liaisons with

c   whomever they wish, but not with their mothers or daughters, nor with their grandmothers or granddaughters. The women will have the same freedom but with the corresponding exceptions in respect to fathers and sons and grandfathers and grandsons. This freedom will be granted with the proviso that should conception result from any of these unions, the fetus shall not be allowed to see the light of day. If a birth cannot be prevented, they must put the child away since it cannot be raised among us.

These all seem like sensible proposals. But how will anyone rec-

ognize his relatives? Who will know her father? Who will know his d
daughter?

None will ever know. But a man will count from his time as bridegroom to the tenth month or as early as the seventh month. All the
male children born in this period he will call his sons; the females
he will call his daughters. And all these will call him father. Their
children, in turn, he will call his grandchildren, and they will call
those who were in his marriage group grandfather and grandmother.
All children conceived during the same mating period will consider
each other as brothers and sisters. This should suffice to keep them e
away from one another. The law will, however, permit brothers and
sisters to sleep together if the lots they draw turn out that way, and if
the oracle at Delphi approves.

Very good.

So much, Glaucon, for the way we shall organize the community
of women and children among the guardians. Next, our argument
must test out these arrangements to see if they are consistent with
the rest of the city's structure and, above all, whether they will serve
the city's best interests. Do you agree?

Entirely.   462

In order to reach agreement in these matters, would it not be
logical to begin the argument by asking what should be the proper
goal of legislators and legislation—and what constitutes for the city
the greatest good and the greatest evil? Then we could ascertain whether
the proposals we have just made will accord with what is good and
not with what is evil.

A fair procedure.

Can a city know any greater evil than to be divided, to be many b
instead of one? Can there be any greater good than what binds the
city together?

None.

Is not the community of pleasure and pain the tie that binds? The
sharing, to the greatest extent possible, of joy and sorrow over the
same births and deaths?

Yes.

But the tie is broken when private concerns displace shared emotional experiences, when the same events in the life of the city and c
among its inhabitants cause some to grieve while others rejoice.

True.

This disaffection, in turn, results primarily from disagreement
among the citizens about such matters as what is "mine," what is
"not mine," and what is "somebody else's."

Exactly.

Then the city will be best ordered where the greatest number of its citizens are in accord about the things that should be called "mine" and those that should be called "not mine."

Right.

So the best city is one whose situation is most like that of an individual human being. If one of us injures a finger, I would assume that the bodily network communicates the event to the governing soul. Because the soul presides over an integral entity, the entire body feels the pain even though only a part of it has suffered injury. This is what we say happens when someone hurts his finger. The same holds true for all the other parts of the human body, whether they are suffering pain or experiencing the delights of pleasure.

Right. And coming back to your previous question, I agree that the best state will be most like the human organism.

Then if any of its citizens experiences anything good or evil, the best state will share the experience as a whole, rejoicing in the pleasure or suffering the pain.

If the city is well governed, it certainly will.

Then it is time to return to our city. We must see whether it exhibits better than any others the qualities we agreed on during the course of our argument.

By all means.

Well, then, in other cities there are rulers and people, just as in ours?

Yes.

And in all of them the inhabitants call each other fellow citizens?

Of course.

But what do the citizens in other cities call their rulers?

In most cities they call them masters. But in democracies they simply call them magistrates.

And the people in our city? What other name do they give to their magistrates besides "citizen"?

They call them benefactors and helpers.

And what, in turn, do the magistrates call the people?

Their employers and supporters.

And what do rulers in other cities call the people?

Slaves.

How do the rulers in other cities address each other?

Fellow rulers.

And in our city?

Fellow guardians.

Have you ever heard of rulers in other cities who commonly refer to some of their fellow rulers as kin while others they call outsiders?

There are many.

And anyone who speaks this way means that the one whom he

considers to be his kin he also considers to be his own, but he excludes   c
outsiders.

True.

But what of our city? Would any of our guardians think or speak
of a fellow guardian as an outsider?

Never. All those he meets will be for him brother, sister, father,
mother, son, daughter, or others of his lineage.

Excellent. But here is another question. Will these all be kin in
name only, or will guardians also behave according to the spirit of
the family? Will there be the customary observances toward fathers?   d
Will parents be respected, cherished, and obeyed? Since any other
kind of conduct would be impious and unjust, would those who
violate these precepts incur the displeasure of both men and gods?
Shall the children be taught these precepts as the common doctrine
of the city? Or shall there be some other kind of teaching imposed
upon the children from birth onward concerning what is due to those
they are taught to call father as well as to other kin?

They must be taught the precepts you cite. Mere lip service with-   e
out performing the deeds of kinship would be preposterous.

In our city, then, more than any other, when a citizen does well
or ill, the others will respond in common with the word we spoke of
earlier: it is "mine" that does well, or "mine" that does ill.

I agree.

And did we not say that such words and such convictions will bind   464
a community together in pleasure and in pain?

We were right in saying so.

More than any others, then, our citizens will be united by a common interest they will call "mine." This unity will cause them to
share pleasure and pain in common.

Right.

And the reason for this, along with the constitution of the state, is
the community of wives and children among the guardians?

That will certainly be the most important reason.

We further agreed that this is the state's greatest good. That was   b
the implication when we compared the well-ordered state to a human
body which experiences and shares the pleasures and pains of its
parts.

Right.

Then the sharing of women and children is indisputably the source
of the state's greatest good.

Right.

And we remain consistent with what we said earlier. You remember that we said the guardians ought not to live in private houses,
nor should they own land or any other private property. Instead they

c   should receive wages for their work as guardians from funds paid in
by the other citizens and spend them in common if they are going
to be true guardians.

Yes.

What I am trying to say is that the arrangements we agreed to
previously and those we have set forth just now will strengthen our
guardians still further in the faithful performance of their duties.
Will they not ward off dissension in the city by preventing the guardians from arguing about what is "mine" and what is not "mine"? Or
from helping themselves to whatever they can lay their hands on and
d   taking it away to their own houses? Or from having women and
children apart from the rest and so intruding private pleasures and
pains into the affairs of state? Instead, they will be united with one
another. They will share common convictions and purposes in governing their household. To the very limits of possibility they will feel
pleasure and pain in common.

That they will.

And because all is held in common, with only their own bodies
remaining to them as private possessions, will not indictments and
lawsuits vanish from among them? Will they not be free of faction
e   insofar as factiousness derives from quarrels about money, children,
and matters of kinship?

Faction must be banished, and this is the way to do it.

Nor would there be a likely cause for lawsuits arising from assault
or bodily injury. For we held that self-defense is right and honorable
between persons of the same age. It follows that all must regard the
conditioning of their bodies as a matter of necessity.

Right.

465   These rules of conduct offer a further advantage. An angry man,
seeking to satisfy his anger within such constraints, will be less likely
to push the quarrel to extremes.

I agree.

Further, the elders will always be in charge of censuring and punishing the younger ones.

Clearly.

Hence, except by command of the rulers, no young man is likely
to strike or do any other violence or dishonor to an elder. There are
two mighty guardians to restrain him: shame and fear. Shame will
b   dissuade him from laying hands on one who may be his parent, and
he will fear that others will come to aid his victim, to whom they are
sons, brothers, or fathers.

That's the way it will be.

Then all these laws will bring peace to the citizens?

A most profound peace.

And being free from faction among one another, the guardians need not fear that the city will rise up in factiousness against them nor divide against itself.

Surely not.

Here I feel hesitant about even mentioning that they will rid themselves of certain troubles so petty that they really ought to be   c beneath notice. I mean such things as the flattery poor men spend upon the rich, the struggle and pain of the poor in raising their children and procuring sufficient money for the life of their households. I mean the borrowing and then the repudiating of debt, and the resort to all sorts of devices to acquire money they then turn over to the stewardship of wives and servants. That these indignities are ignoble and degrading is so obvious they are not worth mention.

Even a blind man can see that.   d

So from all these things, too, they will finally be free. They will live a life happier than the most blessed lives of the Olympic victors.

In what respect?

Olympic honors amount to but a small portion of the tributes paid to the guardians. Theirs is the fairer victory and the greater repute. Their prize and triumph is the deliverance and salvation of the entire   e city. Their crown is the public support of themselves and their children in all the necessities of life. While they live, the city bestows upon them honors and tributes. When they die, they are given an honorable burial.

A fair reward.

Do you remember that earlier on in the argument someone—I have forgotten who—objected that we were not making our guardi-   466 ans very happy because they had the power to take everything from the other citizens, but we allowed them nothing? I believe our response was that we might return to the subject if the occasion should arise but that then we were making our guardians into guardians and our city as happy as possible. That is, our concern for happiness was not limited to any one class.

I remember.

Well, then, if we have shown that the lives of our guardians are better and nobler than the victors at Olympia, surely there is no need to compare them with the lives of farmers, cobblers, and other crafts-   b men?

I shouldn't think so.

Then it may be fair enough to repeat something else I said earlier. If a guardian should strive for any kind of happiness that will be his undoing as a guardian, if he should become discontent with the ways of moderation and security—with the way of life we have described as the best—if he should fall prey to some senseless and infantile misconception that happiness requires him to use his power for the purpose of appropriating everything in the city for himself, then he   c will discover the wisdom of Hesiod, who said that in some respects the half is more than the whole.

My advice would be that he should hold fast to the life of a proper guardian.

Then you will also agree to all we have said about the partnership of men and women in education, in the raising of children, and in guarding other citizens. You would agree further that both within the city and when they go off to war men and women should guard and hunt together like dogs do. Having all things in common, so far as possible, they will do what is best and shun anything contrary to woman's nature in her relationship to man. They will preserve the natural relations of the sexes and not suborn them.

I agree.

What remains to be done, then, is to ascertain whether it would be possible for such a community to be established among men as it is among the other animals, and how that might be accomplished.

You have anticipated the question I was just about to ask.

As far as their wars are concerned, their strategy and tactics are so obvious they hardly merit discussion.

What do you mean?

It is obvious that men and women will take the field together. Further, when the children have become hardy, they will bring them to the battlefield too, so that, like the children of the craftsmen, they will learn what they must do when they are grown. Besides looking on, they must also serve and assist in all the business of war and render aid to their fathers and mothers. Have you ever noticed the like practice in the other arts, how the sons of potters, for example, perform the role of onlookers and helpers for a very long time before they put their hands to the clay?

I have indeed.

Then should potters be more concerned than guardians about educating their children through observation and experience of what is to be their role in life?

Of course not. That would be ridiculous.

Further still, does not every creature in a fight do better in the presence of its offspring?

That is true, Socrates. But this involves great risks. Defeats are also part of war, and should the children be lost along with the parents, what remains of the city will never recover.

True. But would you argue that our first priority must be to avoid all danger?

Certainly not.

If, then, they must run risks, let them be those in which success will make them better men.

Agreed.

Does it make only a slight difference, and one not worth running risks for, whether or not men who are to be warriors observe war when they are boys?

No, it makes a great deal of difference to the issues you are addressing.

Assuming that we shall make the boys spectators of war, we must also take measures to provide them with security. Then all will be well. Won't it?

Yes.

First off, we may suppose that the parents are not blind to the risks of war. We may expect them instead to know, as much as humans can, which expeditions are dangerous and which not.   d

Presumably.

So they will take the boys along when it is safe but not when there is danger.

Right.

And they will not put them under mediocre commanders but will appoint their officers from among experienced veterans qualified to be both their leaders and their teachers.

That would be the way to do it.

Still, it may be objected that things for many men turn out contrary to expectations.

Very true.

To counteract such hazards we must first equip the children with wings. Then if need arises, they may fly away and make their escape.

What do you mean?   e

When very young, we must teach them to mount and ride horses. After that they must be brought to the battlefield, not by mettlesome steeds of war but astride the swiftest and gentlest of horses. This will best enable them to observe the future business of their lives. Should danger intrude, they are also in the best position to follow their elders and escape.

I believe you are right.

But what about the conduct of war itself? How should the soldiers   468
behave toward one another and toward the enemy? Would my assumptions about these matters be right or not?

What are your assumptions?

First, that anyone who deserts his post or throws away his weapons or is guilty of any similar acts of cowardice must be demoted to the ranks of artisans or farmers.

Right.

And anyone the enemy takes alive will be our gift to his captors, who may then do with their victim what they will.

b   Absolutely.

But the man who distinguishes himself and wins the prize of valor shall be crowned first by his comrades-in-arms and then in turn by the youths and the boys.

By all means.

And each will clasp his right hand in greeting?

That, too.

But perhaps you won't approve my next proposal.

What is it?

c   That all should kiss and be kissed by him.

Of course I approve. I would go still further and say that for the rest of the campaign anyone he wishes to kiss may not refuse him. For if anyone be in love with another, whether man or woman, he would be all the more eager to win the hero's reward.

Excellent. We have already said that the good man should have more wives than the rest; moreover, he will often be sought out by others for love affairs. The object, of course, is that as many children as possible shall come from his seed.

We agreed to that.

Let us also call in Homer as advocate of these kinds of honors for
d   the brave among our youth. Homer says that Ajax, having won distinction in the war, received the loin portion as his trophy. For a brave man in the very flower of his youth there can be no more fitting gift than one which both honors his deeds and begets in him still further strength.

That is surely right.

Then in this respect, at least, let Homer be our teacher. At sacrifices and on similar occasions we, too, shall honor the good—if indeed they have proven themselves good—with hymns and those other dis-
e   tinctions we have just been discussing. Men and women alike will be given "seats of honor, meat, and full cups" so that their honors will at the same time be conducive to further training.

Well said.

Let us now consider those who die in the campaign. Is it not so that the first thing we should say of a man who dies gloriously in war is that he belongs to the golden race?

We should.

And should we not believe what Hesiod tells us about the men of this race? When they die,

469
they become good and blessed spirits
abiding here on earth;
watchful guardians of all mortals,
impediments to evil.

We shall believe him.

Then we must learn from Apollo and heed his response concerning the kinds of burial arrangements and distinctions proper for men who have manifested heroic and even godlike qualities.

I entirely agree.

And we shall reverence their graves for all time as befits the remembrance of spirits touched by the divine. Shall we do the same   b
for anyone who has been deemed to be exceptionally good in the ordinary course of life, even though death is due to old age or some other cause?

That will surely be proper.

Next we ought to discuss how our soldiers should treat their enemies.

In what respect?

In respect first of all to slavery. Do you think it just that Greeks should enslave Greek cities? Or would it not be just instead to oppose any such policies? The danger of enslavement by the barbarians should   c
suffice to persuade Greeks to spare Greeks.

That is much the best policy.

Then there will be no Greek slaves in our city, a policy worthy of imitation in the rest of Greece.

Yes, indeed. It would in any case incline Greeks to stand against the barbarians instead of attacking one another.

Now what should we say to the practice of victors who strip the dead of more than their arms? Does this not offer cowards a pretext to evade the ongoing battle by poking about the dead as if they were   d
performing some necessary task? This is simply plunder, and it has deprived many an army of victory.

Very true.

Greed and meanness mark those who desecrate the dead. Only a petty and effeminate spirit will regard a dead body as an enemy when the real foeman has already vanished, leaving behind only the instrument he used to fight with. Do you see any difference between such behavior and that of dogs, unable to get at their assailant, who   e
snarl at the stones he throws at them instead?

An apt comparison.

Then we must desist from the practice of plundering corpses and refusing them burial.

That we must, by Zeus.

Nor will we bring weapons into the temples as offerings to the gods, and most particularly not Greek weapons, if we have any con-   470
cern about preserving friendly relations among Greeks. We should rather learn to fear that such offerings taken from our kin will pollute the temples unless, of course, the god should bid us do otherwise.

Wise provisions.

And what about burning Greek houses and ravaging Greek lands? How shall the soldiers treat their enemies in these matters?

I should be glad to learn your opinion.

b   I think both these practices should be forbidden the soldiers. They should confine themselves to appropriating the annual harvest. Shall I tell you why?

Yes.

I think it is relevant to note that we use *faction* and *war* as two different terms in connection with two different contexts. The one context is characterized by friendly and kindred relations, the other by what is foreign and alien. In the first context strife goes by the name of *faction*. Only with aliens do we use the word *war*.

You have hit the mark.

c   Now see whether I do as well with this point. I assert that Greeks are friends and kin to one another, but barbarians are for them foreign and alien.

Rightly said.

It follows then that when Greeks and barbarians take up arms against one another, they are enemies by nature and that *war* is the proper name for their enmity and hatred. When hostilities break out among Greeks, however, we shall say that by nature Greeks are still friends but that in this particular case Greece is sick and divided by faction.

d   It follows that such enmity should go by the name of *faction*.

I would agree to your formulations.

Then, assume that fighting of the sort we now call faction occurs, and the city is divided against itself. If the contending parties ravish the lands and burn each other's houses, their strife must be condemned as bringing a curse upon the city, and neither side can claim to be true patriots. Otherwise they would never have dared to inflict such outrages upon their nurse and mother. Moderation and reason, on the other hand, would admonish the victors to limit themselves to confiscating the losers' crops and to exhibit the temper of men

e   who expect to be reconciled and not to be constantly at war.

Such a temper is greatly to be preferred to that of savagery.

Now consider this. The city being founded will be a Greek city, will it not?

Necessarily.

Then its citizens will be good and gentle?

Of course.

And they will be lovers of their fellow Greeks. Will they not regard all Greece as their home and take their proper part in caring for the holy places that all the Greeks revere?

Indeed.

Then they will consider Greeks to be their own people and regard any differences among them as factiousness; they will refuse even to consider them as the equivalent of war.

Certainly.

And when quarreling with one another, they will hold fast to the 471 purpose of eventual reconciliation?

That they should.

They will not punish, enslave, or destroy each other. They will not act like enemies but like guardians of the law, chastening others with kindly discipline.

Indeed they should.

Being Greeks, they will not burn houses nor ravage Greek lands. They will never declare the entire population of any city—men, women, and children—to be their enemies. Instead, they will identify only a few as their foes at any one time—those, namely, who are to blame for the quarrel. All these considerations will inhibit them b from destroying houses and laying waste the land since they know the majority to be friends. They will press the conflict only to the point warranted by the sufferings of the innocent and to the extent necessary to bring the guilty to justice.

I am one of those who agree that this is the way our citizens ought to deal with their Greek opponents. The ways Greeks actually behave toward one another now should be confined to our relations with barbarians.

Should we then promulgate this additional law for our guardians: they are not to burn houses or lay waste land? c

Let us so decree. Let us also assume that this and all the previous prescriptions are correct. But, Socrates, if we allow you to go on like this, I fear you will never come to the point of discussing the matters you put aside in order to say all that you have just said. Those matters, you recall, raised the question whether a city such as you have described could ever be a real possibility and how that possibility might be realized. Were your city to be duly constituted, I am among those ready to admit that it would be a boon to its citizens. And I will add what you left out in passing that such a city would be the most successful in war because citizens would be least likely to betray d one another. That is because they know and speak to each other as fathers, brothers, and sons. Should the women join in their campaigns on the front line or in the rear—either to frighten the enemy or as reserves in case of need—all this will make the city still more invincible. On the home front, too, I assume all the benefits you omitted to mention. Let us take it for granted that these and countless other advantages will accrue to the city so constituted. But let us leave off belaboring these points. Excluding all other considerations, e let us now proceed to examine just one thing: whether such a city is possible, and, if so, how it might be brought into being.

472   You are abrupt, my friend. You assault my argument without any regard for my understandable reluctance to press it further. Perhaps you don't realize what you are doing: after I have barely escaped the first two waves, you come along and summon up the third and greatest of the waves, the most formidable of them all. When you have seen and heard my proposal, I am sure you will be lenient with me. At least, you will acknowledge that I had good reason for fear and hesitation about entering into a discussion of so great a paradox.

b   The more such excuses you make, the more we shall insist that you tell us how your city may be realized. So speak out, and don't waste our time.

The first thing we must recall, then, is that we have arrived at this point because we began with an inquiry into the nature of justice and injustice.

What of it?

Oh, nothing. But if we do discover what justice is, must we require of the just man that he meet the standards of justice in every respect and without ever straying? Or should we be content that his behavior

c   should approximate and honor justice more than the behavior of others?

We should be content with that.

Then when we were discussing the nature of absolute justice and injustice—as well as the perfectly just man (supposing that he exists) and the completely unjust man—we were looking for ideals and patterns of instruction. We wanted to bring them into focus as models so that we might judge our own happiness or unhappiness according to the standards they set and according to the degree we reflect them. It was not our purpose to demonstrate the possibility of

d   fully realizing these ideals.

You are right.

Suppose an artist painted an ideally beautiful man, so that his portrait should lack nothing that could contribute to its perfection. Were he then unable to prove that any such man could exist, would that make him any less an artist?

No, by Zeus.

And have we not been trying to create a model of an ideal state in words?

e   We have.

Then do you think our words are any less compelling simply because we are unable to prove that it would be possible to govern a state in accord with what the words prescribe?

No.

Then we have spoken truly. However, if you wish it, I shall strive to show how a real city might most nearly approach the ideal. But you must reaffirm the concessions you made earlier.

What concessions?

Can deeds perfectly match words? Is it not true, whether some   473
deny it or not, that action stands further from truth than speech? How do you stand on these questions?

I stand with you.

Then you won't insist that all the words we have been using so far must find their precise counterparts in practice. But if we can show how a city might be constituted most nearly approximating what we have previously described, then you must concede that we have demonstrated the possibility of its realization. I should be very con-   b
tent with that. Would that satisfy you, too?

It would.

Now we must try to find out what it is that causes our cities to be so badly governed and what prevents them from being governed well. What might be the least change that would transform bad government into good government? It would surely be preferable to manage this with a single change. If not one change then two; if not two, then the fewest and most moderate changes possible.

Proceed.   c

I think there is one change that could bring about the transformation we desire. It is no small change, nor would it be easy to implement. But it is possible.

What is it?

So. At last I come face to face with what I have called the greatest of the waves. But I will speak even if it break over my head and drown me in a flood of laughter and derision. Mark my words.

I am all attention.

Unless philosophers become kings in our cities, or unless those who now are kings and rulers become true philosophers, so that   d
political power and philosophic intelligence converge, and unless those lesser natures who run after one without the other are excluded from governing, I believe there can be no end to troubles, my dear Glaucon, in our cities or for all mankind. Only then will our theory   e
of the state spring to life and see the light of day, at least to the degree possible. Now you see why I held back so long from speaking out about so troublesome a proposition. For it points to a vexing lesson: whether in private or public life there is no other way to achieve happiness.

Socrates, after launching such an assault you must expect to be attacked by hordes of our leading men of learning. They will at once cast off their garments and strip for action—metaphorically speaking,

474 of course. Snatching the first handy weapon, they will rush at you full tilt, fully prepared to do dreadful deeds. If you can't find arguments to fend them off and make your escape, you will learn what it means to be scorned and despised.

It was you who got me into this.

A good thing, too. But I won't desert you; I'll help defend you as best I can. My good will and encouragement may be of use, and perhaps I shall be able to offer more suitable answers than others.

b With such a helpmate at your side you should be able to be at your best in convincing the unbelievers that you are right.

Your invaluable offer of assistance obliges me to try. If we are going to find some way to elude our assailants, I think we must explain what we mean by our daring suggestion that philosophers ought to be rulers. First, we must make clear what it is to be a philosopher. Then, we should be able to vindicate ourselves by explain-

c ing that philosophy and political leadership are inherent qualities of the philosopher's nature, so that it behooves the others to let philosophy alone and to follow the leaders.

It is high time that you come forward with your explanation.

Then let us proceed along the following lines to see if we can clarify our position.

Go ahead.

Need I remind you—or do you remember—that we said if a man loves something, he ought to show his love for all of it? It will not do for him to say that some of it he likes and some not.

d It is well that you remind me because I really don't understand what you are saying.

Such an answer would come from another better than from you, Glaucon. As a lover, you should know how everyone in the flower of youth somehow stirs and arouses emotion in the lover's breast, and all appear desirable and worthy of his attentions. Is that not the way you respond to the fair? You will describe the one with the snub nose as having verve. A hook nose confers on another a royal countenance. He whose nose is neither snub nor hooked is endowed with

e regularity of proportion. To be dark-skinned is manly, while the fair are children of the gods. As for the "honey-colored," what is the term itself but a euphemism invented by some lover who is willing to put up with a pallid complexion if only it is coupled with bloom-

475 ing youth? In short, you will employ any pretense and any fair word rather than risk losing a single one of the young flowers.

If you want to make me your example of a lover's traits, I admit to them for the sake of the argument.

What do you say to the lovers of wine? Do they not do the same thing? Are they not eager to consume every kind of wine on any pretext?

They are.

The same again with men of ambition. If they can't manage to become commanding generals, they are still willing to give commands as lieutenants. If the high and mighty will not honor them, they are willing to accept honors from lesser folk. But honors they must have.

All too true.

Then I have a proposition for you to accept or reject. When we say that a man desires something, do we say he desires all that pertains to it or only one part and not another?

He will desire the whole of it.

So we can say of the philosopher that he loves all wisdom and not just fragments of it.

Yes.

Then any student who is half-hearted in his studies—especially when he is young and lacks the understanding to judge between what is useful and what is not—cannot be called a philosopher or a lover of wisdom. He is like one who picks at his food. We say that he is not really hungry and has no appetite. We say that he is a poor eater and no lover of the table.

Rightly.

But he who is inclined to sample all studies, who gladly addresses himself to the task of learning and cannot get enough of it, he is the one we shall rightly call philosopher and lover of wisdom?

But Glaucon demurred: Not so. You will be conferring these titles on a strange and motley crew. For example, all the lovers of entertainments and other splendors become what they are, I suppose, because they delight in learning something. And those who are always clamoring to hear something new are queer fish to be counted among philosophers. They can't be induced to attend a serious debate or similar entertainment, but they run to all the festivals celebrating Dionysus as if they were paid to lend their ears to every chorus in the land. No difference whether the show is in town or country village, they never miss a one. Are we really to regard these and their like and all the practitioners of the minor arts as philosophers?

No, but they do bear a likeness to philosophers.

Who, then, are the true philosophers?

Those who come to love the spectacle of truth.

That is right. But in what sense do you mean it?

It would not be easy at all to explain it to someone else. But you, I think, would concede this much.

What?

Since beauty is the opposite of ugliness, they are two different things.

Of course.

But since they are two, each is also one?

Agreed.

The same extends to justice and injustice, good and bad, and all other forms. Each in itself is one; yet because each always appears in a great variety of combinations of things and events, it seems instead to be many.

That is true.

And that is how I distinguish those whom you variously described as practical people or lovers of spectacles and the arts from those who alone merit the name of philosophers and with whom our argument is really concerned.

What do you mean?

The lovers of sights and sounds surely delight in beautiful tones, colors, and shapes and in all that art fashions from them, but their mind is unable to recognize and delight in the nature of beauty itself.

That is right.

Then he who believes there are beautiful things but does not believe in beauty itself and who is unable to follow if another tries to lead him to the knowledge of beauty, should we say of him that his life is more like waking or dreaming? Consider: is not the dreamer, whether awake or asleep, one who mistakes appearance for reality?

Anyone who does that is certainly dreaming.

Contrast him with the man who believes that there is such a thing as beauty itself. He is able to contemplate it as well as its parts without confusing essence and things that share in essence. Is he awake or dreaming?

He is very much awake.

Could we not say of the latter that he knows and so has knowledge, while the former makes assumptions and is therefore a captive of opinion?

We would have reason to say so.

But supposing the one who we say is caught up in opinion but who does not realize it becomes angry? Suppose he challenges the truth of our allegation? Can we appease him in any way and try gently to win him over without being so awkward as to tell him he is not in his right mind?

We should try.

Then let us think what we shall say to him. Or should we proceed along the following lines, assuring him that no one begrudges any knowledge he may possess? On the contrary, we should be very glad to discover that he knows something. Let us beg his leave to ask a question: does a man who knows know something or nothing? Would you answer for him?

My reply would be that he knows something.

Is it something that is or is not?

Something that is. How could something be known which is not?   477

Then we can reach a conclusion that will hold however often we scrutinize it: that which entirely is is entirely knowable, but that which in no way is is entirely unknowable.

I agree.

Good. Now if anything is of such a nature as both to be and not to be, would it not lie between what absolutely is and what absolutely is not?

Yes.

Knowledge, then, is of what is and ignorance necessarily is of what is not. If something is really there between what is and what is not, we must find something intermediate that will enable us to see it.   b

Very well.

Do we speak of something called opinion?

Yes.

Is it a force different from knowledge, or is it the same?

Different.

Then opinion pertains to one thing and knowledge to another, each according to its own capability.

True.

So knowledge is naturally related to what is; it is able to know what is and how it is. But before going any further I think we should lay down some definitions and distinctions.

What do you have in mind?

Well, let us consider a class of abilities that enable us—and all   c other things too—to do whatever we (and they) are capable of doing. Examples of such abilities are sight and hearing. Do I make myself clear?

I understand.

Then this is what I think about them. When I focus on abilities, I perceive neither color, shape, nor any other property such as I see when I look at many other kinds of things and am trying to distinguish for myself one from another. When I think about ability, I   d look to one thing only: what purpose it is disposed to serve and what are its effects. This is the kind of scrutiny that enables me to ascertain whether or not something is in fact an ability. And whatever is related to the same purpose and produces the same effects is the same ability, the same power; different purposes and effects prove the presence of a different ability. How about you? How do you see the matter?

The same as you do.

Then let us return to knowledge. Would you say that knowledge is an example of an ability, or would you locate it in some other class of things?

I would call knowledge the most powerful of all abilities.

e   And how about opinion? Shall we call it something other than a capacity?

No. We couldn't do that because opining results from an ability to form opinions.

But you agreed just a little while ago that opinion and knowledge are not the same.

How could any rational person equate what is fallible with what is infallible?

478   Excellent. So we are agreed that opinion is different from knowledge?

Yes. It is different.

Then since each is a different kind of ability, each produces different effects and relates to different things.

Necessarily.

Knowledge presumably relates to reality; it knows what is and how it is.

Yes.

But opinion is the product of beliefs or convictions.

Yes.

Will they be the same thing as the knowledge that knows? Will what is knowable and what is a matter of opinion be the same? Or is that impossible?

According to our previous arguments, it is impossible. If opinion
b   and knowledge are different capacities and if different capacities are naturally related to different things, our reasoning so far rules out any attempt to equate what is knowable with what is simply a matter of opinion.

Then that which can be known is something other than that concerning which there can only be an opinion.

Yes, it is something else.

Is it possible or impossible to have an opinion about something nonexistent? Think about it. When a man has an opinion, does he not have an opinion about something? Or must we reverse ourselves and say that he can have an opinion that is an opinion about nothing?

Impossible.

So opinion involves opining some one thing?

Yes.

c   Further, then, some one thing cannot be equated with what does not exist, for that would be the same as equating it to nothing at all.

Yes.

We earlier related ignorance to the domain of unreality and knowledge to reality?

Rightly so.

Then it follows that opinion has as the object of its attention neither what is nor what is not.

Apparently not.

So then opinion is something different from both ignorance and knowledge.

Apparently.

Then opinion is a capacity distinct from these? Is it more brilliant than knowledge or darker than ignorance?

Neither one.

Do you then deem opinion as something whose light is less than knowledge but brighter than ignorance?

Very much so.

So it lies somewhere between the two?   d

Yes.

Then opinion should be located between the two?

I am sure of it.

Did we not say a little while ago that if something falls into a category that neither is nor is not, it would be located somewhere between what fully exists and what is totally nonexistent? And that the ability to perceive it would be neither knowledge nor ignorance but something in between?

We did.

And now we have before us opinion as an example of such an intermediate category.

We do.

It seems, then, that we still need to discover what partakes of both   e
being and not being—of both knowledge and ignorance—but cannot rightly be called the pure form of either. Once this unknown comes to light, we can properly call it the realm of opinion. After that we shall be able to assign opinion itself to the middle of the spectrum in between knowledge and ignorance. Do you agree?

Yes.

Holding to these premises, let us turn to that good fellow who does   479
not believe that there is anything one could call beautiful in itself, who rejects any idea of beauty absolute and unchanging. He is the same fellow who is the lover of spectacles and who believes in many beautiful things but who cannot tolerate anyone saying that beauty is one, that justice is one, and so on. Now I shall put a question and ask him to answer: my friend, will not any of these beautiful things sometimes appear ugly and base? And of the things that are just, will they not sometimes seem unjust? Of holy things, will they not sometimes seem unholy?

It is unavoidable that sometimes what is beautiful in one perspec-   b tive would appear ugly in another, and so with all the other things you asked about.

And what about the concept of double? Doesn't double look just as often to be half?

As often half as double.

And what of things called great and small, heavy and light? Can they not just as frequently be called their opposites?

Yes. Each will always be identified with its opposite.

Then can each of these relationships be said to be more one thing than the other?

c   You make me think of the jesters who beguile us at banquets with double meanings—also of that child's riddle about the eunuch throwing something at a bat and why he failed to hit it.[1] These kinds of things are also equivocal, and it is impossible to assign them one meaning or its opposite or both.

What to do with them? Can you find a better place to put them than in that intermediate realm between reality and unreality? I should suppose they would not be more obscure, and so less real, than
d   unreality itself; nor would they be clearer, and so more real, than reality.

I agree.

Then we have apparently discovered that many opinions held by many people about such matters as beauty and justice are floating around somewhere in between reality and unreality.

That we have done.

But we agreed in advance that should any such things be discovered, they should be classified as matters of opinion and not as matters of knowledge. They would be denizens of that intermediate zone of flux to which, as we said earlier, the intermediate ability is confined.

That we did.

e   We shall conclude, then, that those who behold many beautiful things but cannot see beauty itself—and will not permit another to guide them to where it is—who observe many just things but do not see justice itself and think this way in all other things, such men have opinions about everything but know nothing of what they profess to believe.

The conclusion is sound.

On the other hand, those who always contemplate things in themselves, things that always remain the same and never change, shall

---

1. An ancient commentator says that the riddle posed was this: a man who was not a man, seeing and not seeing a bird that was not a bird upon a branch that was not a branch, struck it and did not strike it with a stone that was not a stone. The answer is: a eunuch with imperfect eyesight threw a pumice stone at a bat that was sitting on a reed and missed.

we not say that they exhibit knowledge and not merely opinion?

That conclusion also follows.

These latter are the ones that love knowledge and delight in thought, are they not? The others are lovers of opinion? Do you remember that we said they loved and admired beautiful tones and colors and the like but that they could not endure the proposition that there should be reality in the idea of beauty itself? 480

We remember.

Would it be appropriate to call them lovers of opinion rather than lovers of wisdom? Will they be very angry if we say this?

Not if they share my conviction that no one should take offense at the truth.

Then those who in every way welcome true knowledge we shall call lovers of wisdom and not lovers of opinion.

I wholeheartedly agree.

Book VI

So, Glaucon, after we have come a long way our argument has finally made clear to us who are the philosophers and lovers of wisdom and who are not.

Yes, I suppose a shorter way would have proved impassable.

Probably. In any case, I think the whole issue could have been made clearer if it had been our sole concern. But there were so many b other things we were bound to discuss so long as we held to our purpose of distinguishing the just life from the unjust.

Then what comes next?

What's next in order? We have said that philosophers are those capable of comprehending what is eternal and unchanging. Those who are not philosophers lack this capability; instead they wander about inspecting swarms of irrelevancies. So who ought to be the leaders in a city?

How would one give a fair answer to the question?

By deciding who appear competent to guard the laws and the c activities of society: these should be made the guardians.

Agreed.

Should the guardian who is to keep watch be blind or clear-sighted?

That is hardly a difficult question.

Well, then, is there any discernible difference between those who lack knowledge of the true essence of things and those who are physically blind? I mean those whose souls are void of any clear pattern, who have no models to look to as painters do, and so cannot behold d truth, cannot use truth as their measure. Could, then, such as these prescribe laws to serve goodness, beauty, and justice—or guard and preserve those already in force?

No, by Zeus.

Then should we choose the sightless ones as guardians rather than those who have come to know truth and who are second to none in experience and virtue?

That would be a strange choice unless the philosophers prove deficient in other qualities. Moreover, their greater knowledge is itself the warrant of their excellence.

Then what we need to ascertain is whether it is possible for any   485
people to have all the necessary qualities.

True.

As we noted earlier, the first thing we have to understand is the
nature of the persons with whom we are concerned. If we sufficiently
agree about this, then we shall likely agree also that the combination
of qualities we seek is to be found in this kind of person. Then we
need seek no further for guardians for our cities.

How do you mean?

We must first agree that one trait of the philosophical nature is
ever to be in love with knowledge—not the kind caught up in the
never-ending round of birth and death, but the knowledge that dis-   b
closes something of the eternal.

We do agree.

And such a nature loves and wants all of that knowledge. He does
not willingly renounce any part of it, small or large, more valuable
or less. In this he is like those covetous of love and of honor whom
we described earlier.

Yes.

Must not those natures who are to meet our qualifications exhibit
a further quality?   c

Which quality have you in mind?

Truthfulness: an unwillingness to countenance falsehood of any
kind, a hatred of untruth, a love of truth.

Probably.

Not probably, but necessarily. He who is in love cannot help loving all that belongs to the object of his love.

True.

Can you think of anything belonging together more closely than
wisdom and truth?

Impossible.

Then can the same person be a lover of both wisdom and false-   d
hood?

No.

Hence the true lover of knowledge must from childhood on seek
truth in all its aspects.

Yes.

At the same time, we know that when a man's desires strongly
incline to any one thing, they are weaker with respect to other things.
It is like a stream being diverted to another channel.

Yes.

So if a man's desires have been taught to flow into the channel of
learning, he will become caught up in the pleasures of the soul. If
he is a true and not a counterfeit philosopher, he will become indif-   e
ferent to the pleasures of the body.

Necessarily.

Such a man will be moderate and no lover of money. Others may eagerly seek the things money buys, but not he.

That is right.

486   There is still another measure to be used in distinguishing a philosophical from a nonphilosophical nature.

What is it?

Stinginess. Nothing can be more contrary to a soul seeking integrity and completeness in all things, human and divine.

True.

And do you think a mind of true grandeur, fixed on eternity and on all being, will assign much importance to the life of man?

Impossible.

b   Death will not be terrible to such a man?

To him least of all.

Then stinginess and cowardice evidently have no place in true philosophical natures?

I don't think so.

Would a man who has put his soul in order, who is generous and doesn't love money, who is neither braggart nor coward—would he ever be unjust? Would he ever be a driver of hard bargains?

Impossible.

Here is another consideration in distinguishing the philosophical from the nonphilosophical man: whether from youth on he is gentle and just or quarrelsome and savage.

c   That is much to the point.

I also assume you would not fail to consider this.

What?

Whether he is quick or slow to learn. Or do you suppose anyone could really love a task that he found painfully difficult and yielded him little gain for much toil?

He could not.

And if he could not remember what he learned and went about more or less oblivious, his knowledge would simply slip away.

Yes.

And so, having exerted himself for naught, will he not ultimately come to loathe both himself and his failed occupation?

Without question.

d   Lovers of wisdom require good memories. We cannot permit forgetful souls to be counted among their number.

That is right.

What about measure and proportion? Are they not beyond the reach of natures lacking in harmony and balance?

They are.

And truth, in turn, is it not linked to measure and proportion? Or is it rather akin to disproportion?

To proportion.

Then proportion, measure, and grace join our list of requirements in seeking natures whose affinities will unerringly draw them toward reality and truth.

Is there any flaw in the argument so far? Have we not demon- e strated that the qualities we have cited are both necessary and compatible for any soul who would lay claim to a true understanding of reality?

The qualities are clearly necessary to the purpose.

Can you, then, find any fault with a course of study that can be 487 followed only by him whose nature learns quickly and whose memory is long, who displays the qualities of magnificence and grace, who is friend and kin to truth, justice, courage, and temperance?

Momus himself couldn't fault such a combination.[1]

Well, then, when they are matured by education and age, are these not the kind of men who alone should rule the city?

At this point Adeimantus intervened: No one would be able to dispute these statements of yours, Socrates. Nonetheless, when your b listeners hear you argue in this way, they think that because they are inexperienced in your method of question and answer, each question leads them ever so slightly astray until they reach the end of the argument when the sum of these divergences amounts to serious error and self-contradiction. They feel like unskilled players in a game c contending with masters; they are finally cornered and can't make a move. So it is with your game, played with words instead of counters: finally their mouths are stopped, and they don't know what to say. Yet the truth of the matter has by no means been settled. Our present subject of discussion is a case in point. Someone might say that as far as words are concerned, he is unable to contradict you in any of your questions. But when he looks at the facts, he sees that of those who turn to philosophy—not the people who are merely acquiring a nodding acquaintance with it by way of rounding off their education but rather those who linger with the study of philosophy too long— d the majority become cranks, not to say completely debased. And for even the best among them, the studies you yourself prescribe finally render them useless to society.

Do you suppose the men who say this are lying?

I don't know, but I should be glad to hear your opinion.

You shall hear it. I think they are telling the truth.

Then how can it be right to say that our cities will have no respite e

1. Momus is the god of ridicule, censure, or blame.

from their ills until they are ruled by philosophers who, in turn, are of no use to them?

Your question needs to be answered with a parable.

And you, of course, never speak in parables.

You mock me, do you? And that on top of driving the argument into an unmanageable impasse. But hear my parable all the same; you will see once again how greedily I seek after parables.

488

Now, nothing in all of nature can be found to match the cruelty with which society treats its best men. If I am to plead their cause, I must resort to fiction, combining a multitude of disparate things like painters do when they concoct fantastic progeny of stags and goats and the like. Let us imagine, then, a set of events happening aboard many ships or even only one. Imagine first the captain. He is taller and stronger than any of the crew. At the same time, he is a little deaf and somewhat short-sighted. Further, his navigation skills are about on a par with his hearing and and his vision. The sailors are quarreling with each other about who should take the helm. Each insists he has a right to steer the ship though he has never mastered the art of navigation and cannot say who taught him or when he learned. Pushing the matter further, they will assert that it cannot be taught anyway; anyone who contradicts them they will cut to pieces. Meanwhile, they crowd around the captain, badgering him and clamoring for the tiller. Occasionally some will succeed with their entreaties and get the captain's ear, but they will, in turn, fall victim to those who did not and will be put to death or be cast off the ship. Then, after fettering the worthy shipmaster and putting him into a stupor with narcotic or drink, they take command of the ship. Feasting and drinking, they consume the ship's stores and make a voyage of it as might be expected from such a crew. Further, they will use such terms as master mariner, navigator, and pilot to flatter the man who has shown most cunning in persuading or forcing the captain to turn over control of the ship. The man who is innocent of such skills they will call useless. They, in turn, are innocent of any understanding that one who is a real captain must concentrate his attention on the year's round, the seasons, the sky, wind, and stars, and all the arts that make him the true master of the ship. The captain does not believe there is any art or science involved in seizing control of a ship—with or without the consent of others. Nor does he believe that the practice and mastery of this alleged art is possible to combine with the science of navigation. With such activities going on would it surprise you if the sailors running the ship would call the true captain a useless stargazer and lunatic?

b

c

d

e

489

It would not surprise me.

And I presume you perceive my meaning. You won't require that the comparison be put to the proof by demonstrating that the conditions we have just described duplicate the way cities deal with true philosophers?

The parable is clear.

Then teach the parable to anyone who wonders why philosophers are not honored in our cities; convince him it would be the greater b wonder if they were so honored.

I will teach him.

And tell him also that he is right in saying that the best philosophers are of no use to the multitude. But bid him place the blame not on those who are best of men but on those who do not know how to use their skills. For it is unnatural that a pilot should beg his sailors to give him the command—or that wise men should go to the doors of the rich. (The inventor of this last epigram was a liar, of course.) But what is natural is that the sick man, whether rich or c poor, must go to the door of the physician. Everyone who needs to be governed should go to the door of the man who knows how to govern. If he is good for anything, the ruler ought never to entreat his subjects to let him govern them. You will not be mistaken if you liken those now in power to the mutinous sailors we just described and those whom they call useless stargazers, on the other hand, to the true captains.

We are in accord.

Under these conditions, then, we cannot anticipate that the noblest pursuit should enjoy high esteem among those whose way of life is totally contrary to it. But the chief causes of philosophy's ill repute d are those who are its own professed followers. These are the ones you had in mind when citing that critic of philosophers who observed that the majority are rogues and the better sort useless. And I admitted that what you said was true. Isn't that so?

Yes.

Well, have we adequately set forth the reasons why the better sort are useless?

We have.

Shall we now proceed to explain why it is inevitable that the majority should become worthless rogues—and at the same time try to show e that here, too, it is not philosophy that is at fault?

Yes.

Let us begin the discussion by recalling our description of the natural endowments of any person destined to be a man of wisdom. First among his qualities, you will recall, was truth. His fidelity to 490 truth had to be complete and indomitable; otherwise he would be an impostor who would forfeit any share in true philosophy.

Yes, that was said.

In regard to just this quality, is not the prevailing opinion of him clean to the contrary?

It is, indeed.

Can we not fairly plead in his defense that it is in the nature of the true lover of learning to strive mightily toward what really is and that he cannot linger among the profusion of things that men only believe to be real? He will persevere with a passion whose keen edge will not be blunted and with a desire that will not flag until he grasps the essence of each thing by means of the affinity existing between it and a kindred part of his soul. Having striven for reality and now consorting with it, he will beget intelligence and truth, attain knowledge, and truly live and grow. Then he will know surcease from his travail, but not before.

No case could be more fairly made.

Would such a man love falsehood, or would he hate it?

He would hate it.

And with truth leading his way, we need not fear that a chorus of evils would follow in his train?

No. How could it?

But rather a just, sound, and temperate character?

Right.

No purpose would be served in setting out again the ensemble of virtues required of the philosopher. Surely you remember that we cited courage, magnificence, memory, and proficiency in learning? It was at that point that you observed that everyone would have to agree to what I then said, but that if we went behind the words, looked at facts—and looked at the men they describe—we would say some are useless and most are debased. In our search for the cause for these accusations we have arrived at the present question. Why is the majority bad? This question, in turn, prompted us to restate our definition of the real nature of the true philosopher.

That is so.

Then we must consider why the many become corrupt and why a few escape, ending up, as they say, not evil but useless. After that we must examine those who imitate the philosophic nature and so seek to usurp a profession of which they are not worthy. We need to see what kinds of men there are who will set themselves up to pursue a way of life whose requirements are beyond their powers to meet. Finally, we need to identify the discords and inconsistencies in their behavior which bring down upon philosophers and philosophy universal disrepute.

What are the corruptions you speak of?

I shall try to account for them, if I can. First, I think everyone will agree that one perfectly possessing all the qualities of the philosophic

nature we have just described is a rare phenomenon among men and   b
will be found only in a few. Do you concur?

Emphatically.

Now consider how many and powerful are the causes at work to
ruin these few.

What are they?

Most surprisingly, they include those very virtues we have praised—
courage, temperance, and the others—which play their own part in
the corruption of the soul that possesses them and tear it away from
philosophy.

Strange.

Further, those things men call good—beauty, wealth, bodily   c
strength, powerful family connections in the city, and similar attributes—they, too, distract and corrupt the soul. Do you understand
what I am trying to say?

Yes, and I would gladly hear you discuss it in greater detail.

Well, you might try to understand the matter yourself by formu-
lating a general proposition; then the meaning will be clear, and
what I have just said will no longer seem so strange.

How should I proceed?

Consider: we know it to be true of every growing thing, whether   d
seedling or flesh, that when it is deprived of the food, climate, or
location suitable to its growth, it will suffer the greater damage, the
greater its inherent vigor. For evil is a greater enemy of the good
than of the commonplace.

Of course.

So it follows that the superior nature does less well than the inferior, where conditions of nurture are unfavorable?

Yes.

Then, Adeimantus, must we not say the same of men's minds?   e
The most gifted, when exposed to a bad education, turn out the
worst. Great crimes and systematic wickedness are not the products
of half-hearted natures but of the vigorous ones who have been corrupted by their upbringing. Mediocrity will never attain to any great
thing, good or evil.

That is true.

Then the qualities we assumed in the philosopher's nature will   492
necessarily thrive and mature in all excellence, provided he is properly taught. But if sowing, planting, and germination take place in
the wrong environment, the contrary outcome must be anticipated—unless some god comes to the rescue. Or do you, too, sub-
scribe to the popular belief that certain young men are corrupted by
reason of their studies with sophists? Do you think this kind of private
education has so much influence? Is not the populace that is given

b to this kind of talk itself the chief sophist? Are they not the most compelling educators of all, reproducing in their own image men and women, young and old, and succeeding to their hearts' content?
   When do they do this?
   Whenever the multitude convenes in assembly, in courtrooms, at the theater, or in camp or at any other public gathering. There they will make known their approval or censure, but always in excess, producing constant uproar with applause or clamorous protest. The
c volume in which praise and blame are thundered forth is redoubled by the echo from the rocks and the whole surrounding place. In such circumstances, as they say, how do you think the young man's heart will be moved? What private teaching will enable him to hold firm against the current and not be swept away by the torrents of praise and blame until he assents to whatever the crowd says is base or honorable, until he is ready to do as they do and be as they are?
d The pressure will be great, Socrates.
   And we have yet to mention the greatest pressures of all.
   What are they?
   What these erstwhile educators and sophists do when their words fail to convince. Then they turn to deeds and punish resistance with fines, dishonor, and death.
   Yes. They know how to punish.
   So what sophist or any kind of private teaching whatever could prevail against them?
e None, I imagine.
   No. It would be foolish even to try. There is not, never has been, and never will be an education contrary to theirs that could produce a different kind of person and a different virtue. I speak within the human context, of course; where divine intervention enters, all rules are set at naught. Sure it is in the present state of society and govern-
493 ment that if anything can be saved and turned to the good you will not be off the mark by attributing it to god's providence.
   I hold the same opinion.
   Then see if it holds for this as well.
   What?
   Each of these private teachers who charge for their services and are branded sophists and dissidents by the public in fact teaches nothing but the opinions and beliefs the public itself expresses when it crowds into a meeting. Only he calls it wisdom. It is as if he had a great and
b powerful beast in his keeping and sought to learn its desires and moods, how it might be approached and touched, when it was apt to be savage or gentle—and what might induce it to behave in one way or the other. Yes, and then he would learn the several sounds it is prone to utter in each of these attitudes and, further, what sounds

uttered by another will make it tame or fierce. Living with the creature and over time mastering this knowledge he would call it wisdom, distilling from it a system and an art which he would then
proceed to teach. But whether the opinions and desires expressed   c
were honorable or base, good or evil, just or unjust—of this he would
know nothing. Instead he would submit all these issues to the judgment of the beast, calling the things that pleased it good and the
things that vexed it bad. He would have no other measure, calling
just and honorable whatever is deemed necessary, having never
observed how great is the difference between the necessary and the
good and being incapable of explaining it to anyone. Do you not
think, in the name of Zeus, that such a person would be an aston-
ishing educator?

I do.

Would you think that there is any difference between such a person and the man who believes it is wisdom to have learned what   d
amuses or annoys the assembled crowd—whether the matter has to
do with painting or music or politics, for that matter? However a
man associates with the crowd, whether to exhibit his poetry or any
other art, or to offer political service, he will be going out of his way
to make the public his masters, and the proverbial necessity of
Diomedes will compel him to produce whatever things the crowd
likes.[2] But that these things are in fact good and noble—have you
ever heard anyone make such an argument without at the same time
making himself ridiculous?

No. Nor do I ever expect to.   e

With this in mind, let us recall our earlier question. Is it possible
for the multitude to have an understanding for the reality of beauty
itself, or will it be able to perceive only a multiplicity of beautiful
things? Will the many be able to understand the essence of anything
or only the particulars in which essence finds expression?

They will not be able to understand essence.

It follows that philosophy—the love of wisdom—is impossible for   494
the multitude.

Impossible.

Then it is inevitable that the multitude will censure those who do
philosophize.

Inevitable.

And so, too, will those private persons who run with the crowd in
order to flatter it.

Clearly.

2. The origin of the proverb is not known, but the most likely source is the story of the Thracian
Diomedes, who forced travelers to have intercourse with his daughters. Then he killed the strangers.

Taking all this into account, do you see any way that the born
b   philosopher can hope for deliverance? What will help him to be
steadfast in his pursuit and finally to achieve his purpose? Reflect on
what we said before: quickness in learning, memory, courage, and
magnificence are traits of the philosophic nature.

Yes.

Even as a boy among boys, then, will he not be a leader in all
things, especially if his body matches the excellence of his soul?

Of course.

The unavoidable result when he becomes older is that his family
and fellow citizens will want to make use of him for their own ends.

No question.

c   They will fawn upon him. They will present him with petitions
and honors, flattering the power they anticipate will someday be his.

That's the way it usually happens.

How will such a youth behave in these circumstances, especially
if he belongs to a great city, is rich, is well-born, and is tall and
handsome to boot? Will he not give way to unbounded ambitions?
Will he not think himself capable of managing the affairs of both
Greeks and barbarians? Will he not believe himself to be exalted
d   above others? Will he not be haughty in manner, full of pride and
empty of sense?

He surely will.

Supposing someone comes gently to a man in this state of mind
and tells him the truth: that he has no sense and sorely needs it, and
that the only way to get it is to work for it like a slave. Do you suppose
he will easily give ear to this quiet voice when he is surrounded by
iniquities?

Not likely.

Suppose further that one such youth is endowed with a fortunate
e   disposition and is not adverse to admonition. Suppose that he begins
to understand and be drawn toward philosophy. What will be the
reaction of those who think they will be losing him as a friend or a
henchman? They will spare neither words nor deeds to prevent his
being won away from them. In order to persuade him and to ruin
whoever may be teaching him, they will resort to private intrigues
and even public trials.

495   Unavoidable.

Is there any likelihood that he would continue to philosophize?

None whatsoever.

Then we were not wrong in saying that, given deficient nurture
and environment, the very assets of the philosophic nature are somehow causes of its corruption. Their accessories in this process, of
course, are riches and all the so-called goods of this world.

Rightly said.

Such, my friend, is the story of how the best nature engaged in the noblest of pursuits is corrupted and destroyed, a nature, as we have noted, that doesn't turn up very frequently. From this class of men come those who inflict the greatest harm upon cities and individuals—or the greatest good, should the current chance to flow that way. But men with little natures never do great things, neither for cities nor for individuals.

Very true.

So philosophy is left solitary and unwed; those most truly her own abandon her for a life of illusion and error. Now that she is orphaned, their place is taken by others, unworthy suitors who rush in upon her and dishonor her. These are the ones substantiating the reproaches of the critics who accuse some few of philosophy's comrades as being of no account while the rest account for many mischiefs.

That is what people say.

With reason, too. There are other kinds of pygmies, after all, who can see that there is a place that may be empty but one abounding nonetheless in fine words and pretensions. Just as men will make their escape from prison in order to find sanctuary in temples, so these men of little account will blithely abandon their mechanical arts in order to pursue philosophy, especially those most clever in exploiting their meager skills. For even in its present low estate philosophy enjoys a prestige and dignity superior to the other arts. It is the ambition of a multitude of pretenders to have their share in that prestige—never mind that they are unfit by nature, or that their souls are twisted by vulgar pursuits just as their bodies are scarred by the tools of their trade. Is that not certain to happen?

Yes.

Don't they all bear striking resemblance to some bald-headed fellow who tinkered in bronze until he made some money? Silver freed him from his debts; so he went and had a bath and bought himself new clothes that he might play the bridegroom and marry his master's daughter, who had been left poor and desolate.

A close parallel.

And what sort of offspring will be the likely issue of such a marriage? Will they not be baseborn bastards?

Unavoidably.

And so when men unfit for scholarly effort seek to consort with philosophy, their association must be an unworthy one. What kinds of ideas and opinions shall we anticipate from them? Won't they necessarily produce what may fairly be called sophisms but nothing that partakes of reality and true intelligence?

Right.

So, then, Adeimantus, we are left with but a small remnant of those who will worthily consort with philosophy. One such might be

well born and well bred whom exile has disciplined, isolating him from corrupters so that his fidelity to philosophy remains constant. Another might be a great soul born and raised in a small town who despises its parochial values and looks out beyond them. And there may be another few whose natural affinities draw them away from other arts, which they have rightly come to disdain, and into com-
c   panionship with philosophy. The bridle of our comrade Theages may also have acted as a constraint. All the conditions were otherwise at hand to make Theages forsake philosophy, but his sickly body barred his way to politics and so saved him from defecting. My own case is hardly worth mentioning. The internal signals voiced by my *daemon*, I suspect, have been given to very few men before me, perhaps to no man at all.[3]

Those who have been members of this small company know how blessed he is whose pleasant estate is philosophy. They have also come to understand the frenzies of the multitude and have recognized, if I may say so, that there is nothing right or wholesome any-
d   where in today's politics. Anyone who would be a champion of justice will find no ally whose aid could save his cause. He would instead find himself fallen among wild beasts, unwilling to join in their injustices but unable singlehandedly to combat their savagery. Before he could benefit in any way his city or his friends, he would be doomed to perish without having done himself or others any good. For all these reasons the philosopher holds his peace and minds his own business, standing aside and, as it were, seeking a sheltering wall against the storm and blast of dust and rain. Observing others given over to lawlessness, he is content if he can keep himself free of
e   iniquities and evil deeds and depart this life content, at peace, and with blessed hope.

Parting in such a fashion, he would have left behind him no small achievement.

497   Neither would it have been very great unless he had had the opportunity to live in a city congenial to the philosophic nature. Only there would he have been able to attain his full stature and save the city as well as himself.

I think that we have now set forth the reasons why philosophy has been slandered as well as the injustice of the charges—unless you have something more to add.

Not on that subject. But I would like to know which of our current governments you think are suitable to philosophy.

None whatsoever. That is exactly my complaint. Not a single one

3. In the *Apology* (31d) Socrates tells of the inner voice which bids him shun certain activities that would be destructive for him. This sign has continually prohibited him from entering political life.

of today's cities could accommodate the philosophic nature. This is precisely why such a nature is perverted and distorted: just as a foreign seed sown in alien soil tends to lose its identity and yield place to the native growth, so the philosophic nature does not preserve its own quality but degenerates into a deviant type. But if ever a philosopher's own best self finds a counterpart in the best of cities, the   c resulting regime will reveal a true divinity while all others are human in principle and practice. No doubt you will ask me next what this best form of regime is like.

You are wrong. I wasn't going to ask that. I was going to ask instead whether you mean this regime to be the same city we have been founding.

The same in all respects, including one point we made earlier: d there must always be some in the city preserving the same understanding of the constitution as you had when you founded the city.

Yes, that was mentioned.

But it wasn't made plain enough for fear of your own objections. They made it evident that any attempt at explanation would be long and difficult. And now what still has to be said is by no means easy.

What are you getting at?

How a philosophic city can prevent its own destruction. All great things are precarious constructions; as the proverb says, fine things are hard.

In any case, these matters need explanation in order that the inquiry   e be complete.

Certainly it is not lack of will that would hinder us from complying with your wishes. The problem is rather lack of skill. You shall observe for yourself how willing I am and note how recklessly and with what zeal I suggest that the city should cultivate philosophy along lines that are exactly the reverse of what is done today.

In what way?

Nowadays, those who do take up philosophy are youths, just out   498 of boyhood, as a way of occupying the interval before they get on with business and money-making. They address themselves to the most difficult part of the subject (I mean the dialectic)—and then they drop it. These are the ones that pass for model philosophers. When they are older and are invited to attend philosophical discussions by others, they think they have done much if they deign to listen. They treat such matters as a hobby. By the time they reach old age, with very few exceptions, their light is snuffed out more entirely than the sun of Heraclitus—that is, it can never again be   b rekindled.[4]

4. Heraclitus said that the sun was snuffed out each night but was relighted each morning.

What should be done?

The reverse. As boys and adolescents, they should devote themselves to education and culture in a manner suitable to young people. While growing to manhood, they should take good care of their bodies as the basis and support for intellectual life. But as they grow older and the soul begins to reach maturity, let its training become
c   more rigorous. Finally, when bodily strength declines and they are past the age of political and military service, they should be put to pasture. Except for leisure times, let them find true happiness in pursuing nothing but philosophy. When death comes, let their life be crowned with a like destiny in that other world.

You seem to be much in earnest, Socrates. But I think most of your listeners will be even more earnest in their opposition. They will not be convinced, beginning with Thrasymachus.

Now don't try to provoke a quarrel between me and Thrasymachus
d   just when we have become friends—not that we were really enemies before, of course. At any event, we won't abandon our efforts until we convince him and the others, or else at least offer them some assistance in preparing for the next life, when, after being born again, they will confront the same arguments.

You like to deal in short-range forecasts, don't you?

Only moments in the perspective of eternity. However that may be, your assertion that the many will be unwilling to be persuaded is not surprising. The things we have been speaking about here they have never seen put in practice. Eloquence they have heard, and artfully balanced phrases, very different from our kind of unre-
e   hearsed discourse here. But a man balanced in all virtue in word and
499 deed and governing a city as virtuous as himself—that they have never seen. Or do you think otherwise?

By no means.

Nor, my friend, has the multitude ever been seriously inclined to give a hearing to fair and free discussions whose sole purpose is to serve knowledge by searching out the truth, discussions that shun those tricks and subtleties of debate designed to instigate strife in law courts or in private matters.

You are right.

b   These are the kinds of problems I foresaw that made me fear for my earlier proposals. Nonetheless, truth then compelled me to declare that there never will be a perfect state or a perfect man unless some chance obliges the uncorrupted remnant of philosophers now termed useless to take over governance of the state—whether they wish it or not—and constrains the citizens to obey them. Alternatively, by some divine inspiration, an authentic passion for true philosophy must be
c   instilled into the sons of the men now holding power and sovereignty or into the fathers themselves.

Any charge that either or both of these alternatives cannot possibly be realized is simply unreasonable. Only if the charge were true, could we be justly ridiculed as dispensers of daydreams and futilities. Is that not so?

It is.

If, then, at any time in ages past the best philosophers have been obliged to govern the state, or are now governing in some barbaric land far beyond the limits of our knowledge—or will govern at some   d future time—we shall regard our position as vindicated. That is, the constitution we described is put in practice whenever the muse of philosophy holds sway in the state. It is not impossible for such a thing to happen, nor are we speaking of impossibilities. That there are difficulties we readily admit.

I share your opinion.

But—perhaps you were going to say—the multitude does not?

Perhaps.   e

Well, old friend, you ought not to be so severe in criticizing the multitude. They will surely change their opinion if you avoid polemics and gently try to dissipate their antipathy toward the love of learning. Then you can explain to them whom you mean when you speak of philosophers and define their nature and purposes, just as we did a   500 little while ago. That should enable them to understand that you are not talking about the same people they had previously supposed to be philosophers. If they do understand, would you still deny that they would change their opinion and answer differently? Or do you think anyone who is himself gentle and ungrudging will be angry with someone who bears no anger or will begrudge someone who bears no grudge? I shall anticipate your answer: I think that so ungentle and spiteful a temper is to be found only in a few and not in the many.

I very much agree with you.   b

Would you not also agree that philosophy suffers from hostile public attitudes because of the intrusion of bogus philosophers into places where they have no business? Quarreling with one another, they are filled with malice and forever discussing personalities, the very last thing a philosopher ought to do.

The very last thing, indeed.

For surely, Adeimantus, he whose mind is fixed on eternal realities has no time to lower his gaze to a point where he may be lured   c by the petty affairs of men into strife, envy, and hatred. Instead, he keeps his sights fixed on those things that belong to the unchanging and eternal order. Seeing that they neither inflict nor suffer wrong but abide instead in that harmony which reason enjoins, he will try to imitate them. As far as is in him to do so, he will make them his models and assimilate himself to them. Or do you believe it possible that a man would refrain from imitating the things he admires?

That's not possible.

d   Then he who loves wisdom and the divine order will himself reflect that order in the degree that is permitted to men. Nonetheless, he will have plenty of detractors.

That is certain.

So if he goes beyond merely polishing his own intellect and feels under obligation to transfer the patterns he has seen in the divine order to both the public and private natures of men, do you think he will lack the skill to move society toward justice, moderation, and all the virtues of ordinary men in civic life?

He will not lack the skill.

But will the multitude continue to be hostile to philosophers if
e   they perceive that what we have said about philosophers is true? Will they refuse to trust our assurance that a city can be happy only if it is built by architects using measurements from the divine pattern?

501   If they understand these things, they will recant. But tell me, how will these architects go about their work?

First, they will take the record of the city and its citizens and wipe it clean. That will be no easy task, but at least it would set them off from the ordinary run of reformers. Unless they start from a clean slate or clean it themselves, they will neither legislate nor undertake anything else with regard to individual or state.

They would be right.

Next, they would proceed to outline a constitution.

b   Surely.

Their work will frequently require them to look in two directions; they must look at justice, beauty, and temperance in their ideal forms and then again at what they are trying to reproduce in men. They will draw from both sources, blending and tempering until they arrive at a living figure of man like that which Homer himself called the image and likeness of god.

Yes.

c   And as they work, they will be deleting some things and adding others with the purpose of doing everything possible to make men's characters as pleasing and dear to god as may be.

The design, at any rate, is beautiful.

And are we beginning to make any impression on those you said were going to launch a furious attack against us when we asserted earlier that philosophers should rule cities? Will they be in a gentler mood if we now can show them that the philosopher and the political artist we have just been praising as designer of the constitution are the same?

. They will be much gentler, if they are reasonable.

What possible grounds for objection could remain? Will they doubt that the philosopher loves reality and truth?   d

That would be unreasonable.

Or that his nature as we have described it is kindred to what is best and highest?

That would also be unreasonable.

Could they assert that such a nature, properly educated to the tasks he will eventually perform, would not be perfectly good and philosophic in the degree given to human beings? Or will they give preference instead to those we excluded from power?

Surely not.   e

Then will they any longer be angry when we say that until philosophers govern, there will be no end of troubles for cities or for citizens, nor will the constitution we fashioned in words be translated into reality?

I think they will be less angry.

Let us not stop there. May we not say that they will have become altogether gentle and convinced and that, if for no other reason, shame itself will lead them to concur with us?   502

We could say that.

So let's assume they have been persuaded.

Now, could anyone reject the possibility that children of kings and other rulers might be born philosophers by nature?

No one.

And if they were so born, could anyone prove that they would necessarily be corrupted? Certainly we concede that it would be difficult for them to preserve their integrity. But over time's long course, would any maintain that none could be saved?   b

How could they make such a judgment?

And there need be only one such, if his city will obey him, in order that all that now seems distant and unachievable will become real.

One is enough.

If, then, such a ruler promulgates the laws and institutions we have described, surely it will not be impossible that the citizens should be willing to abide by them?

Not impossible at all.

Would it, therefore, be anything strange or unbelievable if others should arrive at the opinions we have already adopted?

I don't think so.   c

And we have also shown sufficiently that the things we have discussed, if they are possible, are also the best.

Yes, the argument has been sufficient.

Then our efforts at legislation have led to the following conclu-

sion: ours is the best constitution if it can be realized, and its realization, while difficult, is not impossible.

So we have concluded.

After having disposed of these difficulties, we must turn to still
another matter. What studies and activities will our constitution makers   d
pursue before their appointment to offices in the city? What are the
appropriate age levels for the various studies they will undertake?

Yes, we need to discuss these things.

My cunning gained me nothing earlier when I tried to omit discussion of those awkward questions about the status of women and
children and the appointment of rulers. I did so because I knew that
any effort to describe what is true and right would provoke dissent
e   and is in any case difficult of attainment. But now I have been compelled to discuss them anyway. We have disposed of those matters
concerning women and children, but the subject of the rulers needs
to be reexamined, I would say, from the very beginning. If you
503   remember, we said that the rulers must prove their love for the city
by surmounting challenges posed by both pain and pleasure, remaining
steadfast under stress of toil, suffering, or any other adversity. We
said that anyone who could not keep the faith would be rejected, but
that he who emerged from each test pure and with virtue intact, like
gold tried in fire, will be garlanded and acclaimed as ruler, and he
will receive honors in both life and death. Our words were something like this, but the argument itself put on a mask and slipped
b   away, fearful that it might otherwise provoke the debate that has
since begun.

That is true. I remember.

Then, my friend, we shrank back from making the audacious proposals that we have since risked. But now let us find the courage to
make the definitive proposal: we must establish philosophers as the
perfect guardians.

Let us assume that has been said.

But note that they will be only a few. All the qualities necessary
for the philosophic nature and education are rarely to be found in a
single individual. Most people come only partially equipped.
c   What do you mean?

Consider those with intelligence, memory, facility in learning,
quickness of apprehension, and the like, together with youthful spirit
and magnificence of soul. You know that few persons of this sort are
also disposed to live a quiet, stable, and orderly life. Instead, their
very energy makes them allies to the whims of chance and renders
them infirm of purpose.

Well said.

On the other hand, those whose temperaments are stable and

steadfast, who are manifestly trustworthy, and who in war are imper-   d
turbable and hardened against fear behave in the same way when at
their studies. They are not easily stimulated and are slow to learn.
An intellectual challenge only seems to make them numb to the
point where they yawn and fall asleep.

That's right.

But we stipulated that unless a man unites both temperaments in
harmonious proportion, he will not be eligible for the highest levels
of education, nor for honors, nor for governing.

And we did rightly.

But don't you think that such candidates will be very rare?

Yes, I do.

That is why we said earlier that its presence must be tested for in
trials of sweat and pain and pleasure. And now we must speak of   e
another matter that came up earlier but that was passed over too
quickly. We must see to it that candidates are trained and tested in
many subjects. And we must observe them closely in order to judge
whether they are capable of mastering the greatest and most difficult   504
studies, or whether they will flinch and slip, as men will sometimes
do in athletic trials and contests.

That certainly seems to be the right procedure, but what do you
mean by the greatest studies?

I suppose you remember that after distinguishing the three parts
of the soul we were then able to set forth definitions of temperance,
courage, wisdom, and justice?

If I had forgotten that, I wouldn't deserve to hear the rest.

And before that—do you remember what was said?   b

What?

I think we said then that only by taking a longer way than the one
we had been pursuing so far could we reach the most precise understanding of these matters and that they would become fully evident
to the one who took it. On the other hand, I added that we could
continue at about the same level of analysis that characterized our
discussions up till then. You said the latter course would suffice, and
it was on this understanding that we continued the discussions. The
result, I think, was a deficiency in precision; but if you were content,
that is for you to say.

Well, I found it satisfying in good measure, and I think the others
did too.

No, my friend, in such matters any measure that falls short of   c
reality is no measure at all. Nothing that is imperfect is the measure
of anything, even though some people sometimes think that enough
has been done and that no further inquiry is needed.

Indolence leaves many in this posture.

A posture least appropriate to a guardian of the city and its laws.

That seems likely.

Then a guardian must take the longer way. He must labor at his
d   studies no less than in gymnastic. Otherwise, as we just noted, he
will never be able to complete that greatest of studies that concerns
him most of all.

So the greatest study is still ahead? There is something still greater
than justice and the other virtues we have considered?

Yes. There are some things still greater. In considering them,
however, we cannot content ourselves with an outline or sketch, as
we have done previously. Instead, we must omit nothing from an
exact and specific elaboration of their nature. After all, it would be
senseless to strive for the greatest possible precision and clarity of
knowledge about comparatively trivial things and then not to require
e   at least the same standards in considering matters of the greatest import.

A trenchant observation. But do you think anyone is going to let
you get away without asking what you mean by the greatest study
and what its subject is?

Go ahead and ask. You have already heard the answer often enough.
Either you have not understood it, or you have made up your mind
to make trouble for me again by attacking my argument. I would
505   guess the latter. After all, you have heard often enough that the
greatest of all studies concerns the idea of the good. It is the one and
indispensable source of what is useful and excellent in justice and
the other virtues. Now, I am almost sure you know what I was going
to say and that I would add, as well, that we know too little about
it—and that however much we may know about other things will
avail us nothing if we do not know this. Neither would any kind of
b   possession profit us if we had not possession of the good. Or do you
think there is any profit in possessing everything except that which is
good? Or in understanding and knowing everything, but understanding and knowing nothing about the good and the beautiful?

No, by Zeus, I don't.

You know very well that for the multitude the good is pleasure.
For those who claim greater refinement, the good is knowledge.

Yes, I know.

And you also know that the latter, after failing to explain what
kind of knowledge they mean, ultimately find themselves forced to
say that it is knowledge of the good.
c   Absurd.

Downright comical: first they taunt us that we are ignorant of the
good and then turn around and talk to us as if we knew what it was
after all. On top of that they assume that we understand the word
good the way they do.

Very true.

Well, are their thoughts any more confused than those who define the good as pleasure? Or are these not also forced into a like contradiction, having finally to admit that some pleasures are bad?

Right.

The result of all this is that both persuasions find themselves using the terms *good* and *bad* for the same things.

Yes.

With the necessary consequence of numerous and vehement disputes?   d

Of course.

Still further: we see that many prefer to seem just and honorable rather than actually to be so. But do we not see it is different with the good? Here no one is content with mere appearances. When it comes to the good, all men seek the reality, and no one is satisfied   e
with less.

Quite.

The good, then, is what every man wants. For its sake he will do all that he does. He intuits what the good is, but at the same time he is baffled, for the nature of the good is something he comprehends only inadequately. Nor is he able to invest in it the same sure confidence that he does in other things. For this very reason the   506
benefits these other things might otherwise yield are lost. Now, in a matter of this kind and importance, I ask you whether we can permit such blindness and ignorance in those best of men we want to govern the city?

Those least of all.

At any rate, a man who does not understand how justice and honor are related to the good won't guard them very effectively. I believe they cannot be understood in themselves without an understanding of this larger relationship.

Your belief is well founded.

Then our constitution can achieve its definitive form only if governed by a guardian who knows these things.   b

Necessarily. But, Socrates, what do you yourself think the good is? Is it knowledge, or pleasure, or something else?

Ah, what a man! You have been making it clear for a long time that you will not be content with the opinions of others in such matters.

That is true, Socrates. It does not seem right to me that someone like you who has examined these matters for so long should confine yourself to recounting the convictions of others but not express your own.

On the other hand, do you think it right to speak about what one does not know as if he knew it?

Of course not. But one doesn't have to claim knowledge; one can simply express opinion and label it as opinion.

No, no. Surely you know that opinions divorced from knowledge are ugly? Even the best of opinions are blind. An opinion can be true, but those who hold it without the requisite knowledge are no different from blind men who have chosen the right direction simply by chance. Or do you think there is a difference?

No.

d   So you want to spend your time with ugly things, with the blind and crooked, when others might tell you about clarity and beauty?

No, by Zeus. But what I do want is that you not retreat at the very moment when we are in sight of the goal. We shall be perfectly content if you explain the good to us in the same way you explained the nature of justice, temperance, and the other virtues.

That would content me, too, my dear friend. But I fear my powers may not be able to reach so far; I fear that my zeal might only make me ludicrous. No, my comrades, let us set aside for a time the nature

e   of the good itself. At the present moment I believe that it is too great a task to attain what it appears to be in my thoughts. However, I am willing to speak of what is most nearly like the good—of what seems to me the child of the good—if you wish. Otherwise, we can let the matter drop.

No, speak. Another time you'll pay what remains due with an account of the father.

507   I wish I could pay the full account today, so that you could receive the principal now and not just the interest. But accept the interest, in any case, together with the child of the good. However, take care that I don't falsely reckon the interest and unwittingly deceive you.

We are on our guard. Speak.

I shall, but only after reaching an agreement with you and recall-

b   ing what I have so often said before during this discussion and on many other occasions.

What?

We assert the existence of many beautiful things, many good things, and many other kinds of things, and to each we give a name.

Yes.

At the same time, we speak of beauty as a single form and of the good in the same way. In these and all other cases, then, we refer to the same things as both many and one. Further, we can integrate the many into a single category and so make them one again, a unity. This unity is what we call a form, something that really is.

Yes.

And we say that the multiplicity of things can be seen but not thought, while ideas can be thought but not seen.

c   True.

And with which of our faculties do we perceive the visible?

With our eyesight.

And with our ears we hear what is audible. Thanks to the other senses we perceive the rest of the sensible world.

That is certain.

Have you ever observed how much the creator of the senses has lavished on vision and the visible?

No. I guess I haven't.

Just look at it this way. Does hearing or voice require another medium so that the one may hear and the other be heard? Without   d such a medium will one fail to hear and the other fail to be heard?

Nothing of the kind is needed.

I think this holds for most of the other senses as well. Do you know any for which it does not?

No, I don't.

Vision and the visible are the sole exceptions. It is they that are dependent on another medium.

How so?

One may have vision in his eyes and try to put it to use, and color may be present in the landscape; but unless a third component is   e present, the eyes will be sightless and color will remain invisible.

What are you talking about?

Light.

I understand.

Then if light is to be assigned proper value, we must recognize that the link between sight and visibility is far more precious than   508 other kinds of links between sense and object.

Light is surely to be honored.

Which of the deities in heaven can you name as author and cause of the light that makes possible both vision and visibility?

Why, the one you and other people as well have in mind. You are talking about the sun.

Then what is the relation of vision to that deity?

What do you mean?

Neither sight nor the eye in which sight is lodged is the sun itself?

Surely not.   b

But together, I think, they are the most sunlike of the sense organs.

By far.

And is the sun's abundance their source of power?

Yes.

Then the sun is not vision but the cause of vision as well as being the cause of sight.

That is right.

So here is the analogy I tried to draw when I spoke about the child

of the good, begotten in the likeness of the good. The relation of the
c sun to vision and its objects in the visible world is the same as the
relation of the good to reason and the objects of reason in the world
of intellect.

What do you mean? Explain further.

You know that when night shades replace the light of day, the
ability of the eyes to perceive color and shape is reduced almost to
d the point of blindness, altogether as if they were bereft of vision.

Yes.

But when the eyes gaze upon objects illuminated by the sun, they
see clearly; they evidently possess vision.

Right.

Now compare the eyes with the soul. When the soul beholds the
realm illuminated by the splendor of truth and reality, it knows and
understands and so appears to possess reason. But when it turns its
gaze to that region where darkness and light intermingle, to the transient world where all things are either quickening or dying, reason's
edge is blunted. The soul becomes mired in opinion; and since opinion shifts from one direction to another, it appears that reason has
vanished.

e It does seem that way.

The idea of the good, then, imbues the objects of knowledge with
truth and confers upon the knower the power to know. Because the
idea of the good is the very cause of knowledge and of truth, it is also
the chief objective in the pursuit of knowledge. Yet as fair as truth
509 and knowledge are, you will be right if you think there is something
fairer still. In our analogy when we proposed knowledge and truth as
the counterparts of vision and light, it was proper to consider the
latter two as sunlike but wrong to assume they are the same as the
sun. In just the same way, knowledge and truth are like the good,
but it is wrong to suppose that they are the good. A still greater glory
belongs to the good.

If the good is the source of knowledge and truth and at the same
time surpasses them both in beauty, you must have in mind a beauty
quite beyond imagination. Surely you cannot be speaking of pleasure?

Be still. Let us consider how the good manifests itself in another
way.

b How?

I assume you would agree that the sun not only confers visibility
on all that can be seen but is equally the source of generation, nurture, and growth in all things, though not itself the same as generation?

I agree.

If we pursue the comparison, the objects of knowledge are not only made manifest by the presence of goodness. Goodness makes them real. Still goodness is not in itself being. It transcends being, exceeding all else in dignity and power.

Glaucon had to laugh. My god, hyperbole can go no further than that!   c

It's your fault. You pushed me to express my thoughts.

Please don't desist. At least elaborate on the metaphor of the sun if there is anything you have been omitting.

I have been omitting a lot.

Well, omit no more, not the least bit.

I imagine I shall have to exclude a good deal. Nonetheless, as far as is practical at this point, I shall not willingly leave anything out.

Please don't.

Recall, then, that we were speaking of two entities. One is the   d
good, governor of the intelligible order. The other is the sun, governing the world of things seen. (I do not say "governing things sun" so that you won't accuse me of playing with words.) In any case, you will keep in mind the visible and the intelligible?

I will.

Let us represent them as a divided line,[5] partitioned into two unequal segments, one to denote the visual and the other the intelligible order. Then, using the same ratio as before, subdivide each of the segments. Let the relative length of these subdivisions serve as indicators of the relative clarity of perception all along the line. Now, within   e
the visible sector the first one of the two subdivisions will contain nothing but images. I mean such things as shadows or the reflections   510
we see in water or mirrored in smooth, bright, and highly polished surfaces. Do you understand?

I understand.

In the subdivision above it are physical objects—the objects casting the shadows and reflections we observed below. I mean the living creatures all about us and all the works of man and nature.

Let it be so.

Would you also agree that the ratio between subdivisions—between shadow and substance—represents the degree of reality to be found in each and that it is also the same ratio dividing opinion from knowledge?

Yes.   b

Now consider how we should go about dividing the intelligible sector.

How?

---

5. Consult the translators' diagram and explication at the end of Book VI.

First, by identifying its own two subdivisions. In the lower one the soul's perception is restrained by a method of inquiry that reduces to images those things we defined as physical objects or models in the subdivision immediately below. Moreover, it operates with the kind of assumptions that lead to conclusions and not to first principles. But in the highest subdivision the soul makes no use of images. It also begins with assumptions and hypotheses but rises to a level where it relies exclusively on forms, a level of intellection that is free from all hypothetical thinking.

I don't think I understand all of what you say.

c   Let's try again. What we have just said will help you understand better as we proceed. Among those who work with geometry and arithmetic and related subjects you know that the odd and the even, the several geometrical figures, the three kinds of angles, and other things related to their inquiries are treated as givens. That is, having adopted them as assumptions, they see no purpose in giving any account of them to themselves or others. They perceive them as self-

d   evident. These premises are for them the starting points of inquiries, which they then pursue in all consistency until they arrive at the conclusions they originally set out to verify.

Yes, I know.

You know as well that they make use of visible shapes and objects and subject them to analysis. At the same time, however, they consider them only as images of the originals: the square as such or the diagonal as such. In all cases the originals are their concern and not

e   the figures they draw. But the objects they draw or construct cast shadows or reflections in water and are therefore real, yet they convert what is real into images. And all the while they seek a reality which only the mind can discover.

511   Yes.

The method of investigation I have just described certainly belongs to the realm of the intelligible, but we must recognize its limitations. First, the method is necessarily dependent upon hypotheses. Because it is unable to go beyond these hypotheses, it is also unable to attain the level of first principles and new beginnings. Second, it transforms into images things that in the visible world below are physical objects. These objects are themselves copied in the visible order, where they are deemed far brighter and more distinct than those below them.

b   I understand that you are discussing things that pertain to geometry and its allied arts.

Then let us go on to understand intelligibility at the highest level. This is the realm that reason masters with the power of dialectic. Assumptions are not treated as first principles but as real hypotheses.

That is, they are not employed as beginnings but as ladders and springboards, used in order to reach that realm that requires no hypotheses and is therefore the true starting point for the attainment of unobstructed knowledge. When reason attains that level and becomes aware of the whole intelligible order, it descends at will to the level of conclusions but without the aid of sense objects. It reasons only by using forms. It moves from forms through forms to forms. And it completes its journey in forms.

I understand you, but not fully. I see that you are describing an enormous undertaking. What I do understand is that you mean to make a distinction between, on the one hand, the realm of reality and intelligibility accessible only to the power of the dialectic and, on the other, the realm of the arts and sciences that depend on unexamined hypotheses. It is true that those who pursue arts and sciences do so with understanding and not by means of the senses. But they do not start from the beginning by going behind their assumptions and examining them; instead they take them for granted. That is why you do not call these men truly intelligent, though the subject matters they investigate would clearly be intelligible to the dialectician. And you seem to call the intellectual efforts of the geometer and those like him understanding and not reason because you consider understanding to be something between opinion and reason.

You have understood me well. And now, let us match the four divisions we have made in the line with these four kinds of cognition in the soul. The highest will be intellection or reason; the next, understanding. The third is belief, and the last, conjecture. Now they must be assigned a space proportionate to the divisions in the line in order to show that each kind of cognition exhibits clarity and precision to the same degree as its cognates manifest truth and reality.

I understand and agree. I shall arrange them according to the order you have proposed.

The Divided Line:
A Diagrammatic Rendering
and an Explication by the Translators

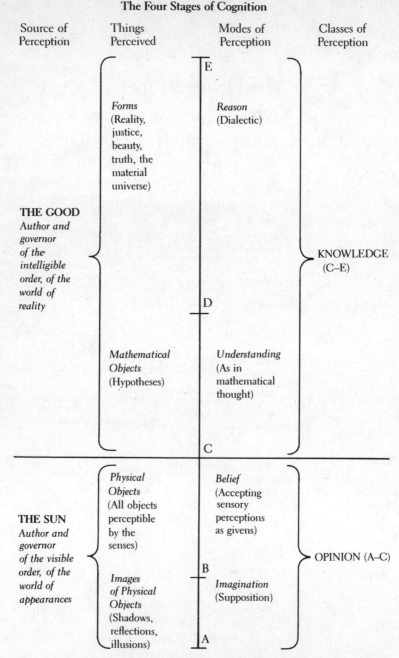

THE DIVIDED LINE
The Four Stages of Cognition

Source of Perception	Things Perceived	Modes of Perception	Classes of Perception
	E		
	Forms (Reality, justice, beauty, truth, the material universe)	*Reason* (Dialectic)	
THE GOOD *Author and governor of the intelligible order, of the world of reality*			KNOWLEDGE (C–E)
	D		
	Mathematical Objects (Hypotheses)	*Understanding* (As in mathematical thought)	
	C		
	Physical Objects (All objects perceptible by the senses)	*Belief* (Accepting sensory perceptions as givens)	
THE SUN *Author and governor of the visible order, of the world of appearances*		B	OPINION (A–C)
	Images of Physical Objects (Shadows, reflections, illusions)	*Imagination* (Supposition)	
	A		

Note: Plato prescribes the lengths of the line's segments at 509d–e and 511d–e.

In the immediately foregoing pages of Book VI (507–511e), Plato employs highly compressed prose to describe in diagrammatic form the various ways in which human beings perceive the world. Tradition has endowed this quasi-diagram with two captions: "The Divided Line" and "The Four Stages of Cognition."

The line contains perhaps the most difficult passages in the Republic. They become less difficult once they are linked to the allegory of the cave that follows directly at the beginning of Book VII (514a–521b) and to the elaboration of the dialectic near the end of Book VII (536d–540c).

The line, the cave, and the dialectic are three different explanations of a single conception: a theory of knowledge that seeks to point the way from the bondage of illusion to the freedom of rational perception. The cave colors the more abstract lessons of the line and the dialectic with drama. It depicts the difficulties, perils, and pain awaiting those who attempt to break free from the illusions of conventional wisdom and to exchange them for the ultimate happiness that true knowledge brings.

All three explanations describe an ascent from darkness into light. The line is illumined by two centers of light. One is the sun, governing the visible world. The other is the good—or goodness—governing the intelligible world. Plato connects the two sources of light and converts them into symbols in order to accent a startling argument: one cannot see visible objects without the sun; neither can one understand reality without the good. The linkage between sun and vision would undoubtedly pass muster with most readers. But the linkage between goodness and understanding must surely raise a host of questions. They are best answered in Plato's own words. Nonetheless, we add a brief explication here.

The link between understanding and goodness is likely to be startling because of the logical inference: at least some kinds of perception cannot be attained without moral as well as intellectual effort. To see and know things as they really are, Plato says, one must be just, one must be good.

The line embodies still more unorthodox doctrine: the universe is neither evil nor ethically neutral. Instead, it is governed—though not without obstructions—by goodness. The proper purpose of individuals and societies is to imitate and reproduce within themselves the order of the universe by pledging fidelity to the governance of the good. This act of imitation and conversion has its origin in the first efforts to move up and out of the lowest confines of the line; its culmination takes place at the line's highest reaches.

The line is a statement of human dependence. The body is dependent on the sun, and the soul dependent on the good. Plato offers this lesson as a way of approaching a realistic and unobstructed perception of life. Those who recognize dependence are realistic; in harmony with the real world, they are also free. Those who disclaim dependence must necessarily become victims of error and bondage.

The line is a vertical course leading to the real world. At the bottom is the realm of shadows, reflections, and images that can be only uncertain and misleading representations of things as they really are. This is the realm of illusion; by definition it obstructs knowledge of the world and knowledge of the self. Governed by illusion, one can only imagine and conjecture about the ways of nature and society.

At the next level of the line one beholds actual objects in the physical world. But Plato argues that here, too, perception is deceptive in so far as what is perceived is taken for granted. That is, without a systematic effort to explain experience in the natural and human worlds one can have only superficial encounters with reality. Lacking techniques of measurement, experiment, and analysis, perceptions are narrowly drawn. It follows that behavior must be unrealistic because it is guided mainly by assumptions and beliefs. With these arguments Plato assigns the two lower levels of the line to the realm of opinion.

Only when perception reaches the two upper levels does it enter the realm of knowledge. Plato chooses to describe the third level as the province of mathematics. Here, use of numbers and exact meaurement begins to transform unreflective perception into reasoning intelligence.

But limitations on comprehension persist. The conflict between reality and appearance continues unresolved since mathematical understanding does not effectively discriminate between real

objects and their representations (510e–511b). More important, mathematics employs hypotheses whose validity it does
not attempt to verify but instead takes for granted. Dependent
on unexamined hypotheses, the mathematics of his day (Plato
argues) cannot yield pure knowledge because it cannot go beyond
conclusions preordained in its own unverified assumptions.

The full exercise of rational perception, Plato concludes, is
reached at the fourth and highest level of the line. Here reason
is able to understand that it must test the validity of any
hypothesis it employs. Such validation requires that each
hypothesis must be measured and analyzed against other and
sometimes conflicting hypotheses. Thus any hypothesis must be
employed as a necessary but still incomplete form of cognition.
These intellectual procedures are the requirements of the learning process Plato called the dialectic.

As dialectical thought attempts to put a universe of hypotheses
to the proof, it will discover their relativity, their incomplete-
ness. At the same time, recognition of both the necessary functions and the shortcomings of hypotheses spurs the intellect to
reach for a level of understanding that conforms to reality rather
than hypothesis.

If one subjects many hypotheses to dialectical examination,
one can arrive at the equivalent of what modern scientific language calls a unifying idea. That is, one can use hypotheses as
disposable vehicles to reach a point of understanding that is
consonant with reality. Once this highest point on the line is
reached, one has achieved the ability to transcend hypothetical
reasoning and to seize some part of reality itself. Only at this
highest level of the line can one find certainty since here alone
is the realm of reality where truth may be discovered. Only in
this realm can one find the types of unifying ideas which
throughout history have been capable of embracing and comprehending the diverse and changeable phenomena of the physical world.

Plato's line thus attempts to point a path to the discovery of
reality, reality in terms of both its spiritual and moral sig-
nificance. Since the path climbs from the concrete to the abstract,
from a familiar world to a strange world, from well-known
opinions to little-known truths, many people prefer to forgo the
journey.

But, Plato argues at 518b–d, all human beings have the

inherent capacity to cast off illusion and discover reality. The learning capacity itself may generate a ferment, rousing the will to change one's mind and make the upward journey. Thus Plato's line is charged with the force of buoyancy. Will to learn is reinforced by the lift and tug of excitement at the prospect of discovery.

But buoyancy is always in counterpoise with the force of gravity. Human imperfection decrees that no one can completely escape the downward pull of illusions; it follows that no one can live a life of uninterrupted rationality at, so to speak, the top of the line. Hence all human beings live their lives at all levels of the line. Those who ascend the heights of the line— those who emerge from the cave into the real world—are not separated from their fellows. They live in the lower world of appearances as well as in the higher world of reality. They are differentiated only in that they spend more of their lives at the higher levels and less at the lower.

The counterpoise of buoyancy and gravity, in turn, holds together the worlds of appearance and reality, of opinion and knowledge, so that mankind remains joined all along the line by the bond of a common humanity.

Book VII

Here allegory may show us best how education—or the lack of it—
affects our nature. Imagine men living in a cave with a long passageway stretching between them and the cave's mouth, where it opens
wide to the light. Imagine further that since childhood the cave dwellers
have had their legs and necks shackled so as to be confined to the
same spot. They are further constrained by blinders that prevent them
from turning their heads; they can see only directly in front of them.
Next, imagine a light from a fire some distance behind them and
burning at a higher elevation. Between the prisoners and the fire is
a raised path along whose edge there is a low wall like the partition
at the front of a puppet stage. The wall conceals the puppeteers while
they manipulate their puppets above it.

So far I can visualize it.

Imagine, further, men behind the wall carrying all sorts of objects
along its length and holding them above it. The objects include human
and animal images made of stone and wood and all other material.
Presumably, those who carry them sometimes speak and are sometimes silent.

You describe a strange prison and strange prisoners.

Like ourselves. Tell me, do you not think those men would see
only the shadows cast by the fire on the wall of the cave? Would they
have seen anything of themselves or of one another?

How could they if they couldn't move their heads their whole life
long?

Could they see the objects held above the wall behind them or
only the shadows cast in front?

Only the shadows.

If, then, they could talk with one another, don't you think they
would impute reality to the passing shadows?

Necessarily.

Imagine an echo in their prison, bouncing off the wall toward
which the prisoners were turned. Should one of those behind the
wall speak, would the prisoners not think that the sound came from
the shadows in front of them?

No doubt of it.

c   By every measure, then, reality for the prisoners would be nothing but shadows cast by artifacts.

It could be nothing else.

Imagine now how their liberation from bondage and error would come about if something like the following happened. One prisoner is freed from his shackles. He is suddenly compelled to stand up, turn around, walk, and look toward the light. He suffers pain and distress from the glare of the light. So dazzled is he that he cannot even discern the very objects whose shadows he used to be able to see. Now what do you suppose he would answer if he were told that

d   all he had seen before was illusion but that now he was nearer reality, observing real things and therefore seeing more truly? What if someone pointed to the objects being carried above the wall, questioning him as to what each one is? Would he not be at a loss? Would he not regard those things he saw formerly as more real than the things now being shown him?

He would.

e   Again, let him be compelled to look directly at the light. Would his eyes not feel pain? Would he not flee, turning back to those things he was able to discern before, convinced that they are in every truth clearer and more exact than anything he has seen since?

He would.

Then let him be dragged away by force up the rough and steep incline of the cave's passageway, held fast until he is hauled out into the light of the sun. Would not such a rough passage be painful? Would he not resent the experience? And when he came out into

516 the sunlight, would he not be dazzled once again and unable to see what he calls realities?

He could not see even one of them, at least not immediately.

Habituation, then, is evidently required in order to see things higher up. In the beginning he would most easily see shadows; next, reflections in the water of men and other objects. Then he would see the objects themselves. From there he would go on to behold the heav-

b   ens and the heavenly phenomena—more easily the moon and stars by night than the sun by day.

Yes.

Finally, I suppose, he would be able to look on the sun itself, not in reflections in the water or in fleeting images in some alien setting. He would look at the sun as it is, in its own domain, and so be able to see what it is really like.

Yes.

It is at this stage that he would be able to conclude that the sun is the cause of the seasons and of the year's turning, that it governs all

the visible world and is in some sense also the cause of all visible   c
things.

This is surely the next step he would take.

Now, supposing he recalled where he came from. Supposing he
thought of his fellow prisoners and of what passed for wisdom in the
place they were inhabiting. Don't you think he would feel pity for
all that and rejoice in his own change of circumstance?

He surely would.

Suppose there had been honors and citations those below bestowed
upon one another. Suppose prizes were offered for the one quickest
to identify the shadows as they go by and best able to remember the
sequence and configurations in which they appear. All these skills,
in turn, would enhance the ability to guess what would come next.   d
Do you think he would covet such rewards? More, would he envy
and want to emulate those who hold power over the prisoners and
are in turn reverenced by them? Or would he not rather hold fast to
Homer's words that it is "better to be the poor servant of a poor
master," better to endure anything, than to believe those things and
live that way?

I think he would prefer anything to such a life.   e

Consider, further, if he should go back down again into the cave
and return to the place he was before, would not his eyes now go
dark after so abruptly leaving the sunlight behind?

They would.   517

Suppose he should then have to compete once more in shadow
watching with those who never left the cave. And this before his eyes
had become accustomed to the dark and his dimmed vision still
required a long period of habituation. Would he not be laughed at?
Would it not be said that he had made the journey above only to
come back with his eyes ruined and that it is futile even to attempt
the ascent? Further, if anyone tried to release the prisoners and lead
them up and they could get their hands on him and kill him, would
they not kill him?

Of course.

Now, my dear Glaucon, we must apply the allegory as a whole to
all that has been said so far. The prisoners' cave is the counterpart of   b
our own visible order, and the light of the fire betokens the power of
the sun. If you liken the ascent and exploration of things above to
the soul's journey through the intelligible order, you will have
understood my thinking, since that is what you wanted to hear. God
only knows whether it is true. But, in any case, this is the way things
appear to me: in the intelligible world the last thing to be seen—and
then only dimly—is the idea of the good. Once seen, however, the
conclusion becomes irresistible that it is the cause of all things right   c

and good, that in the visible world it gives birth to light and its sovereign source, that in the intelligible world it is itself sovereign and the author of truth and reason, and that the man who will act wisely in private and public life must have seen it.

I agree, insofar as I can follow your thinking.

Come join me, then, in this further thought. Don't be surprised if those who have attained this high vision are unwilling to be involved
d in the affairs of men. Their souls will ever feel the pull from above and yearn to sojourn there. Such a preference is likely enough if the assumptions of our allegory continue to be valid.

Yes, it is likely.

By the same token, would you think it strange if someone returning from divine contemplation to the miseries of men should appear ridiculous? What if he were still blinking his eyes and not yet readjusted to the surrounding darkness before being compelled to testify in court about the shadows of justice or about the images casting the
e shadows? What if he had to enter into debate about the notions of such matters held fast by people who had never seen justice itself?

It would not be strange.

518   Nonetheless, a man with common sense would know that eyesight can be impaired in two different ways by dint of two different causes, namely, transitions from light into darkness and from darkness into light. Believing that the soul also meets with the same experience, he would not thoughtlessly laugh when he saw a soul perturbed and having difficulty in comprehending something. Instead he would try to ascertain whether the cause of its faded vision was the passage from a brighter life to unaccustomed darkness or from the deeper darkness of ignorance toward the world of light, whose brightness
b then dazzled the soul's eye. He will count the first happy, and the second he will pity. Should he be minded to laugh, he who comes from below will merit it more than the one who descends from the light above.

A fair statement.

If this is true, it follows that education is not what some professors say it is. They claim they can transplant the power of knowledge into
c a soul that has none, as if they were engrafting vision into blind eyes.

They do claim that.

But our reasoning goes quite to the contrary. We assert that this power is already in the soul of everyone. The way each of us learns compares with what happens to the eye: it cannot be turned away from darkness to face the light without turning the whole body. So it is with our capacity to know; together with the entire soul one must turn away from the world of transient things toward the world of perpetual being, until finally one learns to endure the sight of its
d most radiant manifestation. This is what we call goodness, is it not?

Yes.

Then there must be some art that would most easily and effectively turn and convert the soul in the way we have described. It would lay no claim to produce sight in the soul's eye. Instead it would assume that sight is already there but wrongly directed; wrongly the soul is not looking where it should. This condition it would be the purpose of the art to remedy.

Such an art might be possible.

Wisdom, then, seems to be of a different order than those other things that are also called virtues of the soul. They seem more akin to the attributes of the body, for when they are not there at the outset, they can be cultivated by exercise and habit. But the ability to think is more divine. Its power is constant and never lost. It can be e useful and benign or malevolent and useless, according to the purposes toward which it is directed. Or have you never observed in 519 men who are called vicious but wise how sharp-sighted the petty soul is and how quickly it can pick out those things toward which it has turned its attention? All this shows that we have to do not with poor eyesight but with a soul under compulsion of evil, so that the keener his vision, the more harm he inflicts.

I have seen these things.

Consider then what would happen if such a soul had been differently trained from childhood or had been liberated early from the love of food and similar pleasures that are attached to us at birth like leaden weights. Supposing, I say, he were freed from all these kinds of things that draw the soul's vision downward. If he were then turned b and converted to the contemplation of real things, he would be using the very same faculties of vision and be seeing them just as keenly as he now sees their opposites.

That is likely.

And must we not draw other likely and necessary conclusions from all that has been said so far? On the one hand, men lacking education and experience in truth cannot adequately preside over a city. Without a sense of purpose or duty in life they will also be without a sense of direction to govern their public and private acts. On the other hand, those who prolong their education endlessly are also c unfit to rule because they become incapable of action. Instead, they suffer themselves to believe that while still living they have already been transported to the Islands of the Blessed.

So our duty as founders is to compel the best natures to achieve that sovereign knowledge we described awhile ago, to scale the heights in order to reach the vision of the good. But after they have reached d the summit and have seen the view, we must not permit what they are now allowed to do.

What is that?

Remain above, refusing to go down again among those prisoners to share their labors and their rewards, whatever their worth may be.

Must we wrong them in this way, making them live a worse life when a better is possible?

e   My friend, you have forgotten again that the law is concerned not with the happiness of any particular class in the city but with the happiness of the city as a whole. Its method is to create harmony among the citizens by persuasion and compulsion, making them
520 share the benefits that each is able to bestow on the community. The law itself produces such men in the city, not in order to let them do as they please but with the intention of using them to bind the city together.

True, I did forget.

Consider further, Glaucon, that in fact we won't be wronging the philosophers who come among us. When we require them to govern the city and be its guardians, we shall vindicate our actions. For we shall say to them that it is quite understandable that men of their
b   quality do not participate in the public life of other cities. After all, there they develop autonomously without favor from the government. It is only just that self-educated men, owing nothing to others for their enlightenment, are not eager to pay anyone for it. But you have been begotten by us to be like kings and leaders in a hive of bees, governing the city for its good and yours. Your education is
c   better and more complete, and you are better equipped to participate in the two ways of life. So down you must go, each in turn, to where the others live and habituate yourselves to see in the dark. Once you have adjusted, you will see ten thousand times better than those who regularly dwell there. Because you have seen the reality of beauty, justice, and goodness, you will be able to know idols and shadows for what they are. Together and wide awake, you and we will govern our city, far differently from most cities today whose inhabitants are
d   ruled darkly as in a dream by men who will fight with each other over shadows and use faction in order to rule, as if that were some great good. The truth is that the city where those who rule are least eager to do so will be the best governed and the least plagued by dissension. The city with the contrary kind of rulers will be burdened with the contrary characteristics.

I agree.

When we tell them this, will our students disobey us? Will they refuse to play their role in the affairs of state even when they know that most of the time they will be able to dwell with one another in a better world?

e   Certainly not. These are just requirements, and they are just men. Yet they will surely approach holding office as an imposed necessity, quite in the opposite frame of mind from those who now rule our cities.

Indeed, old friend. A well-governed city becomes a possibility only if you can discover a better way of life for your future rulers than 521 holding office. Only in such a state will those who rule be really rich, not in gold but with the wealth that yields happiness: a life of goodness and wisdom. But such a government is impossible if men behave like beggars, turning to politics because of what is lacking in their private lives and hoping to find their good in the public business. When office and the power of governing are treated like prizes to be won in battle the result must be a civil war that will destroy the city along with the office seekers.

True.

Is there any life other than that of true philosophers that looks with b scorn on political office?

None, by Zeus.

That is why we require that those in office should not be lovers of power. Otherwise there will be a fight among rival lovers.

Right

Who else would you compel to guard the city? Who else than those who have the clearest understanding of the principles of good government and who have won distinction in another kind of life preferable to the life of politics?

No one else.

Should we then proceed to consider how such men might be pro- c duced and led upward to the light in the same way that some men are said to have ascended from Hades to the halls of the gods?

By all means.

This will be no child's game of flipping shells.[1] It is a conversion, a turning of the soul away from the day whose light is darkness to the true day. It is the ascent to that reality in our allegory that we have called the true philosophy.

Yes.

Then we should consider the kinds of studies that will achieve d these things?

Yes.

Well, Glaucon, what kind of study would attract the soul from the world of change to the world of eternal things? A thought strikes me just now as I speak. Didn't we say that these men must be warrior-athletes in their youth?

Yes, we did.

---

1. This refers to a game in which players toss a shell, one side of which is white and the other black, to see which side comes up.

Then the studies we prescribe must satisfy an additional requirement.

What is that?

They must be useful to warriors.

Of course, if possible.

e   We have previously accounted for their education in gymnastic
and music, have we not?

We have.

And gymnastic is that which concerns the development and decline
of the body and hence things that are perishable?

Clearly.

522   So this is not the study we are looking for.

No.

Could it be music as we have so far described it?

No. You remember we said that music is the counterpart of gymnastic and that it employed habit to educate the guardians. Melody
instilled a certain harmony of spirit, and rhythm imparted measure
and grace, but neither was the same as knowledge. It also nurtured
qualities that are related to those in stories that range from sheer
b   fables to tales whose content is closer to truth. But there is nothing
relevant in these studies to your present purpose.

True. Your memory is very precise. But Glaucon, what kind of
study ought we to be looking for then? All the arts seemed to us
mechanical.

They did indeed. But if we exclude gymnastic, music, and the
arts, what remains?

I would say that if we can't locate anything beyond these, we should
consider something that applies to all of them.

What?

c   Virtually the first thing everyone has to learn. It is common to all
arts, science, and forms of thought.

What?

Oh, that trivial business of being able to identify one, two, and
three. In sum, I mean number and calculation. Is it not true that
every art and all knowledge must make use of them?

Yes, it is.

· The art of war as well?

Of course.

d   Well, on the stage, at least, Agamemnon was certainly made out
to be an ignorant general in these matters. In several tragedies
Palamedes, who is said to have invented number, claims to have
been the one at Troy who marshaled troops into ranks and compa-
nies and enumerated the ships and everything else as if nothing had
been counted previously. Agamemnon, he asserts, was literally inca-

pable of counting his own two feet. And how could he if he did not know numbers. But in that case, what sort of a general would he be?

A very queer general.

So reckoning and the ability to number are studies we must prescribe for the soldier.

e

We certainly must if he is to know anything about the ordering of troops—indeed, if he is going to be human at all.

I see something else in this study.

What?

It seems to me arithmetic is one of the studies we are seeking that naturally leads to real knowledge. But no one uses it rightly; no one treats it as something that can truly lead to reality.

523

What do you mean?

Here, at least, is my opinion. Stand by me and take note whether what comes to my mind is relevant or irrelevant. Then either concur or dissent so that we may better test my conjecture.

Explain.

What I mean is that there are two kinds of sense perception. The one is not conducive to thought because the testimony of the senses themselves appears to be sufficient to our needs. In the case of the other, however, the intellect is roused to reflect whenever sensation fails to yield trustworthy evidence.

b

You are obviously referring to the effect on the senses of distance and shadow painting.

No, you have missed my meaning.

What do you mean, then?

I mean that experiences only provoke thought when they are perceived as being contradictory, as manifesting two opposite characteristics with equal clarity, quite independent of their distance from the viewer. I shall try to make my meaning clearer with an illustration. Consider these three fingers: the smallest, the middle, and the index.

c

All right.

Assume that you are seeing them close up. Now consider this point.

What is it?

Each appears to be equally a finger, no matter whether it is the middle one or the one on one side or the other. Nor does it matter whether it is black or white, or thick or thin. Nor do any other features of this kind make any difference. Hence most people do not feel the need to ask the intellect what a finger is, for their perception has never indicated that a finger is at the same time not a finger.

d

That's right.

So it is obvious that a perception of this sort will never provoke thought.

e   Yes.

But now consider size. Can sight satisfactorily measure how small or big objects are? Does it make no difference that one finger is in the middle and another on the side? How about the sense of touch? Does it accurately perceive thickness and thinness, softness and hardness? Are not the other senses defective in what they report? 524 Does not each one of them function approximately as follows: The same sense that discerns hardness necessarily discerns softness as well. Hence it must report to the soul that it perceives the same thing as being both hard and soft.

That's right.

Must the soul not be at a loss concerning the nature of the hard if the sense that reports it at the same time reports it as being soft? The same with light and heavy if the heavy is reported to be light and the light heavy.

b   Yes. These kinds of messages to the soul can be very misleading. They clearly require further analysis.

So these are the occasions when the soul summons up reason and calculation to help it ascertain whether each of the things reported to it is one or two.

Yes.

And if they turn out to be two, each of them is one.

Yes.

Then if each is one and both are two, the soul will think of the two as separate, for what is inseparable can only be one.

Yes.

c   Sight, too, perceives large and small, as we say, not separated but fused. Is that right?

Yes.

In order to clarify all this the intellect is required to do the opposite of what vision does; it must disentangle large from small and perceive them as distinct from one another.

Yes.

And isn't this the point where we first ask the question, what do we mean by large and small, anyway?

Yes.

And this same point prompted our earlier distinction between the intelligible and the visible.

d   Right.

So this is what I was trying to explain earlier when I said some things are likely to provoke thought and some not. Those things are provocative that the senses perceive as contradictory; where no contradiction is evident, there is no cause for reflection.

Now I understand you, and I agree.

To which of these classes do unity and number belong?

I don't know.

Well, what has just been said may help you to find an answer. For if the eye or some other sense could apprehend unity as complete and indivisible, the soul would have no incentive to discover unity's essence, just as in the case of the finger. But if unity is always paired with its opposite so that it appears to be one thing and equally   e something else, there would be an immediate need to judge between them. The soul would be perplexed; it would be compelled to summon up thought and inquire into the true nature of unity. Hence the study of unity will be among those studies that guide and turn   525 the soul to the contemplation of reality.

Well, unity certainly provides a good illustration of how sight can generate contradictory impressions. For we see unity both as one and as infinite multiplicity.

If this holds for unity, then it must also hold for all number?

Yes.

And arithmetic and calculation are entirely occupied with number?

Yes.

Then it looks like they lead us nearer to reality.   b

Very much so.

It follows that they must be among the studies we want to prescribe. Both the soldier and the philosopher must master them: the one in order to marshal his troops and the other so that he may transcend the world of appearances and reach out to the world of reality. Otherwise, he will never be a master of calculating.

True.

And our guardian is both soldier and philosopher?

Yes.

So our laws will prescribe these studies. We should persuade those who are to perform high functions in the city to undertake calcula-   c tion, but not as amateurs. They should persist in their studies until they reach the level of pure thought, where they will be able to contemplate the very nature of number. The object of study ought not to be buying and selling, as if they were preparing to be merchants or brokers. Instead, it should serve the purposes of war and lead the soul away from the world of appearances toward essence and reality.

Well said.

Our discussion of calculation has made me think about the subtlety and charm of its properties and how it can aid us in many   d different ways. All this provided it is turned to the uses of knowledge and not to buying and selling.

What do you mean?

We made the point before that calculation thrusts the soul upward, compelling it to consider pure number. It will resist any attempt to
e link numbers to visible or tangible things. You know, of course, how experts in mathematics behave in discussions about these matters. They laugh at anyone who attempts to argue for dividing up the unity. Indeed, they won't permit it: if you divide it, they will multiply it back again. They stand guard against anyone who asserts that one is not one but many.

You are right.

526 Now suppose, Glaucon, that someone were to say: My good friends, keeping in mind your axiom concerning the nature of the one, the absolute equality of all ones, and their indivisibility, what kind of numbers are you talking about? How do you suppose they would answer?

I think they would answer that they are referring to units that can be apprehended only by thought and in no other way.

Then, my friend, you can see that this is the kind of study that
b appears to be indispensable for us: it compels the soul to apply pure intellect in a quest for pure truth.

It certainly does.

Another point: have you noticed that those naturally skilled in calculation are also quick in most other studies? And that those naturally slow, when trained and drilled in the subject, become quicker and perform better, even if no other benefits are apparent?

That's right.

c I also believe that we could not find many studies in which learning and practice are more demanding then these.

I don't think we could.

For all these reasons, then, this is a study that must not be neglected. It must be part of an education devised for the finest natures.

Agreed.

Having reached accord concerning the study of calculation, we should consider whether the study next following it also fits our purpose.

Do you mean geometry?

Precisely.

d So much as is related to military use is clearly worthwhile. Selecting sites for encampments, securing strong points, deploying troops in column and line as well as in march and battle formations—all these are operations in which a man skilled in geometry would perform very differently than one without such skills.

At the same time, however, these kinds of uses require only a modicum of geometry. What we need to do is to consider whether
e the principal and more advanced part of the subject serves to make

the idea of the good easier to comprehend. We have identified this
effect as common to all studies that compel the soul to turn around
and behold the most joyous part of reality and so attain what the soul
most stands in need of.

I agree.

Then if a study compels the soul to contemplate reality, it is suitable; if not, it is not suitable.

That will be our contention.   527

Well, then, no one with even the slightest knowledge of geometry
will want to deny that this is a science that completely contradicts
the language geometers use to discuss it.

How so?

They can't help it, of course, but what they say is really ludicrous.
They speak as though they were doing something practical, as if their
propositions were designed to be useful in action. All they talk of is
squaring, extending, and adding, whereas the real purpose of their
science is pure knowledge.

That is certainly true.   b

Then we ought to be able to agree on still another point.

What is that?

That the knowledge of which we speak concerns the eternal and
not the temporal and transient.

Agreed. Geometry has to do with unchanging reality.

In that case, my friend, it would tend to draw the soul upward
toward truth. It would produce minds attuned to philosophizing,
elevating those faculties that now wrongfully remain below.

Nothing could be more certain.

It is equally certain, then, that geometry must not be neglected in   c
your fair city. Even its by-products are valuable.

What are they?

What you have already mentioned: its uses in war. Further, we
know that a man who has studied geometry is a better student across
the board than one who has not.

Yes, by Zeus. There is a great difference between the two.

Shall we then prescribe this as the second study to be undertaken
by the young?

Yes.

And how about setting down astronomy as the third such study?   d

I am strongly in favor of it. A heightened awareness of the seasons
and the months and years will be useful both in agriculture and
navigation, and still more in the art of war.

You amuse me, Glaucon. You are so obviously concerned lest
people think you are sanctioning studies that could turn out to be
useless. Nonetheless, I realize your concern is not a trivial one. Only
with greatest difficulty can one understand that every soul has that

e   power of knowing that studies like these can refresh and purify. This holds true even if the soul's habitual behavior has left it blind and corrupt. Such a power is more precious than ten thousand eyes, for it is the only means we possess to see the truth. All who hold this belief will accept these words with deep conviction. But those others who are wholly unaware of such things will naturally call them non-
528   sense, for they can see no profit in them. So you must decide, here and now, to which group you will address your argument. Or will you speak to none of them, pursuing the discussion rather for your own profit, while leaving others free to gain from it what they will?

The latter. I speak and ask and answer questions mainly for my own sake.

I think we ought to back up a little here. We were mistaken about the study we said should follow upon geometry.

What was the mistake?

b   After discussing plane surfaces we failed to consider solids in themselves; instead we immediately went ahead to examine solids in motion. The proper course would have been to proceed from the second dimension to the third, where we would have to consider cubes and all things sharing the attribute of depth.

That's true, Socrates. But this subject seems generally to have gone unexamined.

There are two reasons for that. First, it is a difficult subject, and since it has nowhere found favor, there is little incentive to study it. Second, students need someone to direct them. This is an indispensable requirement, but a suitable director is difficult to find. Further, the way things are now, even were he available, the conceit of
c   those who have talent for this field is so great that they would refuse to accept his guidance. On the other hand, if an entire city should honor and support such studies, these gifted students would more readily submit to his direction. Then continuous and energetic inquiry would discover the true nature of the subject matter. Even now, although the public has no use for it and students are ignorant of the true reasons for studying it, it steadily gains ground against all obsta-
d   cles by virtue of its inherent charm. I shouldn't be surprised if some-day it would be fully understood.

It's true. The subject has a great deal of charm. But explain more clearly what you meant just now. You defined geometry as the study of plane surfaces?

Yes.

And you followed it up with astronomy, but then you draw back.

Because I wanted to explain everything quickly, I lost ground. The proper order would have put three-dimensional studies next. I omitted them because they are so absurdly neglected; then I went on from geometry to astronomy as the study of solids in motion.

That's right.   e

If we assume that a city will sponsor the neglected third study, let us then count astronomy as the fourth.

We could likely do that. This time, Socrates, I shall not discuss astronomy in terms of the vulgar utilitarianism you rebuked me   529 for just now. Instead I shall adopt your principles in its praise. It is evident to everyone that astronomy propels the soul away from mundane matters and toward the contemplation of higher things.

It may be evident to everyone else, but not to me. I don't think it does this.

Why not?

As it is approached by those who currently seek to lead us toward philosophy, it has quite the opposite effect of turning the soul's attention downward.

How so?

You have an overgenerous conception of what is meant by "higher things." Should anyone try to learn something by throwing back his head and staring at the decorations on a ceiling, I suppose you would   b assume he was engaging in intellectual contemplation instead of simply using his eyes. Maybe you are right, and I am being foolish. But in my opinion only the study of unseen reality can draw the soul upward. To anyone who tries to learn about sense objects, whether gazing above or squinting below, I would say he can never really learn because such things cannot be known. I would add that his soul is looking down and not up even though he may be carrying on his studies by   c land or by sea while lying or floating on his back.

A fair retort; your rebuke is just. But if astronomy is to be taught contrary to present practice, what manner of learning will serve our purposes?

One that perceives the sparks lighting the sky simply as decorations on a visible surface. To be sure, they may be properly regarded as the purest and most beautiful of all material things. But we must   d realize that they fall far short of truth. They do not reveal the motions expressed in absolute speed and absolute slowness. Nor do they explain true number and true figures and how they move in relation to one another, nor what they contain and what they carry. These kinds of things can be comprehended not by sight but only by means of intellect and argument. Do you think differently?

No.

Then we must use the ornaments of heaven as heuristic models. They can aid us to understand those things we are looking for, just as if we had unexpectedly come upon some high-precision and richly elaborated diagrams drafted by Daedalus or some other craftsman or   e painter. Anyone knowing geometry and seeing such designs would appreciate the beauty of their workmanship. But he would think it absurd to suppose that by examining them he could discover the true essence of equals or doubles or any other ratio.

How could he think otherwise?

And don't you agree that any real astronomer would think the same way when he looks upward to observe the movements of the stars? He would admire the work of the heavenly craftsman who gave the skies their form and content as a structure of unsurpassed beauty. But it is another matter when it comes to the ratios of day and night, their connection to the month and of the month to the year, and how the stars relate to all of these time spans and to one another. The real astronomer would recognize these things as visible and tangible objects and would therefore count as folly any assumption that they are changeless and eternal. And he would believe that anyone who mistakes such a false assumption for truth is wasting time.

Now that you say so, I will agree.

Then in astronomy, as in geometry, we shall pursue our studies by setting and solving problems, and we shall let the heavens be. Only by practicing the true science of astronomy can we convert the natural and inherent intelligence of the soul from uselessness into something useful.

You set tasks that will require many times the amount of effort now invested in astronomy.

If we are to be of any use as lawgivers, I suspect our prescriptions in other areas will include similar requirements. Now, do you have any other suitable studies to suggest?

Not right now.

Then remember that the general concept of motion finds expression in many forms and not just one. Whoever is wise in these matters could probably enumerate all of them. But between us we could recognize at least two.

What are they?

Add to astronomy its counterpart.

What is it?

We may suppose that as we are given eyes to study the stars so we have ears to hear harmonic movement and that consequently a certain kinship exists between the two forms of knowledge. This is the position taken by the Pythagoreans, Glaucon, and we agree with them, don't we?

Yes.

Then let us consult them since our task is difficult. Let us see what their opinion is and whether they can add to our knowledge. At the same time, we must guard well our own interests.

What do you mean?

We must not permit our students to try to learn things that are imperfect or that do not lead to the results all studies should attain. We just cited shortcomings of this kind in the study of astronomy. Do you know that the same problems exist in harmony? Those who teach the subject attempt to measure sounds and chords within the context of audibility and so repeat the waste of time we discovered in astronomy.

Yes, by the gods, that's right. And they are so absurd, too, with their talk of "dense" notes and the like. They press their ears against the instruments as if they were trying to overhear a voice from next door. Then some claim to detect an extra note between the intervals which should henceforth be accepted as the smallest interval and the basic unit of measurement; others insist that it is no different from the notes already sounded. Both parties prefer their ears to their intelligence.

You are evidently speaking of those worthy musicians who chafe and torment their strings and put them to the rack on the pegs of the instrument. I won't try to extend the metaphor by bringing the blows of the plectrum into the comparison or those complaints of musicians against their strings that they are either too responsive or too resistant. I will simply say that I do not mean these kinds of people. Instead I mean the same people we just now said we would consult about harmony. Their approach corresponds exactly to that of the astronomers. They seek numbers in the accords they hear, but they do not make the ascent to the universal problems of number where they might consider which numbers are harmonious and which not, and why.

The task is beyond human capacity.

Say, rather, that the task is useful in the quest for the beautiful and the good. If undertaken for other purposes, then it is useless.

That is likely.

Still further, my assumption is that if we carry on all these studies to the point where their kinship and affinities with one another are evident, our effort will have contributed to our purpose, and no labor lost. Otherwise, we shall have striven in vain.

I suspect you are right, Socrates, but you are talking about an enormously difficult undertaking.

Do you speak of the prelude, or what? Do we not understand that all this is but prelude to the main themes we still have to learn? Or do you suppose that the experts we have so far been speaking of can have taught us anything about reason and dialectic?

No, by Zeus, excepting only a very few whom I have met.

Further, do you think that men will ever know what we say they

532 must know if they are unable to account for what they say or compel
others to do the same?

Once again the answer must be no.

Then, Glaucon, we confront at last the main theme of dialectic
and of the law that evolves in harmony with it. Dialectic belongs
wholly to the intelligible order, but we also find its counterpart in
the visible order, in that decisive moment when the eyes are able to
see real creatures, then stars, and finally the sun itself. So it is when
a man enters into dialectic, shunning reliance on sense perceptions
and seeking understanding solely by means of rational discourse. He
strives to know each thing in its essence and does not desist until he
b is led by pure intelligence to know goodness itself. Then he will have
arrived at the limits of the intelligible, just as the man of our allegory
reached the limits of the visible.

Exactly.

And is this not the journey we call the dialectic?

Yes.

Now recall the course of liberation from the cave: first from the
chains, then from the shadows, and then from the images that produce them, into the light. There follows the passageway from the
c cave to the sun and, once the passage is completed, the prolonged
inability to look directly at plants and animals and the light of the
sun. In its stead there is the capacity to see reflections in the water
and shadows again—but this time shadows of the divine, not those
produced by artificial images and by an artificial light which, when
compared with the sun, is as unreal as the shadows around it. Observe
the parallel to the course of studies we have just reviewed. These
studies have the power to liberate and raise the soul's best portion to
the level of what is best in the intelligible world. Our allegory showed
in just the same way how the body's most sunlike element may be
d converted to the contemplation of all that is brightest in the visible
world.

I accept this as the truth. It is hard to accept, but it is also hard to
reject. However, since these are words that we shall hear not just this
once but will return to many times over, let us now assume that they
describe things the way they really are. It is time that we consider
the main theme and go through it just as we went through the prelude. So describe to us the character and power of dialectic. What
e are its parts, and what are its ways? These are the things, it seems to
me, that could bring us to the point where we might find some
resting place alongside the road and then, finally, reach our journey's end.

533 My dear Glaucon, you won't be able to follow me any further,
and not because good will is lacking on my part. If I could, I would

no longer show you allegories and symbols but the very truth itself—
at least as I see it. Whether or not I see it rightly I cannot properly
say. But that there is something like this we need to see I cannot
doubt. Do you agree?

Yes.

Can we also agree that it cannot be seen except by way of the
dialectic, and then only by someone experienced in the studies we
have been discussing, and that there is no other way?

We may insist on it.

So much, at any rate, cannot be gainsaid: no other form of inquiry   b
makes a systematic and comprehensive effort to understand what each
thing really is. All the other arts are concerned with human opinions
and desires, with growing things or making them and tending to
them after they are grown or made. Those who pursue geometry and
the allied arts apprehend reality to some degree, as we have seen.   c
But mostly they dream. It is impossible for them to be fully awake so
long as they neglect to examine the assumptions they employ and
fail to account for their use. If one doesn't know his own first principles, if the conclusion and the intervening parts are themselves
barely known, how could any solution that might be put forward
ever be the equivalent of true knowledge?

It couldn't.

Then dialectic remains the only intellectual process whose method
is that of dissecting hypotheses and ascending to first principles in
order to obtain valid knowledge. Even when the soul's eye is sunk in   d
the muddy pit of barbarism, the dialectic will gently release it and
draw it upward, calling upon the studies we recently examined to
support its work of conversion. We should note here that habit has
several times caused us to call these studies sciences. We really need
another word that would connote something more enlightened than
opinion but less pure than science. I believe we used the word *understanding* earlier. But I would think this is no time to dispute over
names while considering things of much greater importance.

Agreed.

Then we shall be content to continue using the terms and classi-   e
fications we set forth previously. Intellection or reason first, then   534
understanding, then belief, and, finally, conjecture. Taken together,
the latter two comprise opinion and so focus on transient things. The
former comprise knowledge and so are drawn to the eternal. These
relationships, in turn, are expressed in a series of ratios: as timeless-
ness is to transience, so is knowledge to opinion, and as knowledge
is to opinion, so is reason to belief, and understanding to conjecture.
But we had better forgo further inquiry into these kinds of cognition
and how they relate to their collateral subject matter. The same with

the arrangement of these subject matters into two classes we call the opinable and the knowable. Otherwise, Glaucon, we shall be involved b in discussions many times longer than those we have already had.

I agree to what you say insofar as I can follow you.

And is not the dialectician one who can explain the reason for each thing's existence? And will you not agree that anyone who is unable to do this because he cannot account for what he says to himself or others lacks the required intelligence?

How could I say otherwise?

And does this not also pertain to the good? A man must be able to c define the idea of the good in his discourse, distinguishing it and abstracting it from all other things. Like a warrior he must run the entire gauntlet of trials, striving to measure everything in terms of reality and not by opinion. He must meet and overcome every obstacle without permitting his reason to falter. The man who lacks this competence, you will agree, can know neither the good nor any good thing. If he perceives any likeness of the good, it will be the d product of opinion and not of knowledge. Dreaming and dozing away his life on earth, he will arrive at Hades before he wakens, and there he will fall asleep forever.

Yes, by Zeus. I will certainly agree to all that.

Now, should the imaginary children we are educating in our discourse ever become your real children, I presume you would not permit them to govern the city or decide matters of great moment while they remain like the irrational lines in geometry.[2]

No, I wouldn't.

Are you, then, prepared to provide by law that they shall give special heed to the discipline that enables them to master the technique of asking and answering questions?

e I shall promulgate such a law, with your help.

Then we shall have established dialectic at the summit of all studies as the capstone above which no other study could legitimately find a place. And with that, our discussion of the course of studies is complete. Do you agree?

Yes.

535 What remains, then, is for us to decide how we shall assign these studies and to whom.

That is evident.

When we were choosing rulers earlier, do you recall the types of men we selected?

Of course.

For the most part, we shall want to choose these same types now.

2. Irrational lines are those that cannot be related to others as one whole number to another.

The most stable and the bravest must be given preference and, so far as possible, the most comely. But at this point we must get additional b
requirements. The rulers must be high-minded and tough, but they must also possess those gifts from nature that equip them to pursue the kind of education we have been discussing.

Be more specific.

To begin with, my friend, they must relish study and must be able to learn with ease. For men's minds will sooner falter when confronting rigorous intellectual work than hard physical exercise because intellection is more specifically a matter for the soul and is not shared with the body.

True.

A good memory, tenacity, and love for labor of every kind are c
further requirements. Without these, how would anyone be willing to follow the prescribed regimen as well as persevere in so difficult a course of study?

No one would unless he was very good-natured.

This is the cause of philosophy's current difficulties and disrepute: the unfitness of those who seek to be her consorts. Instead of true sons they are bastards.

What do you mean?

First of all, the philosopher candidate must not be half-hearted in d
his love of labor, zealous for one side of it and shunning the other. This is what we see in someone who is a lover of gymnastic and the hunt and all manner of bodily exercise but has no love for learning, listening, or inquiry and hates the dicipline such pursuits require. A man who goes to the other extreme exhibits the same flaw.

True.

Likewise, the love of truth ought to be unblemished. But blemish e
there will be if a man scorns the conscious lie—whether he encounters it in others or within himself—yet tolerates the witless lies spawned by ignorance. Should he himself be convicted of ignorance, he shrugs it off, wallowing about like some pig in the muck.

You are right.

With regard to temperance, bravery, magnificence of soul, and 536
the other ingredients of virtue, we must be particularly careful to discriminate between the true sons and the bastards. When the necessary knowledge to make such discriminations is lacking in the individual or the state, the result must be that bastards or defectives will be chosen to be friends or rulers.

So it is.

And so it must be that we take good care in matters of this sort. If we bring men of sound body and mind to undergo so rigorous a b
training and to undertake such difficult studies, justice itself will find

no fault with us. We shall be able to save the city and the government. But if we bring forward men of another sort, we shall achieve just the opposite. We shall deluge philosophy with still more ridicule.

That would be shameful.

Certainly. But I think I have been making myself a bit ridiculous.

How so?

c   By forgetting that we are jesting, I spoke with too much intensity. While I was speaking, I thought of philosophy and how shamefully it has been reviled. It made me angry, and so I spoke with heat and much too earnestly against those responsible.

By Zeus, you were not too earnest for me as a listener.

Too much so for me as speaker. But here let us recall something we ought not to forget. Earlier we chose old men as rulers, but that

d   won't do for the selection we are making now. We mustn't credit Solon's word that in growing old a man is able to learn many things. He is less able to do that than to run a race. All hard labor belongs to the young.

Necessarily.

Then arithmetic, geometry, and all the other preliminary studies that constitute the indispensable preparation for the dialectic must be introduced to the young. But the instruction must not be compulsory.

Why not?

e   Because a free man ought not to be slavish in learning. Compulsion in physical training doesn't hurt the body, but the mind will not retain anything that it is forced to learn.

True.

Then, my friend, we must not keep the children at their studies
537 by force. Instead, we must make learning fun. With this method it will also be easier for us to recognize the natural bent of each.

You have a good point.

You remember we said that the children must be spectators of war, mounted on horseback and brought to the front wherever it is safe, so that even as puppies they might have a taste of blood?

I remember.

Then those who show the greatest aptitude in dealing with studies, labors, and dangers must be selected to join the ranks of the very best.

At what age?

b   When they have finished with compulsory physical training; during the period when it is required, some two or three years, they are simply incapacitated for other activities. Fatigue and sleepiness are the enemies of study. Moreover, athletic prowess will in any case be one of the tests they must pass, and by no means the least.

Right.

Then at the age of twenty those who have been specially selected will be given greater honors than the others. They must return to the studies they pursued in random fashion as children and organize them in such a way that their interrelations and their relevance to reality become manifest.

That is the only kind of education that will endure.

And it is also the most important test available to discern who has the gift for dialectic and who does not. For he who can see the connection between things is a dialectician; he who cannot is not.

I agree.

Then you will want to use these qualities as your criteria for selecting the best from among those who are steadfast in their studies and in war and in all the other duties the law prescribes. From these you will want to make still another selection at age thirty, promoting them to still higher honors. You must test their qualifications in the dialectic in order to see which ones are able to abstract themselves from sight and the other senses and arrive at the place where truth and reality dwell. But at this point, my friend, you must be very careful.

Why?

Haven't you noticed that current practice in the dialectic is causing great harm?

In what way?

Its students have become lawless.

That is true.

But is their behavior any cause for wonder? Can you find no sympathy for them?

Just why should I?

Their situation resembles that of an adopted son raised in a great and numerous family with abundant wealth, all of which has attracted a horde of flatterers. On reaching manhood he becomes aware that he is not the flesh and blood of his adopted parents and that he will be unable to locate his real parents. Can you imagine the difference in his feelings toward his adopted family and toward those flatterers before and after he learns the truth about his adoption? Or should I do the imagining?

You do it.

I would guess that before knowing the truth, he would more likely honor his adoptive parents and family than his flatterers. He would be less likely to neglect the needs of the foster parents and family. It would be improbable that he should think ill of them or act unlawfully against them. In matters of importance he would be more apt to heed them than the flatterers.

Likely enough.

But afterward, I should guess, his sense of honor and devotion to the family would languish. His attachment to the flatterers would grow. He would pay them more heed, openly maintain relations with them, and finally go over to living by their rules. He would have lost all concern for his adoptive family—unless he were of an exceptionally good nature.

Everything you have said seems plausible. But what is the relevance of the story to the students of dialectic?

This. From childhood on we have been brought up with certain convictions about what is just and honorable, and we have obeyed these convictions with the same reverence with which we have obeyed our parents.

That is true.

Then we meet with various kinds of behavior contrary to these convictions. They are pleasurable and seek to reach the soul through flattery and seduction. Men of any decency will resist their blandishments and will continue to honor and obey what their fathers have taught them.

That is so.

But what happens when such a man confronts the question: what is honorable? After giving the answer he learned from the one who taught him the laws, he is refuted in argument. Many and diverse refutations follow, upsetting his faith and making him believe that there is really no difference between being honorable and being base. When he goes through the same thing with justice and goodness and all the things he values most, will he honor and respect them as before?

Impossible.

Then, when he no longer regards the old beliefs as binding, and true principles still elude him, will he not be likely to settle into the life that feeds and flatters his desires?

He will.

Then he will have ceased to be a law-abiding man; he will have become an outlaw.

Necessarily.

Does this not recapitulate the experience of those who enter the dialectic but lack the requisite discipline? Ought we not to be lenient with them?

Yes, and we ought to pity them too.

Very well. However, so that we won't need to pity your class of thirty year olds, we must take the greatest precautions when the time comes to introduce them to the dialectic.

Yes, we must.

Is it not true that the chief safeguard is to prevent them from tasting it too young? Surely you have observed how the first taste of argument provokes lads to misuse it as a kind of sport, that is, they use it competitively. Having been proven wrong in argument, they must go on to prove others wrong. They are like puppies, welcoming all comers to pull and tear at words with them.

Very much so.

And after they have refuted many, and many have refuted them, they rapidly fall victim to a radical distrust of all they formerly believed.   c The result is that they discredit themselves as well as the entire profession of philosophy.

Very true.

An older man, however, will resist such madness. He will prefer to follow the example of someone who wants to use dialectic in the service of truth and not to play games of contradiction. Hence he   d will be more reasonable and moderate, thereby bringing credit rather than discredit to philosophy.

Right.

Hence our insistence on safeguards and precautions just now. We must require that those allowed to participate in argument have developed stable and steady natures. The present practice of admitting any who chance by, whether suitable or not, cannot be countenanced.

I agree.

If a man devotes himself to an exclusive and strenuous study of the dialectic with the same zeal he dedicated previously to gymnastic, would it be enough to require twice as many years for dialectic as we did for gymnastic?

Do you mean six or four?   e

Make it five. In any case, they will afterward have to be sent back down to the cave. You must compel them to take up military commands and other offices suited to youth so that in this kind of experience as well they will be second to none. And while holding these offices, they must continue to be tested to see if each remains steadfast in the face of temptation, or yields instead.

How much time do you allot to this phase?   540

Fifteen years. Then, at the age of fifty, those who have shown their mettle and preserved their integrity through every trial and proven best in all tasks and realms of knowledge must at last be shown the way to the goal. There they must lift up the sunlike part of their souls and behold that which sheds light on all things. Having seen goodness itself, they will adopt it for the rest of their lives as their governor, for themselves, for their city, and for their fellow citizens. From then on each will devote most of his time to the study of philosophy.   b When his turn comes, however, he will take office and toil to serve

the city, understanding it to be an obligation and not an honor. And so, when each generation of guardians has readied those like them in the next to take their places, they go off to dwell in the Islands of
c   the Blessed. The city will decree public memorials and sacrifices in their names. If the Pythian oracle approves, they shall be revered as divinities. If not, they shall be known as divine and happy men.

Done like a sculptor, Socrates. You have given our rulers a marvelous luster.

And the ruling women too, Glaucon. You mustn't think that anything I have said applies any more to men than to women endowed with similar capacities.

That is only right if we are to respect our own commitment that women must have an equal share in everything with men.

d   Well, then, will you agree that our notion of what city and government should be is no mere daydream? Difficult it is, but in some way possible. Not, however, in any other way than we have described. When true philosophers—whether one or many—come to power in the city, they will scorn honors, counting them illiberal and worthless. Their first care will be to do what is right and accept the honors such care merits. They will reform, serve, and maintain the city,
e   and justice will be its chief quality and most indispensable standard.

How will they be able to do all this?

541   By sending out all those over ten years of age into the country. They will take over the children, taking care that they are far removed from the dispositions and habits of their parents. They will be raised according to their own laws and customs in the manner we have been describing. This is the fastest and easiest way to establish the city and the government we have portrayed and to bring happiness and true benefits to its citizens.

b   By far the fastest and easiest, Socrates. And I think you have explained very well how it might come into being, if it ever does.

Then we have said enough about this kind of city and the kind of man who is its counterpart? Henceforth we shall know them.

Evidently. To answer your question, I think we have finished.

Book VIII

Good. We have decided, then, that in the best governed state there must be a community of women and children. Men and women must be educated in common and share common tasks in war and peace. The rulers must be chosen from among those who excel in philosophy and war.

Yes. We agreed to that.

We also agreed that after the rulers have taken office, they must send the soldiers to live in the kinds of houses we described: nothing private and everything in common. In addition to their housing, if you remember, we reached another agreement concerning the kinds of possessions they should have.

Yes, I do remember. We said that they should have none of the things that ordinary men may possess. At the same time, we wanted these athletes of war and guardians to receive in lieu of wages an annual living allowance from their fellow citizens in consideration for their services. In this way they might devote themselves entirely to taking care of themselves and the city.

That's right. But now that we have finished with this subject, we ought to recall that we have arrived where we are now because of a digression. Let us revert to the point where we turned off so that we can resume our former path.

That should be easy to do. You were speaking very much as you are now. You gave the impression that you had completed your discussion of the city and went on to say that the type of city you were then describing you would deem good, together with the corresponding type of man. Subsequently, however, it became evident that you had a still finer man and city to tell about. At any rate, you said that if this city is the good city, then the others are aberrations. Of these aberrant types, you said, there are four whose constitutions and defects are worth examining, and then relating to the corresponding sorts of men. The object was to enable us to observe all of them and to reach agreement about which is the best man and which the worst. Finally, then, we might be in a position to decide whether the best is also the

happiest and the worst the most miserable, or whether the reverse is
b   true. Then just when I was asking what were the four constitutions
you were thinking of, Polemarchus and Adeimantus interrupted. You
picked up their argument, and that's how we arrived where we are
now.

You have a keen memory.

And now, we might borrow from the practice of wrestlers. Let us
resume our earlier positions, and when I put the same question a
second time try to tell us what you were going to say before.

I will if I can.

c   I really am eager to hear about the four forms of government you
were referring to.

That I can easily tell you. The ones I have in mind all have familiar names. First is the frequently admired constitution of Sparta and
Crete.[1] Oligarchy is next in line and second in favor; it is a regime
replete with a horde of evils. Following is its adversary, democracy.
And at the last we come to that glorious thing called tyranny. Worse
by far than all the rest, it infects the city with a mortal illness. Do
d   you have any other type of government to add? I mean one that can
be regarded as a distinct form. There are, of course, dynasties and
purchased kingships and several similar constitutions somewhere in
between. They can be found no less often among barbarians than
among the Greeks.

Certainly there are many exotic types.

Do you realize that there must necessarily be as many types of
human personality as there are forms of government? Or do you
imagine that governments spring from the proverbial oak or rock
instead of from the inclinations that predominate among their citizens, which then tip the scales, so to speak, so that the rest will
e   follow along?

I can't imagine any other source of government.

Then, if there are altogether five forms of government, there would
also be five forms of soul in the human personality.

That is certain.

545   We have already described the man we rightly called good and
just and whose counterpart is aristocracy, the name we use for the
government of the best.

We have.

Our next task, then, is to examine the inferior types of men and
governments: the man who covets honor and insists on victory, the

---

1. Sparta and Crete were dominated by the military spirit. Socrates will shortly describe this kind
of regime as a timocracy (545b).

counterpart to the regime of Sparta; thereafter the oligarch, the democrat and the tyrant. Then, after having beheld the most unjust man, we can contrast him with the man who is truly just. This, in turn, should enable us to complete our inquiry into the way pure justice stands to pure injustice and what each does for the happiness or misery of those who side with one or the other. Then we shall know whether we do better to follow the advice of Thrasymachus and choose injustice or stay with the present argument and choose justice.   b

A good way to proceed.

Shall we do as before, first considering the attributes of the city, where they are writ large, and then of the individual? This way we would examine first the constitution embodying the love of honor. I do not know what to call it other than timocracy, or possibly timarchy. Then we would discuss the man of the same type. We would   c
follow up with oligarchy and the oligarch and with democracy and the democratic man. Finally, we would go to the city ruled by a tyrant and observe it; then we would look into the soul of a tyrannical individual. So we shall seek to make ourselves competent to judge the question before us.

A reasonable way to observe and judge.

Well, then, let us try to explain how aristocracy might yield to timocracy. Does the process not begin according to the simple rule that holds for every type of regime? The rule is that revolution orig-   d
inates in dissensions among the ruling class. But if this class, however small, remains united, innovation is impossible.

The rule applies.

Then, Glaucon, how will dissension arise in our city? How will our rulers and helpers come to disagree and form factions against each other and among themselves? Shall we follow Homer and pray that the Muses will tell us "how faction first befell them," pretending   e
that the mock-heroic tones they adopt to tease little children are to be taken seriously?

What would they say?

Something like this: 546

> Hard it is for a city so constituted to be shaken. But since destruction is the portion of everything created, not even a fabric as strong as this one can endure forever. Surely it will be dissolved, and this is the manner of its dissolution. There is a cycle of bearing and of barrenness in soul and body governing the plants of the earth and also the animals living upon it. As the cycle rotates, so each appears, frequently where the life span is short, less so when it is long. The men you have educated to be your rulers are wise. But even if they apply both reason and sense observation, they will not discover the laws that govern your race nor the   b

times when birth will be auspicious and when it will not. Then will come a time when they will beget children out of season. There is a cycle for divine procreation that the perfect number comprehends. There is also a period of time for mortal procreation when at the first moment multiplication by both roots and squares with three dimensions and four limits of those elements producing likeness, unlikeness, growth, and decline has shown all components to be in proportion and har-
c   mony with one another. All these components have 4/3 as a base, which, joined to a unit of 5, produces a double harmony when raised to the third power. In the first dimension it is equal to the basic unit times 100. The second dimension has an equal base but is oblong—one side being 100 times the measurement of the rational numbers of the whole unit of 5 minus 1, or else of irrational numbers minus 2; the other side is 100 times the cube of the unit of 3. This geometrical figure decides
d   when begetting will be seasonable and when not. When your guardians mistake the figure and unite brides and bridegrooms out of season, the children will not be well favored or fortunate. To be sure, when the time comes, only the best of these will be appointed to office by their predecessors. Nonetheless, they will be unworthy of their fathers. When they come to power as guardians, they will first manifest their negligence toward us, paying too little mind to music and then to gymnastic. The result will be that the education of the younger men will suffer.
e   Those who are appointed rulers from this generation, in turn, will hardly show much aptitude when it comes to distinguishing Hesiod's races—
547   or discriminating between the gold, silver, bronze, and iron of our race. The resulting intermixture of silver with iron and gold with bronze will spawn chaos, inequality, and disharmony. And wherever these appear, enmity and war will always follow. We must know that "this is the ancestry" of faction wherever it occurs.

Let us say that the Muses have given the right answer.

Necessarily. They are Muses.

b   What do the Muses say next?

Once faction appeared, two coalitions were pulling against each other. Iron and bronze were attracted toward money-making and the acquisition of land and houses and gold and silver. The other coalition, gold and silver, not being poor but rich by nature, tried to draw the opposition back to virtue and the inherited order. Thus straining and contending against one another, they came at last to a compromise. They distributed land and houses among themselves to be held
c   in private ownership. Former friends and supporters whose freedom they had once guarded they now enslaved as serfs and domestics. So they kept themselves busy by coercing the subjects they once protected and by making war.

This looks like the beginning of the transformation.

And this new regime would be somewhere on middle ground between aristocracy and oligarchy?

Certainly.

Then we know the cause for the change. But after the change has taken place, how will the city be governed? Since it is an interme- d
diate form, it is obvious that it will imitate the aristocracy in some respects and in some the oligarchy. It will also have some characteristics peculiar to itself.

True.

The city will imitate the preceding regime in many ways. It will honor its ruler. The soldiers will abjure farming, handicrafts, and money-making in general. The provision of common meals will continue, as will the concern for gymnastic and training for war.

Yes.

But there will be aspects specific to the new regime as well. It will fear to admit clever men to office because they will have become e
equivocators instead of being simple and straightforward. It will turn instead to the more ardent and simple-minded types better suited to war than peace. The stratagems and paraphernalia of war will be 548
held in honor, and war will be the leading preoccupation.

Yes.

At the same time, men like these will imitate the oligarchs in their greed for wealth. They will burn with a secret lust for gold and silver, hiding them away in the private treasuries and storehouses with which they will now have provided for themselves. They will build walls b
around their houses, making them into clandestine love nests where they can favor their women and any others they like with lavish expenditure.

Very true.

But they will also be stingy with their own money because they hold it dear and because they are not allowed to possess it openly. The wealth of others, however, they will spend with a prodigal hand in catering to their appetites and in the stealthy enjoyment of their pleasures. They will run away from the law like boys from a father, for they have been educated not by persuasion but by force. This is the behavior that results from neglect of the true Muse of discourse and philosophy and from the preference for gymnastic over c
music.

You offer an apt description of a regime that combines good and bad.

Yes, the elements are mixed. But because of the preponderance of the high-spirited element, one thing alone is its most conspicuous feature: the love of honor and victory.

That is right.

Such is the nature and origin of this form of government. We have only outlined the constitutional structure without further elab-

oration since a sketch should suffice to enable us to see the most just
d   and the most unjust man. Besides, it would be too long a task should
we try to describe all forms of government and all types and dispositions of men without omitting anything.

What of the individual corresponding to this constitution? What
is his nature and origin?

As far as loving victory goes, said Adeimantus, he looks very much
like Glaucon.

e   Perhaps. But in other respects he is quite different from Glaucon.

In what respects?

He will be more self-willed and less cultivated, though fond of
music. He is also fond of listening to argument but lacks skill in
549   speaking. He would be abusive toward slaves instead of simply dis-
daining them as educated men do. But he would be civil in dealing
with the freeborn and obedient to officials. A lover of office and
honor, he lays claim to office not because he has an ability to speak
or anything of the sort but because of his exploits in military exercises
and war. He has a passion for gymnastic and the hunt.

Yes. He really reflects the spirit of the regime.

In his youth such a man would be disdainful of wealth, would he
b   not? But on growing older he would come to love it more as the
greed in his nature asserts itself more strongly. Bereft of the best
guardian, his virtue will not remain unsullied and pure.

What guardian?

A rational and a cultivated mind is the sole guarantor of virtue in
a man's life.

Well said.

Such, then, is the timocratic youth, standing side by side the
timocratic state.

So it is.

c   His origins would likely be of this sort. He might be the son of a
good father living in a badly governed city. The father avoids office
and honors and lawsuits and the bustle that accompanies them. He
will even forgo some of his rights in order to avoid trouble.

But how does the son develop?

Well, in the first place, he hears his mother complaining that her
d   husband is not one of the rulers and that therefore she is held in low
esteem by the other women. She notes that he cares little for money
and is easygoing about it, just as he is in other matters. He will not
fight for money in private lawsuits nor brawl about it in public
assembly. She notes too that he is very much absorbed in himself
and his thoughts. Toward her he is not inconsiderate, but neither is
e   he particularly considerate. All these grievances prompt her to tell

the boy that his father is too slack and lacks courage. She accompanies this with all the other complaints familiar to wives.

Yes. The complaints are very familiar.

You know well enough that the very house servants of such men,
those whose loyalty is not in doubt, will say the same sort of things
to the sons in private. If it comes to their attention that a debtor or
other wrongdoer is not being prosecuted by the father, they urge the
boy to punish the miscreant when he grows up and so prove himself
more of a man than his father. When the boy leaves the house, he   550
hears the same sort of thing. He learns that men who mind their
own business are called fools and held in low repute. Meddlers who
occupy themselves with the affairs of other people, however, enjoy
honors and praise. Hearing and seeing such things, but also listening
to his father and observing his activities at close range while comparing them to that of others, he will be attracted by both. His father   b
will foster the rational part of his soul; the others will stimulate his
appetites and passions. The son is not a bad man, but he has fallen
in with bad company. Subject to two contradictory influences, he
chooses the intermediate ground. He surrenders his soul to the rule
of ambition and high spirit and becomes a man arrogant in manner
and hungry for honors.

You describe the man and his origins exactly.

So now we know both the second regime and the second type of   c
man.

We do.

Should we now follow Aeschylus and tell of "another man set
against another city" or rather hold to our practice of considering the
city first?

By all means, the city first.

Then I think oligarchy would come next.

What do you mean by oligarchy?

A regime based on property ownership in which only the rich hold
office and the poor have no share in government.   d

I see.

Should we begin by looking at how the transition from timocracy
to oligarchy occurs?

Yes.

The truth is that even a blind man ought to be able to see how the
transformation takes place.

How so?

The ruin of timocracy is the gold that accumulates in the coffers
of private persons. First they go about inventing new ways of spending their money. Next they subvert the laws governing expenditure,

e   which they and their wives then ignore entirely.

Likely.

After this, I take it, mutual watchfulness leads to mutual rivalry until the greater number of such people come to embrace these kinds of values.

Also likely.

With time they grow richer and richer, and the more they cherish their fortunes, the less they pay honor to virtue. Might one not think of the antagonism between wealth and virtue as if each were posed on opposing sides of a scale?

Yes.

551   So when the city honors riches and the rich, virtue and the virtuous are honored less.

Clearly.

And whatever men honor they will run after; what is not honored they will neglect.

So it is.

And so the lovers of victory and honor finally become lovers of money and profit. The rich receive praise and respect and public office; the poor are despised.

Very true.

At this juncture they pass legislation specifying the limits of political participation in the oligarchy. They are drawn narrowly or broadly, depending on the tightness of the oligarchy itself. The nub is that no one may hold office whose property does not reach the level of the required valuation. The law is imposed either by force of arms or, before they come to that, by intimidation. Is this not the way it is done?

It is.

In general, then, this is the way oligarchy comes to power.

Yes, but what are the characteristics of this kind of government? What are the defects we were concerned about?

The first defect is the very thing that defines the regime. Suppose the appointment of ship captains was made to depend upon meeting a property qualification? Suppose a poor man were not permitted to navigate even were he a better pilot?

The result would be a sorry voyage.

And would not the same result follow from any government of this sort?

I think so.

Would the government of the city be an exception?

d   Hardly, since governing the city is the highest and most difficult calling of all.

Then here is one very grave defect in oligarchy.

So it seems.

And is the next any less serious?

What is it?

The necessity that such a city must always be two and not one, a city of the rich and a city of the poor. Dwelling together side by side, they never cease plotting against one another.

No, by Zeus. That is no lesser defect.

There is more to criticize: they may be unable to wage war because they shrink from the necessity of arming the multitude, fearing it more than they fear the enemy. But if they make no use of the people on the battlefield, they will find themselves oligarchs indeed, commanding only a few. Further, because they are lovers of money, they will be laggard in putting up the necessary funds.

Reprehensible.

And what about the flaw we noted long before this—the tendency among the citizens of such a city to be busybodies, each wanting to be farmer, money-maker, and soldier all in one? Do you think that is right?

I do not.

Now let us see whether this city is not the first to permit the greatest of all evils.

What is it?

Allowing a man to sell all that belongs to him and another man to acquire it. The seller will go on living in the city but will no longer be part of it. He will be neither money-maker, nor craftsman, nor horseman, nor foot soldier. He will be listed simply as a pauper.

We do see this for the first time here.

In any case, oligarchies certainly do not forbid this kind of thing; otherwise some of their citizens would not be so loaded with money while others are so desperately poor.

Right.

But consider further. In the days when our pauper still had wealth and was spending his money, was he of any greater use to the city in the kinds of things we were just discussing? Or did he belong to the ruling class in name only but in fact was neither a ruler nor a servant of the city? He was merely a consumer.

That's what he was. He seemed otherwise, but he was really nothing but a spendthrift.

Could we say of him that he is like the drone that grows in the cell and then contaminates the hive? He grows up in his own house only to become an affliction to the city?

So he has, Socrates.

All the drones with wings god made stingless, Adeimantus. Of those with legs, however, some he made stingless but armed others

with truly terrifying stings. In old age some of the stingless ones finally
become beggars. From those with stings, on the other hand, come
all whom we call villains.

Very true.

It should be evident, then, that the presence of beggars in a city
indicates that thieves, cutpurses, defilers of temples, and other artists
in crime are lurking nearby.

Clearly.

Well, then, do we see beggars in oligarchic cities?

Except for the ruling class, nearly all are beggars.

Ought we not to assume, then, that there are also many criminals
armed with stings whom the rulers keep under surveillance and hold
down by force?

The assumption is sound.

It is also true the presence of such citizens is the product of bad
education, a corrupt culture, and unjust political arrangements?

We couldn't say otherwise.

Here, then, is the character of oligarchic rule together with
the evils besetting it. There may be still more evils than we have
cited.

Very likely.

Then let us agree that we have finished with our discussion of the
oligarchic regime and with those who rule by virtue of the property
they possess. There remain for consideration the characteristics and
development of the man who typifies the regime.

Yes.

The transition from the timocratic youth to his oligarchic counterpart is something like this.

Like what?

The son born to a timocratic man at first emulates his father and
follows his example. Suddenly, he sees the father run afoul of the
state and founder like a ship on a reef; he and all his possessions are
ruined together. Perhaps the father was a general or held some other
high office only to be entangled in a court action by some servile
flunkies of one sort or another. The outcome was death or exile or
loss of all his property.

Likely enough.

Then, my friend, after seeing and suffering all these things and
losing his patrimony, the son, I suppose, will become timid. He will
banish the love of honor and high spirit from his heart. Humbled by
poverty, he turns to money-making. Greed will make him miserly;
with thrift and hard work he will little by little amass property once
again. Will not such a man now enthrone appetite and avarice in
his heart? Will he not emulate the great king himself, all gorgeous

with crowns and golden collars and girt with the Persian sword?[2]

He will.

Himself in thrall, he will force the principles of reason and high spirit to crouch on the ground on either side of him like slaves. He will suffer the one to calculate and consider nothing but how to make more money from less. The other will be constrained to admire and honor nothing but riches and the rich, his only pride the possession of money and whatever contributes to it.

The conversion is quick and sure: the lover of honor becomes a lover of money.

So this is our oligarchic man.

At all events, he has evolved from the man matching the constitution that produced oligarchy.

Then let us see whether he and that constitution are alike.

Let us do so.

Would the first similarity not be the prizing of wealth above everything else?

Without question.

The likeness would extend to his thrift and hard work. He would gratify only his own most necessary appetites and desires, withholding expenditures for anything else and suppressing those appetites he deemed vain and unprofitable.

That he would.

He would be an odious fellow, ever on the lookout for bigger profits. And he would hoard, a propensity the multitude admires. Doesn't the character of this man coincide with the regime we have been considering?

No question about it. In any case, both the regime and the man put property first.

He is clearly not a man who has valued education.

I should think not. Otherwise he would never have chosen a blind god to be first in honor and to lead his chorus.

Excellently said. Let us go further. Owing to his want of education, the cravings of the drone assert themselves, some marking the idler and some the criminal. Nonetheless, he holds them forcibly in check by dint of his own vigilance and self-control.

Right.

Where must we look if we want to bring under scrutiny the criminal side of such a man?

Where?

Anywhere he can play false with impunity—assuming the guardianship of orphans, for example.

---

2. To a Greek audience the great king is the ruler of the Persian empire.

Of course.

In other matters he may enjoy a good reputation. Calling on some
d   better part of his nature, he forcibly represses other criminal desires
and gives the appearance of being a just man. But he does not rebuke
these desires because he thinks it wrong to indulge them. Nor does
he call upon reason to tame them. He beats them down because he
fears that otherwise he might risk losing his properties.

Exactly.

Yes, by Zeus. In most men of this kind, my friend, you will discover the dronelike appetites whenever they have opportunity to spend
the money of others.

Exactly.

Such a man would hardly be free of dissension. He would not be
one man; in some senses he would be two. Nonetheless, his better
e   desires would generally prevail over the worse.

So it would be.

This is the reason why he would appear to be more respectable
than many others. But the true virtue of unity and harmony in the
soul escapes him and remains far from him.

I agree.

555 Moreover, the stingy man would not be much of a competitor for
victory's honors or any other prizes conferred in the city. He is
unwilling to spend money for fame or in competitions of any sort.
He fears to awaken an alliance between extravagant appetites and
the lone victory. He is a true oligarch. He fights with only a small
part of his resources, he is usually defeated, and he continues to be
rich.

You are right.

Is there any further doubt about the resemblance between the mi-
b   serly and money-loving man and the oligarchic state?

None.

So that we can proceed with our comparisons, we must now consider the origin and nature of democracy.

That would be in order.

Is not the transition from oligarchy to democracy provoked by that
insatiate greed for what oligarchy calls the greatest good, to become
as rich as possible?

How so?

c   Well, since the rulers hold office because of their wealth, they are
unwilling to enact legislation restricting its expenditures. The result
is that there is no limit to what the young prodigals may spend and
waste. The game is that the rulers lend them money on their property and then buy it up so that they become still richer and more
influential.

That's the way it is.

Is it not evident in any city that the worship of riches must be incompatible with a sober-minded and temperate citizenry? One of these must suffer neglect.

d   Evidently.

And the kind of neglect and licentiousness characterizing oligarchies has often enough ruined men whose qualities were by no means ignoble.

That is certainly true.

Armed to sting, these men now wait inside the city. Some are burdened with debt and others disfranchised; some suffer deprivations of both kinds. Hating those who acquired their estates and plotting against them and the rest of the citizens as well, they thirst for revolution.

Yes.

But the money lovers turn their heads away and pretend not to see   e
them. Instead they use their own stings; they use their money to poison any of the remaining citizens vulnerable to usury. The interest they extract augments their capital still further and also swells the   556
number of drones and paupers.

They do know how to multiply.

When all these evils burst into flame, they will do nothing to quench them. They will not pass a law to prevent a man from squandering his substance nor, on the other hand, would they consider another law that would eliminate the abuses of usury.

What law would that be?

It would supplement the first law and compel the citizens to greater virtue. If a law were enacted that each party entering into a loan   b
contract does so at his own risk, there would be less of the shameless pursuit of money in the city and of the evils we have been discussing.

There would certainly be fewer.

But for the reasons we have cited, the rulers use all these methods to subjugate their citizens. At the same time, they and their children become habituated to luxury and idleness, unwilling to exert body   c
or mind and unable to withstand either pleasure or pain.

How could they be otherwise?

Because they neglect everything except their money-making, they are as indifferent to virtue as any pauper.

Just so.

Given their dissonant life styles, what will happen when the rulers and the ruled mingle? The occasion might be on marches or journeys or some public undertaking like a religious festival. Or it may be service in a military campaign as shipmates or soldiers in actual battle. Then, when they observe one another, the rich will not scorn   d the poor. On the contrary, what is likely to happen when a lean and muscular pauper, burned brown by the sun, is stationed in battle beside a pampered rich man burdened with excess flesh and panting from his exertions? Will he not think that fellows of his ilk hold on to their wealth only because the poor are cowards? And when the poor are alone together, will they not pass the word that such men

e are good for nothing and ready for a fall?

I know very well that they talk that way.

We know too that an unhealthy body will fall sick at the slightest upset and be consumed by internal war. Sometimes this happens even with no external cause. Is not a city in like condition similarly vulnerable? Will it not use the slightest pretext to bring in allies from the outside? One faction will recruit from among oligarchies and the

557 other from democracies. But with or without external involvement, the city is sick and will wage war against itself.

A telling diagnosis.

When the poor are victorious, I suppose, a democracy emerges. Some of the opposition are put to death and others exiled. The remainder of the citizens receive equal rights to vote and to hold office, with most of the offices assigned by lot.

Yes. That is just the way democracy is established: either by force of arms or by the use of terror which compels the opposition to withdraw.

Then what will the regime be like, and what will be the citizens'

b way of life? For it is clear that the man will share the qualities of the society; he will therefore turn out to be the democratic man.

That's right.

First of all, then, the people are free. Does not the city resound with freedom and free speech? And doesn't everyone have license to do what he wants?

So they say.

Given this license, is it not obvious that each will pursue a way of life to suit himself?

Yes.

c Then diversity will mark the people of the democratic city more than any other.

Yes.

Hence of all constitutions this is perhaps the fairest. Embroidered with every kind of fancy, it is a many-colored cloak, displaying all varieties of human character. As boys and women see beauty in diversity of colors, so also many would call this regime the most splendid.

You are right.

d And also, my friend, democracy offers a convenient opportunity to choose from among a variety of constitutions.

How so?

Because it tolerates all kinds. Indeed, one could say that anyone who wanted to found a state—as we were just now doing—ought to visit a democracy and there select from a veritable bazaar of constitutions whatever pleases him best. After having made his choice, he could then set up his state.

He surely wouldn't lack for models.

What he would lack is compulsion. The city would impose no obligation to govern, even upon those who are competent to rule. Nor is obedience to authority required unless one chooses to submit: No one is compelled to go to war when the others are making war, nor to keep the peace when the others have concluded peace. By the same token, if some one could fancy public office or want to be a judge, he could declare his candidacy even if there were a law expressly disqualifying him. Is this not a marvelously entertaining way to spend one's time?

For the moment, perhaps.

558

And is not the lenience shown toward some of the convicted criminals truly exquisite? Or have you never seen a regime where men condemned to death or exile nonetheless continue to parade about the city as if they were heroes, and no one sees or cares?

I have seen many.

So it goes with democracy's permissiveness. It exhibits a fine lack of concern for all the requirements we so painstakingly set forth when founding our city. It scorns our judgment that in the absence of transcendent gifts no man can become a good man unless from childhood on his play and all his activities are guided by what is fair and good. All these things are trampled underfoot; the democratic city cares nothing for the past behavior of the man who enters public life. He need only proclaim himself a friend of the people, and he will be honored.

b

A regime of real distinction.

c

Displaying these characteristics and others like them, democracy might appear to be a charming form of government. In its diversity and disorder it proceeds to dispense a sort of equality to equal and unequals alike.

Yes. Everyone knows that.

What about the individual who reflects all this in his private life? Or should we first discuss his antecedents, as we did when we considered the analogous regime?

First the antecedents.

Wouldn't it go something like this? He would be the son of our ungenerous oligarch, trained to follow the example of his father.

d

Exactly.

So he, too, would suppress all those profligate appetites that conflict with money-making—forgoing, that is, those pleasures that are called unnecessary.

That follows.

In order not to clutter up the argument at this point we might do well to define what we mean by necessary and unnecessary pleasures.

Agreed.

e Necessary, then, are those pleasures which by our natures we cannot do without, as well as those pleasures from which we benefit. Nature, in effect, compels us to desire both kinds.

559 True.

So we are correct in terming them necessary?

Yes.

What about those desires from which a man could liberate himself by dint of discipline from youth onward—desires that do the soul no good and might in fact be harmful? Would it be fair to call all these desires unnecessary?

Fair enough.

Let us choose an example of each kind to see if we can classify them according to type.

Very well.

The desire to eat—the desire for simple foods like bread and meat to maintain health and bodily condition—this we would call a necessary desire, would we not?

b I should think we would.

An appetite for bread, at least, qualifies as necessary in terms of both criteria we specified: we benefit from it; and if we cannot satisfy it, we die.

True.

Could we say the same of the appetite for meat if it could be shown to sustain good health?

We could indeed.

c But what about the appetites that go further, whose desires are for other varieties of food? These are the ones that undermine moderation in the soul and bodily good health but that strict training in the younger years can usually eradicate. Are these not rightly called the unnecessary appetites?

Very rightly.

Then they must also be called wasteful. The other kind, however, can be called productive because they are useful to active life.

Very true.

Does the same hold true for sex and the other appetites?

It does.

Then if we revert to the man we recently called a drone, buzzing with appetites and desires, it is he who is governed by the unnecessary desires. The stingy oligarch, on the other hand, is ruled by the desires we call necessary.

Yes.

Now we are ready to ask how the democratic man emerges from his oligarchic counterpart.

Explain.

Recall that in his youth he was denied an education and required to practice strictest economy. Once he tastes the drones' honey, however, he joins up with these fierce and designing creatures, adept at catering to every variety and description of pleasure. This is presumably the point where he turns away from the oligarchic principle to democracy.

Without doubt.

Here we may draw a parallel with the forces that revolutionized the oligarchic city. Forces within the city, you remember, summoned to their aid like-minded allies from outside. So our erstwhile oligarchic youth is undone by importing from his environment cravings that reinforce kindred appetites already within himself.

Of course.

But then, it may be, his father or other kinsmen form a counteralliance to rescue the oligarch in him, with no lack of accompanying reproaches and admonitions. Thus we behold the rise of faction and counterfaction, that is, of internal strife within the man himself.

That follows.

Sometimes, I suppose, the oligarchy regains ground against the democratic elements. Then, as some of his appetites are beaten down and others banished, a sense of shame and a spirit of reverence as well enter the young man's soul to the point where order is restored.

That can sometimes happen.

But sometimes another swarm of desires kin to those that had been cast out are covertly nurtured to take their place. And because the father understands nothing of education, they are allowed to wax strong and become numerous.

That is what usually happens.

The son is drawn once again to the same bad companions. He meets them clandestinely, and a whole new brood of desires is hatched.

Just so.

At last, I suppose, they breach the ramparts of the young man's soul and find it empty. Wanting in all honorable studies and pursuits and in honest discourse, he has lost the watchmen who best guard the minds of those whom the gods love.

Yes, much the best.

False and boastful words and doctrines will crowd into the vacuum and there secure a stronghold in the young man's thought.

They will.

At this point he will return to the Lotus Eaters and live with them openly, will he not?[3] And if any of his kin should still seek to render assistance to the oligarchic dispositions remaining in his character, bluster and boasting will have now become the sentries that hold the gates closed against them. None such is admitted to the castle's keep, d neither ally nor embassy bringing word from old friends. Within, meanwhile, a struggle goes on in which the new guards prevail. Shame they call naïveté, driving it away in dishonor. Temperance becomes cowardice; first they spatter mud upon it and then throw it out. In turn, economy and prudence in expenditures are derided as boorish and ungentlemanly. Finally, the other injurious and unprofitable appetites gang up and push everything else over the side.

That's the way it goes.

e Draining and purging the soul of the captured youth, they put him through a series of extravagant and gorgeous initiation rites. Insolence, anarchy, improvidence, and shamelessness are brought back from exile in colorful array with garlands crowning their heads. In their train is a massive chorus praising them: insolence they call good breeding; anarchy is liberty; improvidence is grandeur; shame-
561 lessness is courage. Does not something like this happen to the youth when he repudiates the training that limited him to the necessary desires and gives free rein instead to the desires that are useless and unnecessary?

That is what happens.

Subsequently, I suppose, such a youth divides his expenditures of time, money, and effort equally between the necessary and unnecessary pleasures. But if fortune favors him so that he does not remain b too long in turmoil, the chief disorders vanish as he grows older. If he welcomes back some of the exiles and expels some of the invaders he is able to establish and maintain a certain equilibrium among his pleasures. He yields to each appetite as it makes its presence felt so that it appears to be a matter of random choice. Then he gives himself over to it until he is satisfied. After that, he turns to some other pleasure, rejecting none and treating all as equally enjoyable.

That he will.

3. The Lotus Eaters were inhabitants of one of the islands Odysseus stopped at on his voyage home from Troy. The effects of eating the lotus are described in Homer's *Odyssey*, Book 9.94–97:

> Whoever of my men ate of the honey-sweet fruit of the lotus no longer wished to return home or to take a message back. They wished to remain there with the Lotus Eaters eating lotus and forgetting their homeward voyage.

At the same time, he lets no word of honest counsel come near the throne. He shakes his head at anyone who tells him that some   c
pleasures are the fruits of good and honorable desires but that others are joined to base affections, so that we should honor and enjoy the former but restrain and subdue the latter. He repeats that one pleasure is as good as another and that all must be accorded equal status.

In his condition that is what he would do.

So he lives his life day by day, indulging each appetite as it makes itself felt. One day he is drinking heavily and listening to the flute; on the next he is dieting and drinks only water. Then he tries some   d
exercise, only to lapse into idleness and lethargy. Sometimes he seems to want to be the philosopher. More frequently, he goes in for politics, rising to say or do whatever comes into his head. If he develops an enthusiasm for military men, he rushes to join them; if for businessmen, then he is off in that direction. His life lacks all discipline and order, yet he calls it a life of pleasure, freedom, and happiness and is resolved to stay the course.

You have reported truly on the man who insists on subjecting   e
everything to the rule of equality.

He is a kaleidoscopic man, a man of many different humors, fair and colorful as the city itself. Many men and women would count him fortunate as the one who displays the greatest diversity in personal qualities and life styles.

Yes.

So this is the democratic man, and we shall pair him with the   562
democratic regime.

Yes.

Now we have still to describe the most splendid of all regimes and men, tyranny and the tyrant.

Necessarily.

Well, my friend, what is the genesis of tyranny? Clearly it is an outcome of democracy.

True.

Does tyranny not spring up from democracy in roughly the same way that democracy emerges from oligarchy?

How so?   b

Is not oligarchy's chief occupation and purpose the acquisition of wealth?

Yes.

The oligarchs' greed for riches and the neglect of all else in their obsession to make money results in their undoing.

Yes.

And does not the passion for what democracy defines as the greatest good also finally result in its destruction?

What is democracy's greatest good?

Liberty. In a democratic city you will hear that this is the most precious of all possessions and for this reason is the only place a truly free man would want to live.

Yes. That is something one hears everywhere.

As I was about to observe, then, does not this excess, this obsession with freedom to the neglect of everything else, revolutionize the democratic constitution and stimulate a demand for tyranny?

How does that happen?

Well, I would suppose that a democratic city thirsting for freedom might choose bad wine stewards at the same time as it becomes drunk from drinking too much of that undiluted wine. Then, if the rulers are not extremely lenient and bland, dispensing liberty with a free hand to all and sundry, they will be denounced and condemned as base oligarchs.

A common occurrence.

Obedient citizens, moreover, will be reviled as no men at all but willing slaves. Praise and honor in public and private go to rulers who behave like subjects and subjects who behave like rulers. In such a city is it not inevitable that liberty should exceed all limits?

It couldn't be otherwise.

And then, my friend, the spirit of anarchy will find its way into the very homes of the citizens and at last infect even the beasts.

What do you mean by that?

I mean that the father will acquire the habit of imitating his children; he will fear his sons. The sons, in turn, imitate the father, showing their parents neither deference nor fear; this kind of behavior persuades them they are free. Citizen and alien resident also consider each other equals, and with the foreign sojourner it is the same.

True.

There are other trifles. In such a society teachers fear and flatter their students; for their part, the students feel contempt for their masters and tutors. All in all, the young mimic their elders, competing with them in word and deed. The old respond by descending to the level of youth. Exuding charm and amiability, they mimic the young in turn so that they may not be looked upon as arbitrary or unpleasant.

Also true.

The outer limits of public liberty are reached, my friend, when the slaves who have been purchased, male and female, are as free as those who bought them. And I nearly forgot to mention the spirit of liberty and equal rights that governs the relations of the sexes.

Is it not time to cite the words of Aeschylus and say whatever comes to our lips?

By all means. I shall do just that. Without seeing it, no one would
believe the degree of freedom enjoyed by the very beasts of the city
compared with anywhere else. The local bitches confirm the truth
of the proverb "like mistress, like dog." Horses and asses have become
accustomed to making their way quite freely and with the utmost
presumptuousness, bumping into everyone they meet who fails to
stand aside. And so, as with everything else here, liberty is bursting   d
out all over.

You are recounting my own memories. I have frequently had that
very experience during my trips to the country.

In sum, you will note that all these things taken together make the
souls of the citizens so hypersensitive that they cannot bear to hear
even the mention of authority. At last they end up by ignoring all
laws, written or unwritten, so that they may be spared the sense of   e
having any master whatsoever.

I know it well enough.

And here, my friend, I believe we have laid bare the hard root of
tyranny.

Hard it is. But what happens next?

Ruin. Democracy is undone by the same vice that ruins oligarchy.
But because democracy has embraced anarchy, the damage is more
general and far worse, and its subjugation more complete. The truth
is, a common rule holds for the seasons, for all the plants and animals, and particularly for political societies: excess in one direction   564
tends to provoke excess in the contrary direction.

Likely.

So an excess of liberty—in the state or in the individual—seems
destined to end up in slavery.

That's probable, too.

It is also probable that the origins of tyranny are found nowhere
else than in the democratic regime. That is to say, the mightiest and
most savage form of slavery results from pushing freedom to the
extreme.

I believe that.

But I believe that wasn't your question. You wanted to know what   b
kind of contagion it is that infects both oligarchy and democracy and
reduces the latter to slavery.

That's right.

What I have in mind is that idle class of men who live extrava-
gantly. The bolder and more energetic among them are the leaders,
and the others follow. All of these we called drones, some with stings
and some stingless.

True.

Both types of drones are a plague to any city they infest; they are

like phlegm and bile to the body. The good lawgiver must play the
role of doctor and prudent beekeeper, taking precautions against them
well in advance. His prime objective should be to prevent their entry
into the city altogether. But if they do make their appearance, they
should be exterminated as quickly as possible, bodies and cells.

By Zeus, you are absolutely right.

Let us now pursue the matter in a way that will help us see our
purpose more distinctly.

How shall we do that?

By conceiving of democracy as a city divided into three classes.
This is, in fact, the actual structure of the city. Want of order is
surely the origin of one of its classes; this is the drone class we have
just now described in oligarchy as well as in democracy.

Right.

But the behavior of this class is far more ruthless in a democracy.

How so?

Because in an oligarchy it is held in disrepute and denied access
to public office. Hence it has no experience in the exercise of authority and is therefore lacking in political vigor. But in a democracy,
with very few exceptions, this is the dominant class. Its most reckless
elements are the chief spokesmen and actors; the rest crowd about
the rostrum, their swarming and buzzing silencing all dissent. In a
democratic regime, then, this is the class that decides virtually everything.

Exactly.

Then there is a second class which is set off from the multitude.

Which is that?

The class of money-makers in which the most disciplined usually
become the richest.

That makes sense.

Here, I suppose, is where one finds the most honey and where the
drones find it easiest to squeeze out for themselves.

Well, yes. One can't look to squeeze much from those who have
little.

Then I suppose it would be fitting to call the rich the drones'
playground.

That's about it.

Now consider the third class, the multitude. These are the people
who patiently cultivate what little property they have and tend to
their own business. When they are assembled together, they form
the largest and most powerful group in a democracy.

True, but they will not often act together unless they think they
can get a share of the honey.

Oh, they share. What happens is that the leaders plunder the rich, keep the lion's share for themselves, and hand out to the people what is left.

Yes, I suppose that in this sense the people share.   b

Next, I would assume that those who have been expropriated would want to defend themselves by speaking in assembly and by doing whatever else is in their power.

Naturally.

The result will be, even though they have no revolutionary intentions, that their opponents will charge them with being oligarchs and plotting against the people.

Of course.

At last, when they observe the people attempting to wrong them—not voluntarily but because of ignorance and because they are misled by slander—they become oligarchs indeed. Willing or not, they too succumb to the evil effects spread by the sting of the drones.   c

That is certain.

The consequences are accusations, arraignments, and litigations of all kinds originating from both sides.

Very true.

And the people—is there not always the propensity to elevate and glorify one man as the people's protector and champion?

Yes.

Then we have located the tyrant's point of entry into the society.   d
The root and foundation of his power in his initial role as protector.

That is clear.

Then what transformation takes place that changes protector into tyrant? It evidently begins with his reenactment of the legend that comes from the shrine of Zeus Lykaeus in Arcadia.

What does the legend say?

That if any man should swallow even the smallest morsel from the entrails of a human being while eating the flesh of other kinds of sacrificial victims, he will be transformed into a wolf. Haven't you heard the tale?   e

Yes, I have.

It describes the people's protector. His docile followers grant him so much free rein that he shrinks from nothing, even shedding the blood of his own kin. He resorts to the customary unjust accusations in order to haul the victim into court and then to take his life. So he murders, and with impious tongue and lips consumes his own flesh   566
and blood. He kills and banishes, but he also hints at the cancellation of debts and redistribution of property. Is it not inevitable—a veritable decree of fate—that such a man should either be slain by his enemies or become a tyrant, and so trade his humanity for the life of a wolf?

Unavoidable.

He is the one who then organizes the faction antagonistic to the rich.

He's the one.

At this stage he may well be driven into exile. But if he is able to return in defiance of his enemies, he will by then have surely become a consummate tyrant.

He surely will.

Now if his antagonists are not able to exile him a second time, nor openly to incite the citizens to do away with him, they themselves
b conspire to assassinate him.

That's the usual scenario.

But then he counters with the classic gambit tyrants use at this stage of the game. He requests a bodyguard so that the friend and protector of the people may be safe.

That's it.

And the people, fearing for the safety of their champion and having no misgivings for themselves, will grant the request.
c Indeed they will.

At this point, any man who is rich—and along with his wealth has the reputation of being a foe of democracy—had better heed what the oracle said to Croesus:

> Flee—flee along the pebbled beach of Hermus;
> stay not, nor be ashamed to be a coward.

He wouldn't have a chance to be ashamed a second time.

So if he's caught, it's the death sentence.

Without question.

Now it is clear that the great man doesn't intend to display his greatness by lying down. Instead, having caused the downfall of many others, he will now stand erect in the chariot of state, transformed
d from a protector into a towering despot.

Why would he choose to do anything else?

Then shall we go on to describe the measure of happiness enjoyed by the city and its citizens when such a creature comes to the fore?

By all means.

In his first days of office he smiles and greets whomever he meets.
e He protests he is no tyrant; instead, he is generous with promises in public and private. He liberates men from debt and distributes lands to the people—and to his friends. During this time his dealings with the citizenry at large are all gentleness and grace.

Necessarily.

In the meantime, I should imagine, he will have become reconciled with some of his exiled enemies and will have destroyed the others, so that he need no longer be concerned about them. His next step, however, so that the people will always be in need of a leader, is to undertake an ongoing search for pretexts to make war.

I dare say.

Moreover, the imposition of war taxes is likely to impoverish the citizenry sufficiently so that they must tend more diligently to earn-   567
ing their livelihood with correspondingly less time to plot against the leader.

A telling observation.

Then, too, I suppose he would suspect the continuing presence of free men in the city who resist his domination. What better way to get rid of them than to send them off to the wars to take their chances with the enemy? All these provide the tyrant with compelling ratio-nales for constantly provoking wars.

They are compelling.

But won't this behavior more readily provoke the people's anger?   b

Of course.

And is there not a likelihood that some of those who helped him establish his power and now share in it will come to disapprove his policies? Of these, will not the bravest speak out frankly among themselves and then even to him?

It is likely.

If the tyrant wills to continue his policies, all these dissidents must be purged, and the purge will be pressed until not a man of worth, friend or foe, remains.

That is certain.

He must watch out to see who is brave, who is magnanimous,   c
who is wise, who is rich. For fate decrees that these will be his ene-mies; so willing it or not, this happy man must conspire against them until there is none left in the city.

A capital purge indeed.

Yes, and with just the contrary results from those that doctors intend when they purge our bodies. They seek to remove the worst and leave the best. The tyrant does the opposite.

If he wants to hold on to his power, this is what he must do.

So necessity leaves him with the pleasing choice between being fated to live only among the vulgar and base, even though they hate   d
him, or ceasing to live altogether.

He has no other way to go.

And the more his behavior offends the citizens, the greater his need for more and more reliable bodyguards?

No question.

But where will he find them? Whom can he trust?

They will come unbidden. They will swarm about him if he offers them a wage.

More drones, by the dog. All sorts and kinds, and aliens at that.   e

Yes. These are the ones I had in mind.

But how about the locals? Would he not raid the domestic market.

What do you mean?

I mean he would free the slaves, take them away from the citizens, and enlist them in his private guard.

He would do that. They are the ones he could trust most.

568   What a blessed fellow is this tyrant whom you so well describe. After having done away with his associates, he is reduced to calling such as these his friends and confidants.

These are indeed the ones he uses as his own.

And such companions, in turn, assure him of their admiration, while the new citizens become his courtiers. All good people, however, hate and avoid him.

What else can they do?

All of which illustrates the vaunted wisdom to be found among the tragic poets, and particularly in Euripides.

How so?

He it was who said, among other profundities, that "tyrants are b   made wise by the company they keep." He evidently meant that the tyrant's associates we have just been describing possess wisdom.

It's true. He and other poets call the tyrant's power "most like god's" and extol tyranny in many other ways.

Being so wise, then, the writers of tragedy will pardon us and all those whose politics resemble ours if we refuse them admittance to our city because they persist in hymning praises to tyranny.

c   I expect that those among them whose minds are subtle will grant us pardon.

Going to other cities, I suppose, they will hire loud and persuasive voices to collect the crowds and move them closer to democracies or tyrannies.

Exactly.

They will be paid and honored for these services, of course. As might be expected, their wards will come chiefly from tyrants, but in the second instance also from the democracies. But the higher these tragedians climb toward the summit of government, the more d   their honor droops, as if shortness of breath prevented it from accompanying them further.

Just so.

But I digress. Let us return to the tyrant and his splendid, iridescent, numerous, and ever-changing bodyguard. Who will pay for its support?

First of all, obviously, the tyrant will sell the city's sacred treasures, if it has any. He will use the proceeds as long as they hold out, together with what he realizes from the confiscated properties of those he has ruined. In this way he will defer having to levy any large contributions upon the people.

But what happens when all these revenues are exhausted?

Ah, then it will be his father's estate that must foot the bills that e he runs up, he and his fellow boozers and their lady friends.

I know. You mean that those people who put the tyrant and his friends in power in the first place must now pay their dues.

Inescapably.

But then what is to be said? What if the people are vexed, protesting that it is not right that a father should support his grown son, that the father should rather be cared for by the son? Supposing they say that they didn't beget and nurture him only to have him grow up 569 and make them be slaves to their own slaves and other riffraff. Instead, they anticipated that with him as their protector they would be liberated from the rule of the rich and the so-called gentlemen of the city. Hence they now bid him and his gang to depart in the same way a father drives his son from the house, together with his rude companions.

Then the people will discover, by Zeus, what kind of monster they b have reared to greatness in their midst. They will learn what it means when the father has become too weak to discipline his son.

What do you mean? Will the son dare to become violent with his father, to strike him if he does not yield?

Yes, as soon as he has taken away his arms.

Your words make the tyrant a very parricide, the cruel nurse of a man's old age. Here is tyranny indeed, openly avowed. People who have fled the smoke of being enslaved by slavery to freemen, as the saying goes, are now consumed by the fire of conquest by their own slaves. In exchange for excessive and unmanageable liberty they now c wear the garments of their own slaves, as it were, in doubly cruel and bitter servitude.

That is precisely what happens.

Well, then, would we be right in saying that we have now adequately described the transformation of democracy into tyranny as well as the nature of tyranny itself?

The description is adequate.

Book IX

We must still consider the tyrannical man himself. How does he evolve from the democratic man? What kind of life does he lead? Is he happy or miserable?

You are right. These are questions we still haven't answered.

I think we have neglected one thing in particular.

What?

We have not yet given a full accounting of human desires, nor have we sufficiently described their nature. We must consider these

b   matters; otherwise our inquiry will remain incomplete.

Don't we still have time to look into them?

By all means. One of their aspects I should particularly like to examine. I think all of us harbor within ourselves unnecessary pleasures and appetites. Some are also lawless. But in some men, when the laws are supported by reason and by the better desires, lawless propensities can be eradicated or at least marvelously reduced in number and intensity. To be sure, in others these kinds of desires remain strong and numerous.

c   What desires do you mean?

Those that stir when the soul is otherwise asleep, when the dominating characteristics of gentleness and rationality slumber. Then the wild and brutish part, sated with food and drink, becomes restless and goes on the prowl in search of anything that will satisfy its instincts. You know that in such a state it will shrink from nothing because it has been released from reason and a sense of shame. It will not hold

d   back from contemplating intercourse with a mother or lying together with anyone else, whether man, god, or beast. Foul murder is no crime, and no flesh is forbidden. In sum, shamelessness and folly have their way.

That is the truth.

On the other hand, I can imagine a healthy man who lives in harmony with himself. He goes to sleep only after he has summoned up the rational element in his soul, nourishing it with fair thoughts and precepts. So he achieves clarity in consciousness of self. So, too,

e   he neither sates nor starves his appetites in order that they may rest and that their related pains or pleasures may not subvert the soul's excellence. Then the soul is left free to reach out and seek to comprehend things as yet unknown to it, things that have been, are now, or are yet to be. And if a man does not permit a quarrel to keep anger awake after he has fallen asleep, he will have tamed the spirited part of his soul as well. Hence he will have calmed two of the elements in his soul and quickened the third where reason governs. You must agree one who goes to his rest in so temperate a manner is most likely to behold truth and is least likely to be visited by dreams of lawlessness.

Exactly.

Well, we have been too much diverted by this issue. But the point we need to keep in mind is this: every one of us—even those accorded the highest degree of respectability—harbors a fierce brood of savage and imperious appetites that reveal themselves most readily in dreams. Reflect on what I have said and see if you agree.

I do agree.

Then recall the personality of the democratic man. He was raised from childhood onward by a stingy oligarchic father who sanctioned only the acquisitive appetites. Unnecessary hankerings after entertainment and ostentation he censured. Is that not so?

Yes.

Driven by hatred for his father's stinginess, the son at first associates with men sophisticated in ways to gratify the horde of appetites we just described. Seduced by their way of life, he is attracted to every form of insolence and excess. But because his nature is better than that of his seducers, he is pulled in two directions and settles for the middle point between them. He enjoys, as he supposes, each in moderation. He considers his life neither illiberal nor lawless. He has been transformed from an oligarch into a democrat.

Our view of this kind of man was and remains the same.

When he is older, let us suppose that such a man has a son whom he raises in accordance with his own way of life.

I follow your argument.

Then suppose that the son repeats his father's experience. Seducers lure him into total lawlessness, which they call total freedom. His father and other kin attempt to reinforce his inclination toward a middle course. But the dread sorcerers and conjurors of tyranny pull in a different direction. If they discover that the young man cannot be persuaded to their side in any other way, they will undertake to inject him with an overmastering urge to protect and reinforce all his idle and profligate desires. So he will come to be enslaved by a great winged drone. Or do you think that desire in such men can end up any other way?

I see no alternative.

Then other desires close in, laden with incense and perfume and wine and garlands to fan the flame of his pleasures and revels. All these buzz around the drone, nurturing its growth and greatness. Finally, they inject this new master of a man's soul with the itch of desire. Stung to frenzy, it chooses madness for its bodyguard and goes berserk. If there are any worthy opinions or desires left in the man—if he is still capable of shame—he will be bled and purged of all these. He will be emptied of temperance, and madness will be imported into his soul.

Your account rings true. We behold the rise of the tyrannical man.

Does not all this help explain why love has so often been called a tyrant?

I should think so.

And can we not say that the drunken man also manifests the tyrannical spirit?

We can.

Still further, the madman, the one who is out of his mind, will he not suppose that he is able to rule over both men and gods and then try to do it?

He will.

Here then, my friend, we have the consummate tyrant, one who by nature or habit—or both—has turned into a creature of drunkenness, lust, and madness.

No doubt of it.

So we have apparently identified the tyrant's origins and personality. Now how about his style of life?

As the wits like to say, you've already got the answer as well as the question.

All right. First off, I suppose, are feasts, reveling, prostitutes, and orgies and like entertainments habitual for those souls wholly in bondage to the despotism of Eros.

All that is certain.

And does not the despot spawn and multiply urgent and terrible desires both day and night?

He does.

With the result that revenues will quickly be exhausted?

Of course.

Next come borrowings and levies on his estate.

How could it be otherwise?

When these resources are also spent, won't the fierce desires he fostered in his soul like young ravens in the nest still cry out for gratification? Won't he be goaded by these and other desires—and especially by passion itself, the commander of his bodyguard—until finally he is in a frenzy and looks about for anyone who owns anything that can be taken from him by fraud or force?

Unquestionably. He must either exact tribute from every possible   574
source or suffer pain and anguish.

An unavoidable choice.

And will not new desires and pleasures spring up within him,
crowding out and displacing their predecessors? Will they not set
him an example? He, the youth, will he not think himself entitled
to bully his own mother and father and, after spending his share, to
seize and spend his father's estate?

That he will.

Should the parents resist him, he will at first try to get his way by   b
deception and theft, will he not?

Yes.

Failing that, he would seize the money by force?

I think he would.

And if the old people tried to hold on to their own and continued
to resist him, what scruples would prevent him from acting the tyrant?

I would fear for the parents of such a man.

But in the name of Zeus, Adeimantus, do you really think that
desire for the casual favors of some newly arrived harlot would suffice
to make him strike his own beloved mother to whom he is bound by   c
the most necessary ties of birth? Or would he strike his old father, so
necessary to his own existence and his oldest friend, for the sake of
some newly blooming and totally dispensable boy friend? Would he
really bring such persons into his parents' house and accord them
precedence over father and mother?

By Zeus, he would.

To bear a son who becomes a tyrant cannot be a blessing.

Never.

What next? After the assets of father and mother are dissipated,
the swarm of appetites in the son's soul continues to grow. Will he   d
not put his hand to housebreaking or snatch the cloak of one who
walks late at night? Will he not ransack a temple? And all the things
he learned in boyhood about what is honorable and what is base,
about what opinions can be accounted just—all these will be over-
ridden by newly emancipated opinions which guard and foster the
prerogatives of lust. These are the same opinions we spoke of earlier
that sleep frees from restraint. Then, however, he still lived subject   e
to laws and still had a father and governed himself according to the
code of democracy. But now as lust's slave, he has become con-
sciously and constantly that which once appeared only occasionally
during sleep. He sticks at nothing: not murder or other atrocity, nor
unhallowed food nor any deed whatever. The passion that rules within   575
drives him to the extremes of anarchy and lawlessness. Controlling
the man like a tyrant controls a city, it will urge him on to every

kind of audacity in order to produce sustenance for himself and his clamorous companions. It is a crowd made up in part of evil associates and in part from the evil habits to which he has given free rein within himself. Will this not be the way he lives?

b   In a city where only a few live this way while the multitude remains generally temperate in its habits, these few will likely emigrate to serve as bodyguards to some tyrant elsewhere. Or they will sign on as mercenaries wherever they find a war. But if they happen to live in a time when peace prevails, they will remain in the city and practice the lesser evils.

What kinds of evils?

Oh, stealing, housebreaking, purse snatching. They will strip people of their garments and strip temples as well. They will kidnap and sell men into slavery. If they are smooth talkers, they play the sycophant. They will bear false witness and take bribes.

c   Lesser evils they may be if there are only a few who inflict them.

That is because small things are small only when compared to the great. All together such petty crimes produce a degree of corruption and evil in the city that, as the saying goes, comes nowhere near hailing distance of the ruin the tyrant brings. But when these kinds of men and their followers become many, when they become conscious of their numbers and fasten on the folly of the multitude, that is the moment of the tyrant's entrance. He will be the one among

d   them who harbors within himself the greatest and most ruthless tyrant of all.

Of course. His tyranny will be absolute.

If the city willingly submits to him. But if the city resists he will punish his fatherland just as he tormented his own father and mother. He will import a new set of companions to help him enslave what

e   he once reverenced as his fatherland or, as the Cretans say, his motherland. These will surely be his intentions.

Exactly.

Is not the public character of such men shaped in private life before they ever come to power in the state? Will they not associate with flatterers ready to stoop to any service? Conversely, should they want

576   favors from others, will they not themselves play the flunky, cringing and fawning while pledging their love? Having once gained their object, however, they behave quite differently.

That is right.

So they live their whole lives without friends. They are always one man's master or another man's slave. Tyrants never learn friendship or freedom.

You are right.

Would we also be right to say that these are men without honor?

We would.

And if our agreement holds true about the nature of justice, could we not say that they are entirely unjust?   b

The agreement surely holds.

Then let us draw some conclusions about the nature of the man who is supremely evil. His waking behavior, I presume, will resemble the traits we observed in his dreams.

I agree.

He is the joint product of his tyrannical nature and his despotic rule, and the longer he rules, the more oppressive his tyranny.

At this point Glaucon took up the argument: Inevitably, he said.

Can we then conclude that the worst man is also the most wretched? Is it certain that the worst tyrant and the one longest in power will also be the most miserable of men? Opinions differ in these matters.   c

That much is certainly true.

Is it not evident that the tyrannical man and the tyrannical state are counterparts? Is there not also a likeness between the democratic man and the democratic state, and so on for the rest of our typology?

Yes.

Then won't the essence of virtue and happiness be the same for men and cities alike?   d

Without question.

With virtue as the measure, how would you compare the tyrant's city with that royal city we first described?

They are direct opposites. One was the best, the other the worst.

I won't ask you to say which is which. That is evident enough. But is your judgment the same when it comes to happiness and misery? And here we ought not to let the presence of the tyrant and the few men around him overawe us. Instead, we ought to familiarize ourselves with the entire city. We must probe into every corner and at all levels. Only after doing all this should we render an opinion.   e

A fair procedure. It should then be plain to everyone that there is no city more wretched than one ruled by a tyrant and none happier than one governed by a true king.

Would it also be fair in applying these criteria to individuals to assert that the only proper judge of men is one who is able to penetrate into the inmost soul and temper of other men? He will not be like a child, dazzled by the pomp of the court which tyrants contrive to deceive outsiders. He will see through it all. Suppose I should make the further assertion that the man we should heed is he who can make these kinds of judgments and has himself lived under the tyrant's roof: the man who has beheld the tyrant's conduct in his own home and has seen with his own eyes how the tyrant treats his intimates when he has stripped off his actor's mask—the man who   577

      b

has also observed his behavior in times of public danger. Is this the man we should ask to report on the happiness or misery of the tyrant in comparison with other men?

All this would also be fair procedure.

Then would you be willing to pretend that we are among those who are able to make such judgments, who have already lived with tyrants and are therefore qualified to answer the questions we will put?

Yes.

c   Let's do it this way. Recall the resemblance between the city and the man; then observe what happens to each.

What happens?

First off, will you say that a city ruled by a tyrant is free or slave?

Altogether slave.

Yet you see free men as well as masters in this very city.

I see that a few are masters. But the many, who are also the most decent, are deprived of honor and shamefully enslaved.

d   Then, if man is like the city, won't these same relationships prevail in him? In the main, won't he be servile and ungenerous? Won't the better parts of his nature be enthralled, while a small part, frenzied and evil, plays the master?

Inevitably.

Will you say that such a soul is slave or free?

Slave.

Will you not also say that the city enslaved by the tyrant is least able to attain what it really wants?

Yes.

So, too, a man's soul, wholly enslaved by its inner tyrant, will be
e   least able to do what it wants. Instead it will be maddened by disorder and frenzy and full of remorse.

Unquestionably.

Will the tyrannical city be rich or poor?

578   Poor.

So then will the tyrannical man be ever in want.

So he will be.

Will not the city and the man resound with terror and alarms?

They will.

Do you think you could find any other city where there is greater pain and suffering, or more complaints and lamentations?

Nowhere.

Will you find any other kind of man more burdened with such ills than the tyrannical man, crazed by his own passions and appetites?

Never.

As far as the tyrant's city is concerned, I take it that all these considerations persuade you that it is the most miserable of all cities.   b

Am I not rightly persuaded?

Indeed you are. And when you behold the same evils in the tyrannical man, what do you say of him?

He is by far the unhappiest of men.

Here we must disagree.

Why?

I do not think he is the most wretched of all.

Then who is?

I have in mind a man whose afflictions you might think are greater
still.

What man is he?   c

A man tyrannical by nature who does not live a private life; he has
the misfortune of becoming a tyrant over the city.

From what has already been said, I suppose you may be right.

Yes, but at this high point of the argument supposing such things
is not enough; they require more serious examination. After all, we
are here addressing the greatest of all questions: the difference between
the good life and the bad.

That is true.

Then see if there is anything in what I have to say. An illustration   d
might help to put the matter in perspective.

What is your illustration?

Consider the private men living in the cities who are very rich and
have many slaves. They resemble the tyrant in that they rule over
many, although the number governed by the tyrant is much greater.

The resemblance is there.

You know that they feel secure, that they are not frightened of
their servants.

What should they fear?

Nothing. But do you know why?

Yes. The private citizen can rely on the entire city to protect him.   e

Very true. But supposing some god should lay hold of a man with
fifty slaves and carry him off together with his wife and children.
Supposing he and all his property and servants were set down in
some lonely place where there were no free men to come to his aid.
What do you think he would fear—how much would he fear—that
he and his wife and children would be murdered by the slaves of his
household?

I think he would be desperate with fear.   579

Would he not at once feel constrained to truckle to some of his
slaves, going against his own will and making them promises and
even freeing them? Would he not be compelled to be the flatterer of
his own servants?

Either that or perish.

But now suppose that the god surrounded him with many neighbors who would not allow any man's claim to be master of another. Could they lay hands on him, he would suffer harsh punishment.

b Then I think his situation would become still more precarious. He would be alone among enemies.

Is this not the kind of prison to which the tyrant is condemned, the man we described with so many fears and so many appetites? He is pleasure-loving and greedy, but alone among the men of the city there is no place he dares go. What all men want to see he may not see. For the most part he lives like a woman, cowering in his house

c and envying those who can enjoy the pleasures of travel abroad.

That is certain.

Such a crop of evils reveals how much more wretched is the existence of the tyrannical man—the very man whom you judged the most miserable. Not only is he ill governed within himself, but once misfortune removes him from private life and establishes him in the tyrant's place, he must try to control others when he cannot control himself. He is like a sick man who is unable to exercise self-restraint and yet is not permitted to pass his days in cloistered privacy; instead,

d he is obliged to engage adversaries in never-ending rivalry and discord.

A telling and exact comparison, Socrates.

Is this not utter misery? Is not the life of the tyrant governing the city more miserable even than that life which you earlier judged to be so wretched?

No doubt about it.

Then he who is completely the tyrant is completely the slave. That is the truth, though some may deny it. More than all the others

e he must cringe and truckle. He must flatter the worst of men. Unable to obtain even a modicum of satisfaction for his desires, he must suffer more deprivation than any other. So he is a poor man, as anyone who knows how to judge souls can tell. He is fear's victim his whole life long, beset by convulsions and tumults. In sum, he resembles the city he rules, and the resemblance holds, does it not?

Yes.

580 Add the fact that power makes him grow steadily worse. It magnifies everything we have said about his person and his public role and thrusts him still further into the realm of envy, faithlessness, and unjust behavior. He becomes ever more friendless and sacrilegious. He is the very source and contagion of wickedness: this supremely wretched man goes about making everyone else as wretched as he is.

No sensible man will dispute you.

b Assume the role of final judge, then, and hand down your opinion, declaring which man is first in happiness and which second, and in what order the others follow. Recall that we have considered five types of men: king, timocrat, oligarch, democrat, and tyrant.

A simple task. I shall rank them in respect to virtue and vice and happiness and misery as if they were choruses, that is, in the order of their entry.

Shall we fetch a herald, or shall I sound the word myself? By proclamation of Ariston's son the best and most righteous man is also the happiest. He is the governor most royal and most royally governs himself. The most evil and most unjust man is also the unhappiest. He is the man who is most given over to tyranny in his own person and so becomes the cruelest of all tyrants to himself and to the city he rules.

Let your words constitute the proclamation.

Shall I add the clause that all these things hold true whether they take place in sight of gods or men or not?

Let the clause be added.

Good. Then we have in hand the first proof for our contentions. Here is another. Tell me what you think of it.

What is it?

I think the second proof can be found in the correspondence between the basic structure of the tripartite city and the tripartite soul.

What do you mean?

In each case the three parts are characterized by three distinctive pleasures and three distinctive desires or appetites. And they are governed by three distinctive codes.

Please explain.

We have already said that one part is that with which a person learns. Another part responds to his passions. We had no particular name for the third because it is composed of so many different elements. Instead we called it the desiring part in recognition of its leading and most powerful element and the intensity of its appetites for food, drink, sex, and the like. We also called it the money-loving part since desires of this sort generally cannot be gratified without money.

That is right.

Were we to say that money is its love and pleasure, we could properly bring these things together under one heading and so clarify our discussion. Then we could understand each other better when speaking of this part of the soul and justify calling it the money-loving or acquisitive part.

As for the element of temperament and high spirit, have we not said that it always seeks conquest, domination, and fame?

Indeed we have.

Then it would be fair to call it the ambitious and honor-loving part?

Fair enough.

The learning part, on the other hand, is wholly directed toward knowledge of the truth. Of the three parts it is least concerned with riches and repute.

That is right.

So we call it the part that loves learning and wisdom.

Yes.

c　And is it not so that in some men this is the part that governs their souls while one or the other of the remaining two parts governs the other kinds of men?

Yes.

So this is why we grouped men into three basic classes: men of wisdom, men of ambition, and men of money.

Yes.

And each of the three classes values a distinct kind of pleasure?

True.

Do you realize that should you ask men from each of the three classes which offers the most pleasurable life, all will give preference
d　to their own class? The man of money will assert that the pleasures of honor or wisdom are vain unless they result in some material gain.

True.

And what about the lover of honor? Does he not disdain the pleasures that money buys as vulgar and beneath his station? As for the pleasure that knowledge brings, he dismisses it as all hot air and nonsense if no sort of honor or distinction is attached to it.

No question.

And what will the philosopher say to these other pleasures when
e　he compares them with the unfailing joys of learning from reality and knowing truth? Would he not say they lag far behind the pleasures he prizes? Would he not simply put them down as necessary pleasures because, in the absence of necessity, he would do without them?

That is certain.

So there is dispute about the several pleasures and about the respective ways of life where they predominate. Let us assume that the dispute concerns not what is better or worse, noble or base. Let the argument be about which yields greater pleasure or pain. How
582　shall we decide which claims are true?

I don't know.

Think about it this way. If things are to be rightly judged, what criteria should we rightly use to judge them? Experience, reason, and inquiry—could we apply any criteria better than these?

None.

Consider, then: which of the three types of men has had the most extensive experience of all the pleasures we have described? Does the

money lover have more experience of the pleasure that comes with
knowing the truth than the philosopher has with material things?   b

There is a vast difference between the two. The philosopher must
necessarily have experienced the material pleasures since infancy.
But the money lover is under no necessity to sample the delights of
learning how things truly are. Moreover, even if he ardently desires
this kind of knowledge, he cannot easily attain it.

Then it must follow that the philosopher is far ahead of the money-
maker in experiencing both kinds of pleasure.

Out of sight.   c

How does the philosopher compare with the lover of honor? Does
he know less of the pleasures of being honored than the ambitious
man knows about the pleasures wisdom brings?

Honor comes to all kinds of men, providing they achieve the goals
they set for themselves. Many honor the rich man; many honor the
brave and the wise as well. Hence all three types know the pleasures
that honor offers. But only the philosopher knows the delight that
comes from seeing things as they really are.

In terms of experience, then, the philosopher must be the best   d
judge of the three.

Clearly.

And he alone is able to add wisdom to experience.

That is right.

Still further, the money lover and the ambitious man lack the
quality essential to judgment; only the philosopher has that.

What quality?

Didn't we say that judgments must be reached by means of reasoned discussion?

Yes.

And this proficiency belongs chiefly to the philosopher?

Of course.

Now if things were best judged by the criteria of wealth and profit,
the money lover's approval or disapproval would offer the most accu-   e
rate verdict.

True.

The same holds true for matters of honor, courage, and victory:
the most trustworthy judge would be the man of ambition.

Clearly.

But if experience, reason, and inquiry are the criteria—

The philosopher's judgment would necessarily be the truest judgment.

Of the three kinds of pleasure, then, the sweetest is that which   583
comes from the learning part of the soul. It follows that the man
whose soul is governed from that part leads the most pleasurable life.

That is certainly true. At all events, when the philosopher judges his own life, he speaks with authority.

And what life and what pleasure does the judge rank in second place?

Those of the man of ambition, the warrior, the lover of honor. He is nearer the first man than the money-maker.

Then the money lover comes off last.

Of course.

b   So the just man has produced two proofs in a row; he is twice victorious over the unjust man. And now, in the Olympian manner, he enters the lists for the third time, in the name of Olympian Zeus the Savior.[1] Observe that in contrast to the man of intellect, pleasure for the others is neither entirely true nor wholly pure. Instead, it is a kind of painted façade, as I think some wise man once told me. Nevertheless, this third contest will be the most difficult and will decide the match.

Surely it will. But what do you mean?

c   I shall find out if I ask and you answer my questions.

Ask them.

Tell me, have we not said that pain and pleasure are opposites?

We have.

And that there is a midpoint unaffected by pain or pleasure?

Indeed there is.

And it is here between the two that the soul finds a certain repose? Or do you see it differently?

No.

Can you recall the kind of things men say when they are sick?

What things?

d   That nothing, after all, is more precious than health. But until they became ill they had no idea that health is the greatest of all pleasures.

Now I remember.

Have you not heard those who suffer saying that nothing gives more pleasure than relief from suffering?

Yes. I have heard them.

So we should be able to cite many cases in which people suffering pain pay no attention to the idea of enjoyment but instead prize relief from pain as the greatest pleasure.

e   Yes. In such cases a respite from suffering is a welcome pleasure.

Conversely, when pleasure ends, pain will take its place?

Perhaps.

1. This seems a combined allusion to two separate practices. First, there were three falls in a wrestling match at the Olympic games. Second, the third of the ritual libations before a banquet was to "Zeus the Savior."

Then, as we just said, the midpoint of repose between the two offers both pain and pleasure?

Apparently.

But is it really possible for something that is neither pain nor pleasure to be both?

I don't think so.

Consider further: the soul must perceive both pleasure and pain as a kind of motion. Is that not true?

Yes.

Still further, we just now agreed that the soul is in an intermediate 584 state of repose when it experiences neither pain nor pleasure?

We did agree.

Then can it be right to assert that the absence of pain is pleasure and the absence of pleasure pain?

Surely not.

You are right; the assertion is illusory. It is true that when repose b displaces pain, it seems like pleasure. The same is true in reverse: when repose displaces pleasure, it seems like pain. But these illusions are all a kind of sorcery; they tell us nothing about the reality of pleasure.

Our discussion so far would confirm your argument.

Then in order to avoid the mistaken notion that pleasure is not merely the absence of pain and pain the absence of pleasure, one must identify pleasures that do not proceed from pain.

Where should I look? What pleasures do you mean?

There are many such pleasures. Consider the pleasures that derive from the sense of smell. They are pleasures unrelated to any previous pain and yet can quickly attain a marvelous intensity. Moreover, when they depart, they leave no pain behind.

Very true.

So we shall reject the proposition that the absence of pain is pure c pleasure and the absence of pleasure pure pain.

Agreed.

Nonetheless, this proposition applies to most of the pleasures transmitted from the body to the soul—including those that are most tense. That is, they function as a kind of relief from pain.

Yes. They do.

And this same function is apparent when one is anticipating pleasure or pain?

Yes.

But do you know their nature and what they resemble most? d

What?

Do you agree that there are in nature such things as up, down, and center?

I do.

Do you suppose that anyone who is moved to the center from below could imagine other than that he had moved up? At the middle point, then, if he should look back down whence he came, would he not think that he is now on top since he doesn't know what is really above?

By Zeus! I don't see how he could think anything else.

e   But should he descend again to where he was before, he would suppose—and correctly—that he had moved downward?

Certainly.

And all that he experiences results, in turn, from his inexperience of what is really up, down, and center?

Clearly.

Then is it any wonder that those without experience of truth have false notions about pleasure and pain and what lies between, and about many other things as well? When they are brought down by

585   pain, their impressions are realistic enough; they know they are in pain. But when they move upward again to the middle point, they are persuaded that they have reached the ultimate in pleasure. It is as though, in the absence of white, they were comparing black with gray. Similarly inexperienced in true pleasure, they are persuaded that pleasure is the absence of pain.

By Zeus! I wouldn't be surprised if that were so. I would certainly be surprised if it weren't so.

Consider further: are not hunger and thirst and their like perceived by the body as deficiencies, as a kind of emptiness?

Very much so.

b   And are not ignorance and folly, in turn, an emptiness of the soul?

Yes, they are.

So both the man who obtains food and the one who attains wisdom will have filled the emptiness?

Surely.

And which fills more truly and fully, the greater reality or the lesser?

Surely the greater.

Then what fulfillment will offer the greater reality? Will it be food and drink, with all their embellishments, and nourishment in general? Or will it be true opinion, knowledge, and reason, and all the

c   things whose sum is excellence and virtue? Think of it this way. Will it be the thing that most really is, the thing that holds fast to what is always the same, to truth and immortality, and therefore becomes like that to which it is attached? Or will it be what is joined to things that are mortal and never the same and so also becomes like that to which it is attached?

Closeness to what does not change brings one far closer to reality.

And does not the essence of the unchangeable attain the same degree of knowledge and reality?

It does.

And the same with truth?

The same.

So that if it shared less in truth, it would share less in reality?

Necessarily.

Generally speaking, then, could we say that the things that tend   d
the body's needs are further from truth and reality than those that tend the needs of the soul?

Much further.

Will we find the same disparity if we now make a direct comparison between body and soul?

Yes.

And when something is nearer to reality and is itself more real, will it not experience greater fulfillment than something less real and filled with unrealities?

Of course.

Now if pleasure is enjoying an abundance of those things agreeable to our nature, the enjoyment of real things yields the greatest and most lasting pleasure. Conversely, attachment to unreal things removes   e
us further from reality. There pleasure is diminished and uncertain.

Unquestionably.

So it is with those who have no experience with wisdom and virtue   586
but constantly busy themselves instead with feasting and like activities. First, they seem to have been swept down to the bottom and then up again as far as the middle; then they roam and drift between the two points all their lives. Confined to these limits, they never look up to what is truly above them; nor have they been borne upward. Never have they been refreshed with reality's essence; never have they tasted pleasure that is pure and cannot deceive. Always they look down with their heads bent to the table. Like cattle, they graze,   b
fatten, and copulate. Greed drives them to kick and butt one another with horns and hoofs of iron. Because they are insatiable, they slay one another. And they are insatiable because they neglect to seek real refreshment for that part of the soul that is real and pure.

Socrates, said Glaucon, you describe the life of the multitude exactly in the style of an oracle.

So they must live with the façades and illusions of true pleasure: their pleasures must be mixed with pain. It is this juxtaposition of sensations that gives to each its color and intensity, driving fools into   c
frenzies of self-love. And all these deceptions are fought over in the same way that Stesichorus recounts the fighting at Troy for the ghost

of Helen by men who didn't know the truth.[2]

It will necessarily be something like that.

Won't the same hold true for the spirited part of the soul and for the man who caters to its needs? Won't the cause be the envy that love of honor provokes? Or the violence fired by love of victory? Or anger born of ill humor? All these—honor, victory, and anger—he will seek to attain or appease, and all without consulting reason or discretion.

Then the same things must befall him also.

At the same time, let us boldly give expression to a sense of confidence concerning the desires that belong to the money-loving and ambitious parts of our nature. Those desires that submit to the rule of reason and are indulged only with the pleasures that reason approves will discover true pleasure—at least to the limit of their capacities—because they are enlisted in the service of truth. So they will receive what is properly their own, if what is best for each thing may properly be said to be its own.

Indeed, it will be most truly its own.

So when the entire soul submits to the government of the wisdom-loving part, it will be liberated from internal dissension. The result will be that each of the parts will mind its own business and not interfere with the others. Each will enjoy the pleasures proper to it; these will be the best pleasures and the truest.

Very true.

But when one of the other parts seizes control, it will be unable to discover the pleasure it desires. And it will drive the other parts to seek out pleasures alien to their needs. Hence they will pursue false pleasures.

You are right.

And this effect will most likely be produced by desires most removed from philosophy and reasoned discourse?

Yes.

And what is most distant from reason is most distant from law and order?

Clearly.

Did we not find at this most distant point of desire the man of lust and the tyrant?

We did.

Whereas the man of discipline and the king are closest?

They are.

---

2. Stesichorus, a lyric poet, wrote a poem apologizing for Helen on the grounds that she herself was never at Troy, but that the Trojan War was fought for her ghost by men who were unaware of this until after the war was over.

Then if we consider the pleasures proper to them, I suppose the tyrant is furthest separated from true pleasure and the king is nearest to it.

Necessarily.

The tyrant's life will know the least pleasure and the king's life the most?

That also follows.

But do you know by how much the tyrant's pleasure falls short of the king's?

If you tell me, I shall know.

Well, there seem to be three kinds of pleasure, one genuine and two false. Shunning law and reason, he even disdains the limits set c for the false pleasures. He goes beyond them, gives himself over to certain slavish and mercenary pleasures. It is no easy task to measure his debasement, except perhaps in the following way.

How?

The tyrant, you remember, stands third from the oligarch. The democratic man stands between.

Yes?

So his illusionary pleasures are thrice removed from those of the oligarch—that is, if what we said before is true.

It is true.

Now if we agree that king and aristocrat are one and the same, we d can place the oligarch at third remove from the king.

Third is right.

Then the tyrant must be separated from pleasure by a number that is three times three.

So it seems.

In that case the tyrant's illusion of pleasure, measured in terms of length, is a plane number.

Quite.

Finally, the square and the cube define the true distance separating the tyrant from pleasure.

All that is obvious to one skilled in mathematics.

Then turn it around and say how far the king is removed from the e tyrant in terms of true pleasure. When we are finished with multiplication, it will be evident that the king experiences 729 times more pleasure than the tyrant. The tyrant's pain may be measured by the same number.

Your calculations concerning the distance between pleasure and pain for the just and unjust man overwhelm and baffle us.

But if days and nights and months and years have relevance to 588 men's lives, the number is relevant and true.

Surely it is.

Then if the good and just man is pleasure's victor by so wide a margin over the man who is bad and unjust, won't his triumph be far greater in beauty, grace, and virtue?

A prodigious victory, by Zeus.

Having reached this point in the argument, we should do well to return to the things we said first of all and thanks to which we have managed to come this far. Someone, I recall, said that the unjust man will find injustice profitable providing he has a reputation for justice. Was that not said?

Yes, it was said.

Now that we have agreed on the nature of just and unjust conduct, let us try to reason with the one who made that assertion.

How?

By describing the soul in such a way that he will understand the meaning of his words.

What kind of description?

Something like we find in ancient fables about the Chimaera, Scylla, and Cerberus. Many others, too, tell how a multitude of forms grow naturally into one.

That's right. They do.

Imagine, then, a single figure of a multicolored creature with many heads. The ring of heads consists of both tame and wild beasts springing forth from the parent creature, which can produce them and change them at will.

The work of a clever dissembler. Still, speech is more easily twisted than wax and other materials. So let the figure stand.

Then another figure: choose an idea and make it into a lion. Choose still another and make it a man. Make the first far larger than the second.

That is easier. The work is done.

Then unite all three in one in such a way that they will naturally grow together.

I have united them.

Next, encompass them about with the single likeness of a man. Do it so that it looks like one animal, a human being, to anyone who looks only at the surface and is not able to see beneath.

The outer casing is now in place.

Now let us turn back to the one who tells this man that it pays to be unjust and that he will find justice inexpedient. Let us say that all his assertions amount to no more than a recommendation to gorge and exalt the many-colored beast and the lion and all that the lion symbolizes. They offer a recipe that will starve the human being within him to the point where he can be dragged wherever the other parts of his soul want to go. Never do they speak words of friendship and reconciliation; rather do they provoke a man's parts to bite and fight and devour one another.

When a man praises injustice, this is what he really means to say.

His opposite is the man who asserts justice is the more profitable. He tells us that in thought and deed the inner man must govern the entire man. He must deal with the many-headed beast like a farmer who nurtures and cultivates his crops but prevents the growth of weeds. The lion's nature must become his ally, and he must care for all the beasts in common. First he must be friends to all of them and then make them friends to one another. This is the manner in which he must bring them up.

When a man praises justice, this is what he really means to say.

On every count, then, the man who praises justice speaks truth. The man who praises injustice lies. By whatever standard we apply, whether pleasure, profit, or reputation, the friend of justice speaks truly. But the unjust man does not even understand what he dishonors.

No. He cannot understand it.

But he does not willingly choose error. Should we not try to persuade him with gentle questions? "Friend," could we not say, "there is some reason in the distinctions law and custom have made between fair and foul? The grounds are these: fair and honorable are those things that subject the brutish part of our nature to the human part or rather, perhaps, to the divine. But foul and base is that which makes the gentle nature captive of the wild." Would he agree to that or not?

If he would listen to me, he would.

Will anyone believe that he could profit by taking gold unjustly after considering this further argument? The moment he takes the gold, he will have enslaved the best part of himself to the worst. Or, if he took gold in exchange for enslaving his son or daughter—and to fierce and vicious men at that—there could be no profit for him no matter how much he pocketed. Enslaving the most divine part of himself to what is most unclean and shameful, would he not know terrible anguish? Should he take the golden bait, will he not bring about his own ruin, more dreadful by far than Eriphyle suffered when she sold her husband's soul for a necklace?[3]

Far worse, indeed, said Glaucon, if I may speak on his behalf.

Don't you think that some of these concerns are linked to the ancient odium attached to licentiousness? Is it not dissolute behavior that unleashes that dread, huge, and many-headed beast?

---

3. Eriphyle was bribed by a necklace to persuade her husband, Amphiaraus, to join six others on a military expedition. He was killed in battle; her son Alcmaeon killed her in revenge.

Clearly.

b   And do we not frown upon stubbornness and bad temper because together they drive the spirited element to excess and exalt the lion and the serpent in us?

Yes.

Conversely, we reproach luxury and softness for making the very same element go slack so that it becomes weak and cowardly.

Yes.

And is he not odious who permits his own sordid desires and his taste for flattery to subordinate his spirited part to the moblike beast? Who exposes it to insult in order to get money to feed the beast's insatiable appetite? Who trains it from youth onward to behave in such a way that instead of a lion it becomes an ape?

He is odious indeed.

c   But why do you suppose the laboring man who works with his hands should be regarded with disdain? Shall we not say that reproach is deserved only if the best in him is so weak that he cannot govern the beasts within himself? If instead he is their servant and unable to learn anything except what flatters them?

All that is likely.

Shouldn't such kinds of men be governed in the way that the best man governs himself? This is what we mean when we say that they

d   should be slaves to the best man who has the divine principle within him. We do not intend to say, as Thrasymachus did, that subjects must be governed to their own detriment. Our purpose is different. It will be best if all are governed by what is intelligent and divine. Preferably each will establish this kind of government within himself. If not, however, let it be imposed from without, so that, as far as possible, we may all be friends and kinsmen because we are all guided by the same principle.

That's right.

e   Such is the clear intent of the law as the ally of all classes in the state. The same purpose must guide us in raising our children: before we set them free, we must, in effect, establish a government within

591   them. The best in ourselves must foster the best in them. And we shall not let them go until we confirm in them this authority and guardian. Then they may go free.

Plain words.

Well, then, Glaucon, is there any way we could support an argument asserting that it is profitable to be base, licentious, or unjust? All these things make us worse even if they bring with them wealth and power.

We could not sanction them.

Or could it be profitable to commit an injustice undetected and
so escape the penalty? Doesn't the man who goes unpunished become   b
still worse? On the other hand, consider the one who is caught and
suffers the penalty. Will not the beast in him be calmed and tamed
and the tame part set free? Won't his entire soul return to its better
nature, attaining temperance, wisdom, and justice? And because the
soul is more precious than the body, won't his achievement be still
greater than the body's exploits in reaching a state of health, strength,
and beauty?

That is certain.

The wise man will devote all his life to these ends. He will begin   c
by pursuing studies conducive to his purpose and thrust aside the
others.

Of course.

He will not turn over the body's habits and training to brutish and
irrational pleasures, nor will he turn his gaze in that direction. Neither will he make health his life's chief aim. He will count health,
strength, and beauty important only insofar as they serve to make
him more temperate. In sum, he will always care for the harmony
of his body in order to further the harmony of his soul.   d

These are the things that will make him a true musician.

And will he not seek the same order and harmony in his management of money? What the multitude worships leaves him unim-
pressed. So he will refuse to engage in the pursuit of limitless wealth,
with the result that he will avoid limitless evils.

He will.

Instead, his attention will be constantly directed to the internal   e
government of his soul. He will take care that nothing disturbs it,
neither an excess nor a deficiency of property. This is the principle
he will apply in so far as possible and add to or subtract from his
wealth accordingly.

That is precisely what he should do.

When it comes to honors, his purpose will be the same. He will   592
gladly accept those he believes will make him a better man. But any
private or public honors that threaten the internal government of his
soul he will reject.

If these are his purposes, he will not want to enter politics.

Yes, he will, by the dog. Perhaps not in the city of his birth, unless
some divine contingency should intervene. But he certainly will in
his own city.

I understand. You mean he would only take part in the politics of
the city we have founded and built with our words. For I don't believe
it can be found anywhere on earth.

b   It makes no difference whether such a city now exists or ever will. But perhaps its prototype can be found somewhere in heaven for him who wants to see. Seeing it, he will declare himself its citizen. The politics of this city would be his politics and none other.

That is likely.

Book X

Indeed. And many other things about our city convince me that we   595
have built it truly. When I say this, I think particularly of the role
we assigned to poetry.

What do you mean?

We barred any kind of poetry that is imitative; under no circumstances can it be admitted to the city. The reason for excluding it
should be still more evident than before now that we have examined   b
the soul's several parts.

What do you mean?

Well, don't go tattling to the tragic poets and all the other mimics.
But, between ourselves, it appears to me that their art corrupts the
minds of all who hearken to them, save only those whose knowledge
of reality provides an antidote.

What do you have in mind when you say that?

My love and reverence for Homer since I was a boy makes me
hesitate. Yet I must speak out: he seems to have been the first teacher
and originator of all these beautiful tragedies. Honoring truth must   c
take precedence over honoring the man. Hence my conviction that
one must speak his mind.

That much is certain.

Then listen. Or, rather, answer.

Then ask.

Could you tell me in general what imitation is? I myself am hardly
able to understand its nature and purpose.

Then how should I be able to understand it?

Nothing to wonder at. You know that men with duller vision often   596
see things before those with keener sight.

True. But in your presence I find myself unwilling to say just
anything that occurs to me. So speak up yourself.

Very well. Shall we begin the inquiry by following our customary
procedure? I think we have generally followed the practice of sub-
suming multiplicities under a single form or idea and then calling
them collectively by a single name. Do you understand?

I understand.

Then consider some multiplicity of your choice. For example, there are many beds and tables.

Of course.

But among these furnishings, I suppose, there are only two forms: one of a bed and one of a table.

Agreed.

Is it not also our custom to say that the carpenter who makes a bed or table or some other piece of useful furniture looks to the form of each? Presumably no craftsman produces the form itself. How could he?

He could not.

Now, what would you call this next kind of craftsman?

What kind?

The one who can make all the things that each class of artisan considers its own specialty.

I would call him a clever and wonderful man.

Wait. Soon you will say even more. Not only is this craftsman able to construct all practical contrivances. He also breeds all plants and animals, including himself. Still more, he creates the earth and sky, the gods and all things in heaven and in Hades under the earth.

Now I would call him a wonderful sophist.

Are you skeptical? Tell me, do you think no such craftsman could exist? Or do you think it possible that in some sense there could be one who makes all these objects but in another sense not? Or don't you realize that in a certain way you yourself could be the maker of all things?

And what way is that?

The way is not difficult. It can be quickly managed anywhere on earth—most quickly if you are prepared to carry a mirror with you wherever you go. Quickly you will produce the sun and the things of heaven; quickly the earth; quickly yourself; quickly all the animals, plants, contrivances, and every other object we just mentioned.

But only in appearance; not in reality.

Excellent. You advance the argument at just the right moment. Now, the painter is one kind of craftsman, is he not?

Of course.

I suppose you will say that what he creates is unreal. Still, in a certain way, he does make a bed, doesn't he?

Yes. He makes something resembling a bed.

Once again, how about the carpenter? Weren't you just saying that he also does not make a real bed? He simply makes a particular bed and not what we call the real bed, the form of a bed.

Yes. I said that.

Then he is not making something real but only a facsimile. That is not reality. So if someone should say that the carpenter's work (or that of other artisans) is the same as reality, he could hardly be called truthful.

At least, that would be the view of people who devote their time to these kinds of arguments.

· No wonder, then, that the one who makes beds also offers only a   b
dim reflection of the truth.

No wonder.

Shall we now apply these examples to aid us in finding out what an imitator really is?

If you wish.

Well, then, it turns out there are three kinds of beds. One exists in nature. I suppose we would say god created it. Who else could?

No one else, I should think.

And then the bed the carpenter made.

Yes.

And the one made by the painter. Right?

All right.

So we have the painter, the carpenter, and god. These three produce three kinds of beds.

Three. Right.

God, then, whether he willed it or because he felt some constraint   c
not to make more than one bed, did in fact make only one bed, the real bed. Never were two or more beds made by god, nor would they ever be.

Why not?

I shall explain. Even if he had made only two beds, a third would unavoidably appear. That would be the real bed, of which the other two would only be copies.

Right.

God, I suppose, knowing this and wishing to be the real creator of   d
the real bed and not some particular craftsman making some particular bed, wrought in nature only one bed.

Apparently.

Shall we call him something like its true and natural creator?

That would be fitting since he has created this and everything else in nature.

What about the carpenter? Does he not make a bed?

Yes.

And the painter? Does he not also create a bed?

Certainly not.

Then what relationship does he have with the bed?

e   I think it would be most fair to call him an imitator of things that others create.

So one who makes something at third remove from nature you call an imitator?

Indeed I do.

And the maker of tragedies is also thrice removed, as it were, from the king and the truth. He is therefore an imitator like all other imitators?

It seems so.

Then we agree about the imitator. Now let us return to the painter.
598   Is it his habit to imitate the original in nature or the craftsmen's products?

What the craftsmen make.

As they are or as they appear to be? This is a distinction still to be made.

What do you mean?

This. If you look at a bed from the side or the front or from any other angle, is it any different? Or does it remain the same in fact but different in appearance—and does this not hold for everything else?

b   The latter is true. It looks different, but it's not different.

This, then, is the point we want to consider. Does painting imitate reality or appearance? Does it imitate illusion or truth?

Illusion.

Then imitation is surely far from truth. This probably explains why the imitator will put his hand to anything; he grasps only a small fragment of whatever it is he works with, and even that is unreal. The painter, for example, will portray a shoemaker, a carpenter, or
c   other craftsmen without any understanding of the arts they use. Nonetheless, if he is a good artist and displays his portrait of the carpenter from a distance, he would deceive children and unreasoning men into believing that they were seeing a real carpenter.

Why not?

At any rate, my friend, I think this is what we should keep in mind in all such matters. When anyone tells us that he has met some person who knows all the arts and everything else known to man— that there is nothing he does not know better than everybody else—
d   we must tell him that he is gullible and must have met a magician and been deceived. He was duped into thinking such a person omniscient because of his own inability to test and verify the difference between knowledge, ignorance, and imitation.

That is certain.

Now let us consider tragedy and Homer as its master. Some say the tragic poets know all the arts, all things human, all things pertaining to virtue and vice, all things divine. They claim that the good poet writing good poetry must know what he is writing about; otherwise he would not be able to be a poet. Therefore we must ask whether those who talk this way may have been keeping company with imi- 599 tators who deceived them; whether, in consequence, they looked at the works of poets but did not understand that they were thrice removed from reality and could easily be produced without any knowledge of truth. For poets contrive appearances and not reality. Or is there something in what they say? Do good poets really know what many think they say so well?

The question certainly requires examination.

Then if a man were able to produce both realities and illusions, do you think he would choose to work with illusions and devote himself to them as the best that life could offer?

No.   b

I would suppose, if he actually knew the things he imitates, he would do those things and leave off imitating. Would he not try to leave as his memorial a tangible record of many splendid deeds? Would he not rather be the one who is praised than the one who praises?

I should think he would. In deeds there is far greater honor and profit.

Well, let us not demand an accounting from Homer or any of the other poets whether any of them were really doctors or whether they   c merely copied off medical language. Nor will we ask whether any poet, past or present, has ever healed men as Asclepius healed them; nor whether he has left behind heirs to his medical knowledge the way Asclepius did. And we shall forgo questions about any of the other arts. But surely it is fair to inquire of Homer concerning the   d greatest and most estimable things he undertook to speak of: wars, military skills, the governing of cities, and the education of men.

"Beloved Homer," we could say, "if your words about virtue are not at third remove from the truth, if you don't fit our definition of the imitator as an inventor of dreams—if you are instead next neighbor to truth and can identify the kinds of behavior that make men better or worse in both private and public life—then tell us what city has ever been better governed thanks to you. Sparta owes thanks to Lycurgus. Many other cities, small and great, owe a similar debt of   e thanks.[1] What city gives you credit for having been a good lawgiver or benefactor? In Italy and Sicily, Charondas is so credited; among us it is Solon. Who credits you?" Will there be any he can name?

1. The next several lines contain the names of a series of lawgivers who gained fame for their success in designing successful constitutions.

I don't suppose so. Even Homer's followers have never mentioned any.

600   Can we recall any war in Homer's time won under his command or as a result of his advice?

None.

What about the inventions and practical devices that we expect from men skilled in crafts? Thales the Milesian and Anacharsis from Scythia are credited with many.[2] How about Homer?

None.

Well, if Homer has no record of public service, what report do we have of him as a private educator around whom men gathered because b   they cherished his teachings? Did he and they pass on to posterity a kind of Homeric way of life after the manner of Pythagoras?[3] Such a legacy is counted among Pythagoras's greatest achievements. Even now his successors use the term *Pythagorean* to denote a certain way of life that many of our contemporaries look upon with respect.

Once again, Socrates, there is no report. To look on his companion Creophylus as representative of Homeric culture might turn out to be a more promising subject for ridicule than the name Creophy-
c   lus itself.[4] For if the things said about Homer are true, he was neglected by that child of the flesh during most of his lifetime.

So tradition tells us. Don't you suppose then, Glaucon, that if Homer had really been able to educate men and make them better because he was a man of real knowledge and not an imitator, he would have had many companions and been loved and honored by them? After all, Protagoras of Abdera and Prodicus of Ceos and others are able to attract many of their contemporaries to their private lessons, where they impress upon their listeners that without instruc-
d   tion from them they will be able to govern neither their cities nor their own homes. This is the wisdom that makes them so beloved that their students all but carry them about on their shoulders. If Homer had helped men to achieve excellence, surely his contemporaries would not have let him and Hesiod live as itinerant reciters of poetry. Would they not sooner have parted with gold than with their poets? Would they not have insisted that they stay with them
e   and dwell in their homes? Failing that, would they not have followed and attended them until they were able to receive from them an adequate education?

2. Thales and Anacharsis are both counted among the seven sages of antiquity. Thales was a philosopher, statesman, and mathematician; his most famous exploit was his calculation of an eclipse that occurred on May 28, 585 B.C. Anacharsis is reported to have invented the anchor and the potter's wheel.
3. Pythagoras based his philosophical and religious beliefs on mathematical formulations. He provided an education for his followers based on his "way of life." In southern Italy he founded a religious brotherhood in the city of Croton.
4. Creophylus literally means "of the beef tribe"; he is supposed to have been a friend of Homer and an epic poet.

I think your questions are to the point, Socrates.

Then we should be prepared to declare that the entire tribe of poets—beginning with Homer—are mere imitators of illusions of virtue and imitators as well of the other things they write about. They don't lay a hand on truth. Instead, as we said a moment ago, they are like the painter who knows nothing about cobbling but who cre- 601 ates what seems to be a shoemaker in the eyes of those who also know nothing of the subject and who judge simply in terms of shape and color.

You are right.

I suppose we may say the same of the poet himself. He only knows how to imitate, daubing the several arts with words and phrases but understanding nothing. His imitations speak to those who are equally ignorant and who see things only through words. The poet will use meter, rhythm, and harmony; and no matter whether his subject matter concerns generals or shoemakers, his hearers will call everything praiseworthy. It is true that these embellishments have great charm. But once the poet's words are said alone, without the accom- b panying music and color, I think you know what kind of showing they make. Surely you have observed for yourself.

I have.

Are his words not like faces that once were young but never beautiful and from which youth is now departed?

Exactly.

Now consider still another proposition: The imitator, the one who c creates illusions, does not understand reality but only what reality appears to be. Would you agree to that?

Yes.

All right. But we mustn't leave the matter at midpoint. It ought to be discussed fully.

Go ahead.

Well, we might say that the painter paints reins and a bit.

Yes?

But they are manufactured by a cobbler and a smith?

Of course.

Does the painter know the true characteristics of reins and bit? Or is it not true that even the artisans, the cobbler and the smith, fail to understand their nature? Is it not true that only the horseman understands how to use them?

That is true.

Then we can say that the same holds true for everything.

What? d

Everything finds expression in three arts: the art that uses, the art that creates, and the art that imitates.

Yes?

But judgments about what is true, beautiful, or good in any living thing, any human action, or any human art ought to be made only in terms of the use that nature or the artisan intended them for.

True.

e   Then the conclusion must necessarily follow that he who uses anything is the one who knows most about it. He draws on his experience in reporting its merits and defects to the maker. For example, a flutist will tell the flute maker which of his flutes performs best in concert; he will order accordingly, and the flute maker will do his bidding.

You are right.

He who possesses knowledge, then, will make judgments concerning the degree of excellence of the flutes; the other will heed him and make the flutes accordingly.

Yes.

So the user will have true knowledge. But the maker will also trust his own judgment concerning the merits and defects of the instru-

602   ment because he associates with, and hence is compelled to listen to, the man who knows.

True.

But what about the imitator? Will experience or application teach the painter what is beautiful and real? Were he compelled to keep company with the man who knows and who tells him what to paint, would he be persuaded?

No.

Then neither knowledge nor opinion can help the imitator to arrive at valid judgments about his own imitations.

It seems not.

So far as understanding his own work, then, the situation of poet and imitator must be truly delightful.

Not at all. Quite the reverse.

b   Nonetheless, he will keep on imitating, and never will he understand why something is bad or good. And what he will imitate is all too evident: whatever pleases the ignorant masses.

Of course.

So it seems that we are all but agreed on these matters: the imitator knows hardly anything about the things he imitates; imitation is a kind of game and not to be taken seriously; and those who write tragedies, either in iambic or heroic verse, are the most extravagant of all the imitators.

Agreed.

c   By heaven, then, it follows that imitation must be concerned with things at the third remove from truth.

Agreed.

And which part of man responds to imitation's power?

What do you mean?

Let me illustrate. I assume you would agree that the mass of any magnitude looks different when viewed from near and then from far?

I agree.

And that straight things appear bent when seen underwater? And that color can distort our vision so that concave becomes convex? The source of all these illusions is plainly to be found in some part of our souls. There is where we shall find the flaw in our nature that the imitators exploit, where they manipulate light and dark so that their conjuror's tricks and marionette shows appear to be nothing short of magic.

True.

Now the full beauty of man's capacity to weigh, to measure, and to number comes to light. All are antidotes to error. They liberate our souls from illusory perceptions of what is greater or less or more or heavier, so that we may be governed by those things that we can weigh, measure, and reckon.

That is unquestionably true.

And these would obviously be functions of that part of the soul that reasons and calculates.

Clearly.

But when the reasoning part measures and demonstrates that some things are equal, some are larger, and some smaller, won't it often be contradicted by appearance, by the way these same things seem to be?

Yes.

And didn't we judge it impossible that one could simultaneously hold contradictory opinions about the same thing?

We did, and rightly so.

Then that part of the soul that rejects the evidence of measurement and the part that affirms it cannot be the same.

True.

Further: the best part of the soul is that which relies on calculation and measurement?

Clearly.

And the contrary part is to be found among the lesser elements of the soul?

Necessarily.

This is the point I was getting at when I said that the works produced by painting and imitation are generally far from truth. Such arts appeal to that part in us which is far removed from intelligence. They cannot be our companions or friends for any good or healthy purpose.

Very true.

Hence imitation is a defective art. It mates with what is also defective, and so it produces defective offspring as well.

Apparently.

Does all this apply only to vision? Or does it also apply to hearing and hence to poetry?

It probably applies to both.

c   But we ought not to rely only on the plausibility of the analogy we drew from painting. Let us instead consider directly that part of the mind to which imitative poetry makes its specific appeal. We must discover whether this part of the mind is superior or inferior.

We have an obligation to try.

Put it this way. Let us say that imitation simulates the actions of human beings, whether the acts be freely willed or performed under compulsion. It also reports the actors' judgments whether the results were good or ill, and whether they felt joy or sorrow. Is there anything else to say?

Nothing.

In all of this, then, is any man of one mind? Or are confusion and contradiction evident here just as they were when we were discussing the phenomenon of vision? Is a man ever of two minds about the

d   same thing? When it comes to action, is he divided against himself? Does he experience internal strife? But I realize that there is now no need for us to come to an agreement about these matters. We found sufficient agreement in previous discussions that our souls are always teeming with ten thousand such contradictions.

We were right in making the agreement.

e   Yes. But I think we omitted something then that must be considered now.

What is it?

We surely said it before this: a good man who has the misfortune to lose a son or suffer some other kind of loss of something most dear to him will bear what he has to bear with greater composure than others.

Of course.

Now consider this. Will he feel no pain? Or, since that could not be, will he be temperate in giving vent to his grief?

The latter is closer to truth.

604   Now tell me this. When will he make the greater effort to fight back and endure the pain? When he is among others or when he is by himself?

His struggle will be greater when he is seen by others.

But when he is alone, I should think he would dare to utter many things he would be ashamed of were others to hear them? He would do many things that he would rather not have others see him do?

True enough.

Do not law and reason sustain the will to endure? Is it not the suffering itself that goads a man to give way to his grief?   b

Yes.

So when we observe two contradictory impulses simultaneously at work within a man, must we not infer the presence of two distinct motives?

Clearly.

One of which is ready to follow the precepts of the law?

What do you mean?

The law, I should imagine, admonishes us to maintain our equanimity in adversity, insofar as that is possible. It bids us shun discontent because we cannot know what is truly good or evil in such situations. No one benefits from despondency, and nothing in mor-   c
tal life deserves that much concern. Finally, grief prevents us from attaining the thing we need the most and as quickly as possible.

What is that?

Thought. We need to think about what has happened to us. One must accept the way the dice fall and then order one's life according to the dictates of reason. One ought not to behave like children who have stumbled, wasting time wailing and pressing one's hands to the injured part. Instead, the soul should learn to remedy the hurt forth-   d
with, to restore what has fallen, and to remedy the complaint with the appropriate medicine.

Surely that is the best way to deal with whatever chance may bring.

The best part of us, we have said, is willing to follow these rules of reason?

Clearly.

Then must we not also say that the part of us which leads us to dwell on past sufferings and positively revels in lamentation is our idle and irrational side and the very author of cowardice?

We will say that.

Then that part of our personality given to despondency presents   e
many and diverse occasions for imitation. Much different is our disposition to be reasonable and intelligent. It remains relatively constant and is not easy to imitate. Nor would the imitation be easy to understand (especially by some disorderly mob in a theater) because it would be reflecting a disposition alien to the crowd.

Very true.

It should be evident that the imitative poet is far removed from   605
the better disposition of our souls. Since he covets applause from the multitude, his pursuit of wisdom leads in a different direction. He devotes himself to unstable or choleric characters because they are easier to imitate.

That is also true.

Hence we would be justified in laying hold of the poet and setting him down as the counterpart of the painter. Like the painter, his works are distant from reality. Poet and painter also resemble one another in their appeal to the inferior part of the soul and their neglect of the best part. At last, then, we have arrived at a justification for not admitting the poet to a well-ordered state. Because he calls forth the worst elements in the soul and then nourishes them and makes them strong, he destroys the soul's reasoning part. All this finds a parallel in any city where someone makes the wicked mighty, appoints them the city's governors, and corrupts the city's best elements. The imitative poet has exactly the same impact on the private individual. He corrupts the individual's character with fabrications far removed from reality and panders to the soul's fool that cannot even distinguish big from little.

Well said.

But the gravest indictment remains to be discussed. The poet's power to corrupt even the best men—with rare exceptions—is surely the most serious cause for alarm.

If the effect is what you say, it surely is.

Listen and consider this. When Homer or one of the other tragic poets imitates a grieving hero and causes him to utter extended lamentations or has him chant and beat his breast, you know that even the best of us enjoy it. We are held captive by the imitation; we suffer with the hero, and whoever can most powerfully evoke this mood in us we call the best poet.

Of course. I know that.

When we experience personal sorrow ourselves, however, quite the contrary occurs. We pride ourselves if we are able to maintain our equanimity and bear the burden. We reckon this to be a man's behavior. But what we found favor with just now in the poem we generally consider to be the behavior of women.

I recognize that.

Is it right that we should respond in this manner? We see a man impersonate the kind of character that we would despise and reject in ourselves. Yet we do not disapprove; instead, we enjoy ourselves and praise the performance.

By Zeus! That certainly doesn't seem reasonable.

It will seem reasonable enough if we consider what follows.

What?

Consider how in our own misfortunes we forcibly constrain that part of our soul that hungers for tears and the satisfaction of a cry. This is the part whose nature it is to desire these things; this is the part that finds satisfaction and enjoyment in the poets. And the best

part of us, when it observes the suffering of others and has not been   b
sufficiently educated by either reason or habit, will relax its control
over the sentiments. After all, there is no disgrace in comforting and
pitying what is evidently a good man when he gives way to an excess
of grief. Instead, to do so would be counted as a vicarious pleasure
and pure gain, something one would not willingly forgo by disdain-
ing to hear the whole poem. That happens, I suppose, because only
a few men will reflect that the vicarious enjoyment of other people's
sufferings has an effect upon one's own. Lavishing pity on others
makes it hard to contain pity when it comes to our own sufferings.

That is true.   c

Must we not apply the same principle to the things that make us
laugh? Are there not jokes you would be ashamed to repeat but which
provide you with much amusement when you hear them privately
or at a comedy? In these circumstances you see no disgrace in laughing at them just as in the other example there seemed no cause for
disgrace in giving vent to pity. Here, too, your reason is at work
admonishing the comic in you so that you will not gain the reputation of a buffoon. But when others joke, you let your comic sense
run loose. Indulging it, you return to your own affairs and discover
that you have unwittingly become a comic poet.

Right again.   d

Sex, anger, and all the desires, as well as all the pleasures and
pains that make their presence felt in whatever we do—on all these
poetry has the same effect. It makes them grow great instead of drying
them up. It establishes them as our governors when instead they
should be the ones governed if we are to become men who are better
and happier instead of worse and more miserable.

I can't dispute you.

So then, Glaucon, when you encounter admirers of Homer who   e
say that this poet is the tutor of Greece, that to study him is to refine
human conduct and culture, and that we should order our entire
lives in accordance with his precepts, you must welcome them and
love them as people who are doing the best they can. You can cer-   607
tainly agree that Homer is the greatest of poets and first among tragedians. But you must hold firm to the position that our city will
admit no poetry except hymns to the gods and fair words about good
men. Once entry is permitted to the honey-tongued Muse, whether
in lyric or epic form, pleasure and pain will become kings of the city,
law will be displaced, and so will that governing reason which time
and opinion have approved.

I concur.

Having returned to the subject of poetry, let us make her an apol-   b
ogy: we acted properly when we exiled her from the city earlier on.

Reason constrained us to do so. And lest we be convicted of a certain harshness and parochialism, let us remind her that there is an old quarrel between philosophy and poetry. "The bitch that yelps and bays at her master," "great in the conversation of simpletons," "a company of overwise fools," and "refined thinkers who are really beggars"—these and many other reproaches mark the ancient antagonism.[5] Even so, we shall declare that if poetry that is imitative and aims to provide pleasure can show cause why it should find a place in a well-governed city, we should be glad to welcome its return from exile. We, too, are very aware of its charms. Of course, we must not be guilty of impiety by betraying what we think is true. But don't you yourself feel the magic of poetry, especially when Homer is the poet?

It affects me deeply.

Then if poetry, in turn, would make her defense in lyric or some other meter, would it not be just if she should return to us from exile?

It certainly would be.

And we would certainly offer her partisans—not poets themselves but those who love poetry—an opportunity to plead her case in prose without meter and to argue that poetry is not only delightful but also a blessing to the life of men and well-governed cities. And we shall hear them kindly, for we shall surely be the gainers if the case can be made that poetry is a source of goodness as well as pleasure.

It would be a very great gain.

But, my friend, if the verdict goes the other way, we must be like men who once loved but now know that their love has played them false. Hard though it is, they will hold themselves aloof. So we, loving this kind of poetry bred into us by the education we have received from our noble cities, will rejoice if poetry appears at its best and truest. But so long as she is unable to offer a tenable defense, we shall chant to ourselves the arguments we have already considered. They will serve as a talisman to protect us from being seduced once again by the rude passions of the masses. In any case, we have learned that this kind of poetry does not deserve to be taken seriously in any meaningful effort to seek truth. On the contrary, one who listens to it must fear for the governance of his soul and must hold to all we have said about poetry.

You are right. I agree.

My dear Glaucon, we are engaged in a great struggle, a struggle greater than it seems. The issue is whether we shall become good or bad. And neither money, office, honor, nor poetry itself must be allowed to persuade us to neglect justice or any other virtue.

5. The identity of these poets who attacked philosophers is unknown.

After all that we have discussed I am ready to join you in saying that. I should think anyone else would do the same.

But we have yet to discuss virtue's greatest rewards and honors.   c

If they are greater than those already considered, they surpass anything I am able to imagine.

Then think of something great that can take place in a very short time. The life of man, for example, from childhood to old age, is only an instant when compared with all of time.

In truth, it is nothing at all.

So we must ask whether an immortal being won't want to pay more attention to all of time than to an instant.   d

I should think so. But what do you mean by that?

Have you never sensed that our soul is immortal and never dies?

He looked straight at me with wonder in his face: No, by Zeus, I haven't. Is it really in you to say this?

Justice requires me to. You could think so, too. It's not hard.

It's hard for me. But I would be glad to hear from you that it is otherwise.

Listen.

Speak.

Do you call some things good and some evil?

Yes.

Do you understand them in the same way I do?   e

How do you understand them?

Evil corrupts and destroys. Good purifies and preserves.

I agree with that.

How about this? Would you say that each thing is marked by a particular good and evil? As examples, ophthalmia afflicts the eyes,   609
sickness the whole body, mildew spoils grain, rot eats away the wood, rust gnaws at bronze and iron. Would these not suggest that nearly everything is vulnerable to a particular infirmity or evil?

They would.

When anything is infested by one of these evils, does it not become diseased and finally fall victim to dissolution and destruction?

No question about it.

Then only the evil and vice inherent in each thing can cause its destruction. If it is impervious to them, nothing else could destroy it. For it is clear that what is good will not destroy; nor will that   b
which is neither good nor bad.

No. They could not.

Now suppose we observe something together with its peculiar evil. It suffers because of the evil, but it is not destroyed by it. Must we not conclude that in this case we have to do with something indestructible?

Likely.

Then how about the soul? Are there any things that can corrupt it?

There certainly are. They are all the things we were discussing c just a little while ago: injustice, dissolute behavior, cowardice, and ignorance.

Do any of these actually destroy and negate the soul? Here let us reflect a moment so that we won't be deceived by supposing that the soul of an unjust and foolish man who is caught in an unjust act will then be destroyed by the injustice within him. Instead, let us think about it this way. The body's evil is disease. It wastes and destroys until the body is a body no longer. So with the other things of which we were just speaking. The evil specific to each infests it and takes d over until nothing is left. Isn't that right?

Right.

Let us examine the soul from the same perspective. Does the presence of injustice and all the other vices attending it reduce and corrupt the soul to the point of death and to the separation of soul from body?

No. That is certainly not what happens.

And surely it is unreasonable to suppose that anything can be destroyed by some alien evil and not by the evil specific to itself.

Yes. That would be unreasonable.

e   Then observe, Glaucon, that neither do we consider it correct to say that the body is injured by the bad foods it ingests, whether they are stale or rotten or otherwise unwholesome. Instead, if the ingestion of bad food is followed by bodily illness, we say that the food activated the disease specific to the body which functions, in turn, as the real agent of destruction. The body is one thing; food is another. 610 Bad food can never destroy the body. All it might do is to activate the specific evil to which the body is subject.

Quite right.

The corollary must be that the evils afflicting the body cannot afflict the soul. If the soul is to be destroyed, its destruction must be accomplished by a defect specifically its own. Evil cannot prevail against something that is alien to it.

Your point is reasonable.

But if it is mistaken, we should turn around and refute it. If not, b however, we should never concede that the soul could be destroyed by fever, by any other kind of illness, or by murder itself, even if the body were to be chopped up into little pieces. So we shall hold to our argument that none of these things is able to propel the soul one jot closer to destruction unless someone can prove that bodily defects directly cause the degeneration of justice and purity in the soul. When

a defect particular to one thing appears in another but does not acti- c
vate the other's own special defect, we shall not countenance anyone
saying that the soul or anything else can be destroyed in this manner.

Surely no one could dispute you. No one can prove that death
will make the soul more unjust.

Those who want to dodge the issue of the soul's immortality might
be so bold as to challenge that argument and assert that death does
make a man less pure and more unjust. But we have an answer. For
if their assertion is true, then it must follow that injustice is like a
disease, like a canker that kills its victims. The extent of corruption d
present in each case will determine whether death comes late or
early, but in every case injustice will itself be the killing agent. On
this premise, unjust men would die under very different circumstances from the way things are now. Now they may die, but only
because other men impose a penalty on them.

But—by Zeus! If injustice is fatal, it will not seem so terrible a
thing to the one it infects, for it will release him from all his troubles.
In any case, however, I think it will appear to be something quite
different. Others injustice may kill, but for the man already unjust
it is the very source of his energy, an energy so potent that he never
needs sleep. So I have to conclude that death and injustice are far e
apart from one another.

Well said. For if the soul's own peculiar infirmity and vice cannot
destroy it, cannot end its life, then an evil designed to destroy some
other thing can hardly kill the soul or anything else except its own
predetermined target.

Hardly. Indeed. Probably.

So if no evil can destroy the soul, neither the evil intrinsic to it or 611
some other evil, then the soul must be indestructible, and if indestructible, then immortal.

A necessary inference.

Then let us infer it. But if the inference is correct, it follows that
souls must always be the same. If none is destroyed, their number
could not decrease. Nor could it be augmented because the numbers
of immortal things could come only from the ranks of the mortals.
The end result would be that everything would end up being immortal.

True.

But we should reject this conclusion because it contradicts the
argument. By the same token, we should not suppose that the soul's b
true nature abounds in diversity, contradictions, and anomalies.

How am I supposed to understand that?

It is hard to imagine something immortal whose composition is
the product of diverse elements and whose construction is less than

the best. Yet the way we discussed the soul just now, that is how it appeared to be.

Dubious reasoning.

Nonetheless, both our recent and previous discussions should suffice to persuade us that the soul is immortal. But the soul must be
c   seen as it truly is. It must not be distorted as we find it when it is hinged to the body and its miseries. The light of reason must enable us to discover the soul in its pure form, where its beauty is far more radiant. Then one's understanding of justice and injustice and all the other things we have spoken of will be much more precise. When we first discussed the matter, we were certainly realistic in describing the soul as it currently appears to us. We are like those who catch a
d   glimpse of the sea god Glaucus. They are hard put to imagine his original nature. He has suffered dismemberment of some parts of his body, while others have been mutilated or worn down by the waves. At the same time, such things as shells and seaweed and rocks have grown upon him, so that he appears more like a beast than what nature first intended him to be. In the same way, countless wounds distort our vision of man's soul. And so, Glaucon, we must look elsewhere to see truly.

Where?

e   To the soul's love of wisdom. We must mark what it knows. We must disclose the yearning that links it to the immortal and divine and so to eternal being. We must discover what it would become if it gave itself wholly to what it yearns for, and if this impulse should thrust it up from the ocean's depths where it now lies. We must see how it looks with those rocks and barnacles scraped off which have
612   accumulated during the course of its earthly feasting and that now cling to it in stony and disordered profusion as evidence of that same feasting that men call happiness. Then one could see its true nature, whether complex or simple, and the patterns of its being. But by now, I suppose, we have given a fair description of the forms the soul assumes and suffers in human life.

That we have certainly done.

Then we have met all the demands the argument might require,
b   except that we omitted mention of the rewards and repute that you said Homer and Hesiod had promised to those who behave justly. Instead, we have demonstrated that justice for its own sake is what is best for the soul. We have proved that the soul ought to do justice whether it possesses the ring of Gyges or not—or, for that matter, the helmet of Hades.[6]

---

6. In the *Iliad*, Athena put on the helmet of Hades in order to be invisible (Book 5.844 f.). Hence the coupling with the ring of Gyges, which also conferred invisibility on its wearer (*Republic*, Book II. 359c–360b).

True.

In that case, Glaucon, no one could object if we now add to what we have just said by finally restoring to justice and all of virtue what c is rightfully theirs. I mean the power to confer upon the soul rewards both human and divine, in all their quantity and quality, both in a man's lifetime and thereafter.

I see no possible objection.

In that case, will you now return what you borrowed from me during the argument?

What?

I acceded to your proposition that the just man should seem unjust and the unjust man just. That's what you asked me to do. Even if it were impossible to conceal the deception from gods and men, you thought it right that the concession be made for the sake of argument so that one might arrive at a judgment between absolute justice and absolute injustice. Or don't you remember that?

If I didn't, I would be most unjust myself.   d

Since the judgment has now been made, I ask you on behalf of justice to restore to her the repute that she in fact enjoys among gods and men. I also ask that we acknowledge the purpose served by her repute: that she may also acquire those prizes gained from merely seeming just, so that these, too, she may confer upon the truly just. She has already proven that her gifts are real gifts; they are gifts that do not deceive those who are true to her.

What you ask from me is fair.   e

Then return this first: an affirmation that the gods will not be deceived about who is just and who is not.

We will return that.

Next, as we agreed at the outset, if the gods are not deceived, they will hold the just dear and declare the unjust enemies.

True.

Further: shall we not agree that all that is best is given to the man whom the gods hold dear, with the exception of any evil necessarily due him from some previous offense?   613

By all means.

Then these must be our conclusions concerning the just man: whether he experiences illness, poverty, or anything else accounted evil, all will turn out well for him in life and in death. For surely the gods will never neglect the man who yearns to be righteous and b who pursues virtue in a quest to become as like god as a man can be.

It is probable that like will not reject like.

And must we not think the contrary of the unjust man?

We must.

Then those would be some of the prizes the gods bestow on the just man.

In my opinion, anyway.

What, then, does the just man receive from his fellow men? If we now concern ourselves with reality, must we not say the following? Aren't those who are clever and wicked like runners who run well at the start but fall behind after the turn? After briskly seizing the lead they end up scorned and uncrowned and looking like imbeciles with their ears dragging on their shoulders. But the true runners finish the race, take the prizes, and receive their crowns. Is this not generally the experience of just men? At the completion of every action, of every association, and of life itself, do they not achieve honor and harvest the prizes that men bestow?

So they do.

Then you will bear with me if I say of just men exactly what you said of the unjust. For I am about to say that it is precisely the just, when they grow older, who will hold office in their own city if they choose. They will marry into the families they favor and likewise marry off their children into families of whom they approve. Thus, all you said about the unjust I now say of the just. As for the unjust—even if most of them escape detection in their youth—they will be caught and scorned at the end of the race. In old age they will be mocked and made miserable by their townsmen and strangers alike. They will suffer the lash, fire, and the rack and all those brutalities you rightly said were unfit to recount in polite conversation. Assume that I have enumerated everything they suffer. Consider whether what I have said is credible.

It is credible. What you say is just.

Now we know the ways, gifts, and prizes that gods and men give to the just man during his lifetime. They are companions to the blessings which justice herself confers.

They are awards that are both sure and enduring.

In quantity and greatness they are nothing compared with what awaits each man when he is dead. We should know about these things so that we shall be able to return in full measure what our argument owes to both the just and the unjust.

Then tell us about them. There are few things I would rather hear about.

I won't tell you the kinds of tales told to Alcinous.[7] I want to tell you the tale of a brave man. His name is Er, son of Armenius, and a Pamphylian by race. Once upon a time, he was killed in battle.

---

7. In Books 9 through 12 of the *Odyssey*, Odysseus tells Alcinous, the king of the Phaeacians, the story of his wanderings, one of which is a trip to the underworld.

When the corpses were collected on the tenth day, they were already decayed, but his was untainted. Having been brought home, he lay on the pyre where on the twelfth day, as he was about to be buried, he revived. After returning to life he related what he had seen in the world beyond.

He said that when his soul parted from his body, he found himself in a vast company journeying to a mysterious place. Here he saw c two openings in the earth next to one another, and directly above each of them two other openings reaching into heaven. Judges sat between them. After each judgment they bade the just to continue their journey to the right and upward into heaven. Each was marked d in front by tokens of the judgment passed. The unjust were bidden to proceed with their journey to the left and downward. Trailing behind them was evidence of everything they had done.

When Er himself went forward, they said he was to be the messenger to mankind who would report back his observation of the other world. They told him he should look at and listen to everything about him. He watched at one opening into heaven and one into earth and saw the souls leaving through them after each had been judged. As for the other pair of openings, souls emerged from the earth below in dust and dirt while those from the one above descended clean and pure.

All those in the constant flow of arrivals looked as though they had e been on a long journey. With delight they went to rest in a meadow and set up camp as if anticipating a public festival. Acquaintances greeted one another. Those souls who came from below put questions about the way things were above, and those from heaven asked about what it had been like below.

So they told their stories to one another. Those whose journey took them beneath the earth for a thousand years wept and lamented 615 as they recalled the burden of their manifold sufferings. Those from above tried to describe the inconceivable beauty they saw and experienced in heaven.

To try to tell everything, Glaucon, would take too much time. But this was how Er summed it up. For every unjust deed they had inflicted and for every man who suffered wrong at their hands, they paid the penalty tenfold in each case. That is, for each injustice they were punished once every hundred years. Assuming this figure to be b the span of human life, they could be punished ten times for each crime. So if some men had caused many to die, either by betraying cities or armies and sending people into slavery—or were guilty of any other wrongdoing—they suffered for each of their misdeeds tenfold. On the other hand, those whose deeds were kindly and who c had been just and holy in their conduct were rewarded in like measure. He also spoke of those newly born who lived only briefly, but what he said isn't worth repeating.

Er told of still greater rewards and punishments for piety and impiety toward the gods and toward one's parents, and for suicide. For he said he stood close by when someone questioned another: "Where is Ardiaeus the Great?" Now Ardiaeus had been tyrant of a certain city in Pamphylia just a thousand years earlier. It was said that he had killed his old father and his elder brother and was guilty of many
d   other evil deeds.

Er said that the one questioned about Ardiaeus replied, "He has not come; because of one of the most terrible sights we have seen, I know he will not come. That is, after we had suffered everything and were nearing the mouth of the opening and were about to go up,
e   suddenly we saw him along with others. Almost all were tyrants, but some were private men who had committed great crimes. They all supposed they were about to emerge from the opening, but the mouth would not let them pass. It roared whenever someone tried to get out who had not yet paid the full penalty for his crimes or whose evil was incurable. There were men stationed there, he said, fierce men and incandescent from the fires within them. On hearing the sound
616 of the roar they seized some of the souls and led them away. But Ardiaeus and others they bound hand and foot and head as well, throwing them down on the ground and stripping off their skin. They dragged them by the side of the road so that the thorns pierced their flesh. To all who came by they explained the reasons for the spectacle and announced that their charges would finally be led away and thrown into Tartarus."[8]

Many were the fears of all who had been below, Er said, but what each feared most was that the roar might sound when he was about to rise from the opening. Great was the joy of each if there was
b   silence. These were the kinds of judgments and penalties imposed. Rewards were of a contrary nature.

When each group had remained on the meadow seven days, they were required to leave on the eighth and resume their journey. After four days they arrived at a point where they could see a light straight as a pillar stretching through heaven and earth. It most resembled a rainbow, but its light was brighter and purer. Another day's journey
c   brought them to the center of the light. There they saw the ends of the bindings stretched from heaven, for the light was what bound together the rotations of heaven in the same way that the undergirders support a trireme. The spindle of Necessity was firmly fastened to these ends so that it was the axis for all the heavenly orbits. Its

8. Tartarus is the underworld.

shaft and its hook were made of a diamond-hard substance. The whorl that weighted it at the bottom was made of the same substance as the spindle alloyed with others. Its shape was like the whorls we d use, but from Er's description we must understand it to look like one great empty whorl completely scooped out and containing another smaller whorl closely fitting inside it—just like bowls that fit inside each other. In the same way a third, a fourth, and four others nested inside.

There were thus eight whorls in all set within one another, show-ing their rims as circles when seen from above; but from beneath it e looked like a single whorl clasping the shaft, which was driven through the middle of the eighth. The circle of the rim of the first and out-ermost whorl was the broadest, second broadest was the sixth, third broadest was the fourth, fourth broadest was the eighth, fifth broadest was the seventh, sixth broadest was the fifth, seventh broadest was the third, and eighth broadest was the second. The rim of the largest was spangled; that of the seventh was the most brilliant; that of the 617 eighth reflected the color of the seventh. The circles of the second and fifth were like one another yet yellower than the others; the third had a white color; and the fourth was reddish. The sixth was not as white as the third.

The shaft revolved as a unit in a circle with the same motion; the eighth and outer circle moved most swiftly. Within the revolving whole the seven inner circles were borne gently in a direction oppo-site to the whole: the fifth, sixth, and seventh moved together with b each other but more slowly; the fourth was next in speed in its cir-cling as it appeared to them; after these came the third followed by the second.

The spindle itself was turned on the knees of Necessity. Atop each of the rims stood a Siren being carried in a circle, sending forth one sound, one note; from all eight arose a symphonic harmony. Three others, seated on thrones set at equal intervals, were the Fates, c daughters of Necessity: Lachesis, Clotho, and Atropos. They were robed in white, and they wore garlands on their heads. They sang in unison the hymn of the Sirens: Lachesis of the past, Clotho of the present, and Atropos of the future. Clotho, touching the outer cir-cumference of the spindle with her right hand, helped in turning it. Now and then she paused. Similarly, Atropos rotated the inner cir-cles with her left hand; Lachesis, placing one hand here and the d other there, gave aid in turn to both her sisters.

When the company of souls arrived at this point, they were imme-diately told to appear before Lachesis. A prophet marshaled them into orderly ranks. Then he took from the lap of Lachesis lots and life styles, after which he ascended a towering platform and spoke:

"This is the word of Lachesis, maiden daughter of Necessity. Souls that abide for a day, now begins another cycle of the mortality that ends in death. The gods will not choose a spirit to guide you; you shall choose that spirit yourself. He whose lot bids him choose first must, like all souls, select a life to which he will be bound by necessity. Yet virtue is not bound by any master, so that each will possess as much virtue or as little as he does honor her. The blame belongs to him who chooses. God is blameless."

Then the prophet cast the lots among them, and each picked up the one that fell beside him, Er excepted. He was not permitted to take part in the drawing. Each read the number of his lot. Next, the prophet flung out the life styles and patterns on the ground before them in far greater numbers than the souls assembled there. The variety was enormous, for they included the lives of all the animals as well as human lives. There were tyrants among them, some who had prevailed to the end but others who were ruined midway through life and ended up beggars in exile and poverty. There were men famed for their beauty and bodily strength and for their prowess, for their high birth, or for the virtues of their ancestors. There were some defective in these same virtues. It was just the same with the lives of women. But in none of them was there any fixing of the quality of the soul, since each soul develops differently according to the life it chooses. Otherwise all things were mixed together: wealth and poverty, health and sickness, and every intermediate state.

I believe, dear Glaucon, that this moment of choice is the time of man's greatest peril. It admonishes each of us—even if we neglect all other studies—that a man should be concerned first of all with searching out and studying that which enables him to discern the good. He must seek out those who will give him the capacity and knowledge to distinguish the good life from the bad, so that he might always and everywhere make the best choice conditions allow. He must take into account all the things we have been discussing and reckon how they severally or jointly affect the goodness of his life. He must know the good and bad effects of beauty when joined to poverty or wealth and coupled with any of the several habits of the soul. He must know the interrelated effects of high birth or low, of private life and public power, of strength and weakness, of quickness or dullness in learning and of all other things a soul acquires or inherently possesses.

These are the requirements for reasoned inference and choice in the matter of the better life and the worse. Fixing on the nature of his own soul, a man will call worse anything that brings the soul closer to injustice and better that which brings it closer to justice. Everything else he will renounce, for he knows that this is the supreme choice in life as in death. He will be adamant in carrying his conviction even into the house of death so that he will not be seduced by wealth and all the other trivia to be found there. So will he be armored against embracing tyranny and other vices that would cause him to inflict irreparable evils on others and suffer still greater evils himself. 619

So he will learn how to shun excess. He will choose a life that avoids the extremes both in this world, as far as that is possible, and in all life to come. For this is how a man will find his greatest happiness. b

The messenger from the other world then reported still further words from the prophet: "Even the man who comes last is not fated to an evil life. If he chooses wisely and conscientiously, he will live agreeably. He who has first choice ought not to be reckless; he who is last ought not to be disheartened."

After these words from the prophet, Er said that the man who had drawn the first lot rushed to claim the greatest tyranny as his choice. In consequence, he failed to realize that it fated him to eat his own children and to do and suffer many other horrors as well. Once he realized his plight, he began to beat his breast and bewail the choice that failed to heed the prophet's admonition. But he did not blame himself for his misfortune. He blamed fate and the gods and everything except himself. He was one of those who had come down from above. In his former life he had lived in a well-governed city, and his virtue was a product of habit and not of philosophy. c

One might say of those who came down from heaven that not a few got caught up in similar circumstances because they had lost touch with the experience of suffering. But those who came up from the earth below were well acquainted with suffering in themselves and in others. Hence they were less inclined to make hasty choices. For these reasons, together with the factor of chance in the lot, most souls found themselves exchanging good for evil as well as the reverse. d

Yet on the basis of the reports we receive from there, we may affirm this probability: if a man has a healthy love for philosophy and does not draw his lot from among the last, each return to this world will find him happy. Not only that, but his journey to and from this world will not take him on that rough and subterranean road; he will follow smooth heaven's path instead. e

Er said the way many souls selected their lives was a sight to behold: pitiful, ridiculous, and sometimes wonderful. For the most part, the choice of the new life was determined by the habits and experiences of the old. He saw Orpheus's soul select the life of a swan.[9] Because 620

9. Orpheus, the great singer in Greek mythology, was killed when he was ripped apart by Thracian women. Thamyris was another singer who boasted that he could defeat the Muses themselves in a contest; for this boast the Muses blinded him and took away his art. Ajax committed suicide

of his death at the hands of women, he hated all womankind and was unwilling again to be conceived and born of a woman. Er saw the soul of Thamyras choose the life of a nightingale; then he saw a swan making the choice to become a human being. Other musical animals did the same. The soul that drew the twentieth lot chose the

b life of a lion; this was Ajax, son of Telamon. Remembering his loss of Achilles' armor, he rejected becoming human again. Next was the soul of Agamemnon, whose sufferings at the hands of men generated the same hatred of humankind. His soul chose to be an eagle.

The soul of Atalanta drew one of the middle lots. Catching sight of the honors that come to a male athlete, she could not pass them

c by but snatched them up for herself. After that he saw the soul of Epeus, son of Panopeus, taking on the nature of a woman artisan. Way in the rear he saw the buffoon Thersites getting himself into the body of an ape.

Chance would have it that Odysseus's soul drew the last lot of all. Memory of all his labors had made him renounce ambition. When it came time for choice, he searched for a long time for the life of an ordinary man who would mind his own business. With some

d difficulty he found it lying where others had disregarded it. He chose it gladly and said that even had he drawn the first lot, he would have done the same. So, in similar fashion, beasts assumed men's lives and exchanged with one another: the unjust into the savage and the just into the tame, and there were all kinds of combinations.

When all the souls had chosen lives in the order determined by

e the lots, they went to meet Lachesis. She sent with each as a companion the spirit he had chosen to be guardian of his life and destiny. The spirit first led the soul to Clotho, where her hand turned the spindle and ratified the choice made and the fate to follow. Then

621 the soul was led to where Atropos was spinning the web of destiny so as to make it irreversible. Then, without a backward look, they passed under the throne of Necessity. When all had passed under, they journeyed together to Oblivion's plain, where the heat was stifling and terrible and neither trees nor plants grew. At evening they camped by the river of Forgetfulness, whose waters no container can hold. All were required to drink some of the water. Those who were

b imprudent drank more than the measure, and each as he drank forgot everything. Then they went to sleep. When it was midnight, there was the sound of thunder and of the earth quaking. Suddenly

---

when he was not awarded the arms of Achilles because of a political deal. Agamemnon was murdered on his return from Troy by his wife and her lover. Atalanta agreed to marry the man who could beat her in a foot race; myth has it that Melanion or Hippomenes threw three golden apples in her path, and she lost the race by stopping to pick them up. Epeus is the builder of the Trojan horse. Thersites was a lower-class soldier who was beaten into silence for reviling Agamemnon (*Iliad* Book 2.211–277).

they were carried off, each in a different way, up to their births, like shooting stars.

Er said that he himself was not permitted to drink of the water. He could not say how he was returned to his own body, but suddenly he recovered his sight and saw it was morning, and he was lying on the funeral pyre.

And so, Glaucon, the tale has been saved and not lost. If we believe c it, it will save us, too, and we shall make a safe crossing of the river of Lethe and keep our souls undefiled. But if I am also able to convince you when I affirm that the soul is immortal and able to bear every evil and every good, we shall always hold to the upper way and in every way practice justice with wisdom. So shall we be friends to the gods and to ourselves both in this life and when we go to claim d our rewards, like the victors in the games go forth to gather their prizes. So shall we fare well here and during that thousand-year journey whose story I have now told you.

Glossary of Names and Places
in Plato's *Republic*

Achaeans: a Homeric name for the Greeks.

Achilles: the son of the mortal Peleus and the goddess Thetis. He was the greatest of the Greek warriors at Troy and the hero of Homer's *Iliad*.

Adeimantus: along with his brother Glaucon, he is the chief respondent to Socrates throughout the *Republic*. He and Glaucon are, in fact, brothers of Plato.

Aeschylus: fifth-century Greek tragedian (525–456 B.C.) whose most famous plays are the *Oresteia* and the *Prometheus Bound*.

Agamemnon: king of Mycenae and leader of the Greeks during the Trojan War. The *Iliad* begins when he refuses the appeal of the old priest Chryses to ransom his daughter, whom the Greeks had captured on a raid. When Agamemnon returned home, he was slain by his wife, Clytemnestra, and her lover, Aegisthus (see Aeschylus, *Agamemnon*).

Ajax: the son of Telamon, he was reckoned the second best warrior at Troy after Achilles; but after he failed to be awarded the armor of the dead Achilles, he committed suicide (see Sophocles' *Ajax*). At *Republic* 468d there is reference to the occasion when he was given the honorific cut of meat at a banquet after he fought Hector in single combat (*Iliad* Book 7.321 f.).

Alcinous: the king of the Phaeacians who heard Odysseus relate the story of his wanderings, including such episodes as his blinding of Polyphemus, his resistance to Circe's temptations, and his journey to the underworld (*Odyssey* Books 9–12).

Apollo: the god of music and prophesy. His oracular temple was at Delphi.

Archilochus: one of the earliest Greek lyric poets. Some of his poems contain animal fables.

Argos: the realm of Agamemnon in the northwest corner of the Peloponnese.

Ariston: father of Plato, Adeimantus, and Glaucon.

Asclepius: the god of healing.

Athena: daughter of Zeus and goddess of wisdom.

Atreus: father of Agamemnon and Menelaus.

Atropos: one of the three Fates cited in the myth of Er (*Republic* 614b ff.). She spins the web of destiny and so is the governor of mankind's future.

Attica: the region of Greece in which Athens is located.

Bias of Priene: a statesman and one of the legendary Seven Sages of Greece, a group to whom many wise statements were often anachronistically attributed.

Cephalus: father of Polemarchus, Lysias, and Euthydemus. He is a wealthy old man, living in the Piraeus, in whose house the discussion in the *Republic* takes place.

Cerberus: the monstrous dog who guards the entrance to Hades. He has fifty heads and a "voice like bronze."

Chimaera: a monster whose head was a lion, whose middle section was a she-goat, and whose tail was that of a serpent.

Chiron: a Centaur, a being half man, half horse. He is described as a wise teacher of medicine and other arts to Achilles (*Iliad* Book 11.828 ff.).

Chryses: a priest of Apollo whose daughter, Briseis, was taken as booty by Agamemnon during the Trojan War. Chryses came to the Greek camp asking to ransom his daughter but was rebuffed by Agamemnon. This incident is the beginning of Homer's *Iliad*.

Cleitophon: the son of Aristonymus whose name Plato used as the title of a short dialogue discussing Socrates' method of teaching and contrasting it with that of Thrasymachus.

Clotho: one of the three Fates cited in the myth of Er (*Republic* 614b ff.). She records and so makes irrevocable the choice of each person in the underworld at the time when he or she is scheduled to select a new life and return to earth. So doing, she is the symbolic governor of the present.

Cocytus: one of the nine rivers of the mythological underworld.

Croesus: last king of Lydia and proverbially wealthy (see Herodotus, *The History of the Persian Wars* Book 1.6–91).

Daedalus: legendary inventor, artist, and craftsman who designed the Labyrinth at the palace of Minos among other masterworks.

Damon: a writer on music and meter who was reputed to be a teacher of Pericles. Plato cites him as an authority on the ethical effects of rhythms and scales (*Republic*, 400a–c and 424c).

Diomedes: one of the Greek warriors in the Trojan War and a major character in Homer's *Iliad*.

Dionysus: the patron god of an ecstatic form of Greek religion. He was celebrated and worshiped yearly at various dramatic festivals in Athens and throughout the Greek world.

Eros: god of sexual love.

Euripides: a Greek tragic poet of the fifth century (ca. 485–ca. 406 B.C.). His most famous tragedies were *Medea, Hippolytus,* and *The Bacchae.* He is satirized by Aristophanes for his sophistical cynicism.

Eurypylus: a Greek warrior who was wounded in Book 11 of the *Iliad* and cared for by Patroclus.

Euthydemus: a son of Cephalus and brother of Polemarchus and Lysias. He is an interlocutor in the dialogue of Plato which bears his name.

Glaucon: along with his brother Adeimantus he is the chief respondent to Socrates in the *Republic*. He and Adeimantus are, in fact, brothers of Plato; Xenophon, *Memorabilia* Book III.vi, reports another discussion between Socrates and Glaucon.

Glaucus: a fisherman who became immortal by eating a magical herb. He threw himself into the sea, where he became a sea god (Ovid, *Metamorphoses* XIII.920–965).

Gyges: first of the Mermnad dynasty of Lydian kings who reigned from ca. 685–657 B.C. (see Herodotus, *The History of the Persian Wars* Books 1.8–14).

Hades: the king of the underworld (see *Iliad* Book 15.185–193).

Hector: the son of Priam and the most valiant of Troy's defenders. He was slain by Achilles, who then gave vent to his anger by lashing Hector's body behind his chariot and dragging it around the tomb of Patroclus (see *Iliad* Book 24.1–54).

Hellespont: the waterway that divides Europe from Asia, and the site of Troy. The Greek navy drew up here, and the Greeks camped along its shores throughout the ten-year Trojan War.

Hephaestus: the craftsman of the gods. He designed the throne that captured Hera in its chains when she sat down and the bed that caught Ares and Aphrodite while in the act of adultery. When he tried to protect his mother Hera from Zeus, the latter threw him down to earth; he walked with a limp thenceforth.

Hera: wife of Zeus and queen of the gods.

Heraclitus: an Ionian philosopher of the late sixth century B.C. who believed the world to be the product of a process of constant change.

Hermus: the major river of Lydia, a region on the western coast of Turkey facing Greece, flowing to the Aegean Sea.

Herodicus: one of the first Greeks to study scientifically the beneficial effects of exercise and diet.

Hesiod: a poet and contemporary of Homer (ca. 725 B.C.). He wrote on the origin and nature of the Greek gods and celebrated the just man as the best adapted to the demands of the Greek world (see his *Theogony* and *Works and Days*).

Homer: the great classic poet of Greece (ca. 725 B.C.), author of the *Iliad* and the *Odyssey*. Both epics were still used as standard instructional materials in the Greek schools of Plato's time, four hundred years after Homer composed them. Students had to memorize them since they were regarded as authoritative commentaries on Greek history and relations among men and gods; they were also the most extensive repository of maxims deemed appropriate to the conduct of human affairs.

Hydra: a monster with many heads; as soon as one was cut off, two or three others grew in its place.

Ida: a mountain near Troy where Zeus had a sanctuary.

Inachus: a river in Argos, the area in the northeast Peloponnese where Agamemnon ruled.

Islands of the Blessed: islands located at the ends of the earth, where many heroes dwelt in the afterlife.

Ismenias: a Theban who took money from the Persians to stir up war among the Greeks (see Xenophon, *Hellenica* Book 5.2.35).

Ithaca: an island on the west coast of Greece and the home of Odysseus. This is the island that Odysseus struggles to reach throughout the first half of the *Odyssey*.

Lachesis: one of the three Fates cited in the myth of Er (*Republic* 614b ff.), ruler of the past. She distributes the lots determining the sequence in which humans may choose a new life in the underworld.

Lethe: the underworld river of forgetfulness.

Lysias: a son of Cephalus and brother of Polemarchus and Euthydemus. He was a well-known speech writer, one of whose discourses is reported in Plato's *Phaedrus*.

Menelaus: brother of Agamemnon and husband of Helen. Helen's abduction and subsequent adulterous life with Paris in Troy and Menelaus's determination to recover her and revenge himself constitute the classic prologue to the Trojan War.

Midas: the king of Phrygia with the legendary "golden touch."

Musaeus: a mythical singer and seer who is reputed to have been the son of Orpheus.

Muses: nine deities who are the patrons of intellectual pursuits, including literature, music, dance, and astronomy.

Nemesis: a goddess of retribution who punished human presumptuousness.

Niceratus: son of Nicias, the commanding general during the Peloponnesian War. Niceratus was killed under the rule of the despotic Thirty Tyrants in 404 B.C.

Odysseus: the hero of Homer's *Odyssey* who visited fabulous countries and even the underworld during his ten years' journey back to Ithaca and then defeated 108 suitors to regain his wife and throne.

Olympia: the sanctuary of Zeus in the middle of the Peloponnese. The Olympic games originated here in 776 B.C. and took place every four years thereafter. Victors in these games were celebrated as the finest athletes in Greece.

Orpheus: the famed singer of Greek mythology who founded the Orphic religion, with its mystic cult and doctrine.

Palamedes: one of the cleverest heroes at Troy. He is credited with the discovery of both the alphabet and numbering.

Pamphylia: an area on the southern coast of Turkey.

Patroclus: son of Menoetius and comrade of Achilles. He was slain by Hector at Troy, and in revenge Achilles dragged Hector's corpse around Patroclus's tomb.

Perdiccas: Perdiccas I and Perdiccas II were kings of Macedon.

Periander: tyrant of Corinth (ca. 625–585 B.C.).

Phocylides: sixth-century B.C. poet, well known as the author of proverbs.

Phoebus: another name for Apollo.

Phoenix: Achilles' guardian at Troy. In a famous scene in Book 9 of Homer's *Iliad*, Phoenix advised Achilles to accept the gifts offered by Agamemnon and return to fighting for the good of the Greeks. Achilles rejected this advice, continued to stay away from battle, and more of the Greeks were killed.

Pindar: fifth-century B.C. lyric poet of Thebes who wrote odes in honor of the Olympic victors, celebrating both physical and moral excellence.

Piraeus: the seaport of Athens, lying about six miles south of the Acropolis.

Pittacus of Mytilene: a sixth-century B.C. statesman and one of the Seven Sages, a group to whom wise statements were often attributed.

Polemarchus: a son of Cephalus and brother of Lysias and Euthydemus. He is the heir to his father's discussion with Socrates early in Book I of the *Republic*.

Polydamus: an Olympic victor in 408 B.C. in contests featuring a combination of boxing and wrestling (pancration).

Priam: king of Troy. When he saw his son Hector killed, he gave way to frenzied bursts of grief and lamentation. Later he ransomed Hector's corpse from Achilles (see *Iliad* Book 24).

Prodicus of Ceos: a Sophist and contemporary of Socrates who specialized in finding the precise meaning of words and using them correctly. He charged high fees for his lessons.

Protagoras of Abdera: a Sophist who offered instruction in virtue or the correct conduct of one's life. He is best known for his statement "Man is the measure of all things."

Pythagoreans: the followers of the philosopher Pythagoras, who founded a religious society in Croton in southern Italy that imposed a strict code of behavior. Pythagoras studied ratios between numbers on the basis of musical intervals and discovered consistencies from which he derived geometrical and astronomical systems.

Pythian oracle: the oracle of Apollo at Delphi, the most famous oracular seat in Greece.

Sarpedon: the son of Zeus who was fated to be killed by Patroclus at Troy. Zeus laments his coming death in the *Iliad* Book 16.433 ff.

Scylla: a sea monster with six heads—each containing three rows of teeth—and twelve feet (see *Odyssey* Book 12).

Scythia: a broad expanse of territory north of the Black Sea occupied by a tribal warrior society.

Seriphus: a small island off the eastern coast of the Peloponnese.

Simonides of Ceos: a lyric poet born in the sixth century B.C.

Sirens: bewitching singers who were half woman, half birds (see *Odyssey* Book 12).

Solon: Athenian constitutional reformer and poet of the early sixth century B.C. who was honored in Athens as the greatest exemplar of political wisdom.

Sophocles: Athenian tragic poet (496–406 B.C.). He had a long and successful career writing for the theater. Among his most famous plays are *Antigone*, *Oedipus the King*, and *Oedipus at Colonus*.

Styx: one of the nine rivers of the mythological underworld by whose authority the gods took their oaths.

Syracuse: a Greek colonial settlement and the leading city in southern Italy during the fifth and fourth centuries B.C.

Theages: a young pupil of Socrates whose ill health made him unsuited for a political career, but was also the cause of his remaining a philosopher. There is a short dialogue bearing his name among the works attributed to Plato.

Themis: a goddess who summoned the council of the gods in which Zeus permitted the gods to join in the fighting at Troy on whichever side they wished (see *Iliad* Book 20.20–30).

Thetis: a goddess who married Peleus, a mortal, and became the mother of the ill-fated Achilles.

Thrace: a broad area north of the Aegean Sea occupied by a collection of tribes dominated by an aristocratic class of warriors and hunters.

Thrasymachus of Chalcedon: a young Sophist who taught his students how to increase their persuasiveness by appealing to the emotions and who equated justice, in effect, to power.

Troy: a city located on the shores of the Hellespont in northwestern Turkey. It was also the scene of the Trojan War.

Xerxes: the great king of Persia (485–465 B.C.).

Zeus: the king of the Olympian gods.